**The Jessie and John Danz Lectures**

**The Jessie and John Danz Lectures**

# The Uses of Ecology

*Lake Washington and Beyond*

W. T. Edmondson

UNIVERSITY OF WASHINGTON PRESS

*Seattle and London*

*Library of Congress Cataloging-in-Publication Data*

Edmonson, W. T.
    The uses of ecology : Lake Washington and beyond / W. T. Edmonson.
        p.    cm.—(The Jessie and John Danz lectures)
    Includes bibliographical references and index.
    ISBN 0-295-97024-3 (alk. paper)
    1. Water—Pollution—Washington (State)—Washington. Lake.
2. Water—Pollution—United States—Case studies.    3. Lake ecology–
–Research—United States—Case studies.    I. Title.    II. Series.
TD224.W2E36   1991                                        90-47158
363.73'94—dc20                                            CIP

The paper used in this publication meets the minimum requirements
of the American National Standard for Information Sciences—
Permanence of Paper for Printed Library Materials,
ANSI Z39.48-1984.

This book is dedicated to

**G. Evelyn Hutchinson**

who wrote nearly fifty years ago:

"The writer believes that the most practical lasting benefit science can now offer is to teach man how to avoid destruction of his own environment, and how, by understanding himself with true humility and pride, to find ways to avoid injuries that at present he inflicts on himself with such devastating energy."

## The Jessie and John Danz Lectures

In October 1961, Mr. John Danz, a Seattle pioneer, and his wife, Jessie Danz, made a substantial gift to the University of Washington to establish a perpetual fund to provide income to be used to bring to the University of Washington each year "distinguished scholars of national and international reputation who have concerned themselves with the impact of science and philosophy on man's perception of a rational universe." The fund established by Mr. and Mrs. Danz is now known as the Jessie and John Danz Fund, and the scholars brought to the University under its provisions are known as Jessie and John Danz Lecturers or Professors.

Mr. Danz wisely left to the Board of Regents of the University of Washington the identification of the special fields in science, philosophy, and other disciplines in which lectureships may be established. His major concern and interest were that the fund would enable the University of Washington to bring to the campus some of the truly great scholars and thinkers of the world.

Mr. Danz authorized the Regents to expend a portion of the income from the fund to purchase special collections of books, documents, and other scholarly materials needed to reinforce the effectiveness of the extraordinary lectureships and professorships. The terms of the gift also provided for the publication and dissemination, when this seems appropriate, of the lectures given by the Jessie and John Danz Lecturers.

Through this book, therefore, another Jessie and John Danz Lecturer speaks to the people and scholars of the world, as he has spoken to his audiences at the University of Washington and in the Pacific Northwest community.

# Contents

# Illustrations

Sweet are the uses of adversity,
Which, like the toad, ugly and venomous,
Wears yet a precious jewel in his head
And this our life exempt from public haunt
Finds tongues in trees, books in the running brooks,
Sermons in stones, and good in everything.
I would not change it.

*As You Like It*, act 2, scene 1

# *Preface*

In June 1986, within a few minutes of receiving an invitation to deliver the Danz lectures, I had created a title for the series and decided the sequence of topics. To convert the ideas into lectures took six months; to develop the lectures into the manuscript of this book has taken much of my working time for more than three times that long. There is a great deal to say about the topic, and three lectures gave time for only a fraction of it. For this written version I have expanded the scope of everything discussed in the lectures and added some topics not included in them.

I will use a question for the central theme of the whole book: What can an ivory-tower, egghead ecologist do to help people understand and solve problems of environmental deterioration? Now I myself am an ivory-tower, egghead ecologist and I know something about that. In my opinion, the Ivory Tower is one of the strongest pillars of our society.

Ecology is a field of basic biological science having to do with the organization of nature: populations, communities, and ecosystems. During the 1960s when environmental deterioration was coming to public attention, the word ecology was misappropriated and redefined in various ways, such as "the science of environmental deterioration" or "the science of survival." Even now newspaper pictures of a troop of Boy Scouts picking up trash along a stream may be labelled "an ecology project," and a raid by members of the Greenpeace organization on a whaling vessel has been described as an action by a group of ecologists. It is of course imperative to control the disposal of solid waste and the extermination of species, but that is not what ecology is about. In this book I hope to show by example what the science of ecology is about, but my main goal is to show that knowledge of ecology is an essential foundation for effective solutions to our increasing environmental problems. This is not a textbook. I give plenty of information, but make no attempt to survey everything that is known about any topic. My own field of ecology is limnology, the scientific study of inland waters. Here I emphasize lakes, but do not limit my attention to them.

The book starts with an account of a widely known local success story, the pollution and recovery of Lake Washington. I use the Lake Washington experience as a sort of model against which I can compare other environmental problems. I emphasize that the lake has been a very attractive object for basic scientific research. When pollution was seen to be damaging it, our scientific studies enabled us to understand exactly what the problem was and how it could be fixed. The reaction of people in the region to the predicted deterioration of the lake and the nature of the public action taken to protect it form an important part of the story.

Chapter 2, "Lake Washington in Context: How Communities Work," introduces some basic ecological ideas and terminology that will be helpful in understanding the problems to be described.

Part 2, "Lessons from Lake Washington," presents examples of environmental problems that can be illuminated by knowledge derived from the Lake Washington experience. Although Lake Washington is physically connected with Puget Sound, the pollution of the sound will not be the next topic. It is more useful to discuss another topic first—the vigorous controversy about detergents that came to a climax in the early 1970s and still continues. This introduces a recurring point: the choice, or balance, that must often be made between quality of environment and quantity of corporate profits. It also illustrates how special interest can lead to creative misinterpretation of data.

Not all environmental problems arise from pollution. Mono Lake and the Panama Canal (chapters 5 and 6) expose special problems that result from different ways of using water. Chapter 7 includes four quite different topics that are united by the fact that they depend upon the atmosphere as an effective, chemically reactive transporter of materials. All involve enormous financial interests and the possibility of enormous environmental damage.

Since most environmental problems take time to develop before they are perceived and time to recover after protective action, research in environmental ecology has taken on a special character, dominated by the necessity for continuing study. Long-term ecological research, or sustained ecological research, as it is coming to be known, is the focus of part 3, a series of examples selected to demonstrate that aspect of the field and the difficulties of managing sustained projects. The final chapter of the series describes the special kinds of effort and support required for genuine long-term projects, based on the examples given in the preceding five chapters. It includes a scrutiny of the current state of support by granting agencies.

In part 4 I try to make sense of the whole thing and take a look ahead. The word *pollution* is used frequently in the environmental literature, but I think the concept needs to be clarified, and I make an attempt in chapter 14. The use of expert witnesses in legal actions or on investigative panels draws attention to the problem of knowing what to do when two "experts" give conflicting testimony. Chapter 15 includes this point and the educational background needed by environmental experts. In chapter 16 I comment on a number of themes that pervade the book, with special reference to environmental protection and environmentalism. Finally, in chapter 17 I introduce the biggest problem of all, population, at which point we reach the edge of the scope of this book.

Authors are supposed to consider the audience for whom they are writing, and adjust their language accordingly. I have written for a very diverse audience, and the book therefore is a chimera. Primarily it is written for the kind of people who attend Danz lectures, certainly a diverse group in itself. In addition it is directed to people in all professions who are involved in handling environmental problems: engineers, lawyers, legislators, corporate managers, and scientists. After writing the preceding sentences, I finally realized that really I was writing the book for myself. I valued the stimulus to organize my thoughts in a way that would not be appropriate for the scientific papers that I usually write. For that reason, there are patches here and there in which I take advantage of this opportunity to express opinions to fellow limnologists about matters that have been debated among us and need to be resolved for more effective application of our research. It is important to know that professionals can disagree about basic concepts. Some sections also serve as a personal record of my own activities and interests. Some information is presented for the first time in print in this book. I invite readers to scan selectively and read what interests them.

Some of the examples, such as Lake Washington and Puget Sound, are of local interest, and I give more detail about them than about most of the others. But every environmental problem is of local interest somewhere. While each case has its own special features, some features are common to many situations, and we benefit by comparison. My major examples are given in enough detail to permit such a comparison with others.

Now some housekeeping details. For those who want to read further I have included extensive documentation. Each chapter has its own bibliography, and all are collected at the end of the book. To avoid clutter, I use a simple reference system. Publications that document specific points are usually identified in the text simply by the name of the author and publication date in parentheses. In addition, the bibliographies include other useful sources of information. Their significance is indicated by the title or by notations. The bibliographies are not intended to be complete, up-to-date compilations of pertinent literature. The references either have been especially useful to me or illustrate a point particularly well. They should enable one to find almost all published information used.

In general, English units are used for dimensions and the metric equivalent is given in parentheses, rounded to a convenient number.

It has been impracticable to keep the manuscript up to date between October 1988, when the draft was finished and the summer of 1990, when the final revision was completed. Almost every day something appears in the newspapers, magazines or on television that is pertinent to the book. I am reminded of a discovery made by Professor Donald F. Poulson when I was a student. Poulson's Principle states: "the day after you give a lecture on some topic, a very important publication on the same topic arrives in the mail." Very recently there have been some momentous environmental events; some advances, some retreats. I have taken notice of only a few of them, without full treatment. One is especially significant in terms of the severity of the damage that can be created by careless industrial operations and in terms of what we can learn about the responsiveness of the perpetrators to environmental concerns. It must rank close to the Chernobyl nuclear disaster in illustrating these points, if not in human destruction. That is the oil spill in Prince William Sound, Alaska in March 1989.

Danz lecturers are guided by a phrase in Mr. Danz's will. They are to be scholars "who have concerned themselves with the impact of science and philosophy on man's perception of a rational universe." As the reader will see, I present examples of the best and the worst thought as it has been applied to the way we deal with our environment and the other species with which we share it.

# Acknowledgments

M any people have contributed to the production of this book, both by helping me to acquire the experience that enabled me to write it, and by responding to my requests for specific information to include. My thanks go first, of course, to Jessie and John Danz for establishing the lectureship which has made such a great contribution to life at the University of Washington, and to the Danz family for their continued interest. Professor Charles D. Laird and Professor Robert T. Paine of the Department of Zoology had the thoughtfulness and patience to prepare my nomination; I am grateful to them, and to the Danz Lectureship Committee for agreeing with them. Without the invitation it would never have occurred to me to write a book like this. Any zoologist would be happy to join a parade headed by Sir Julian Huxley, the first Danz lecturer and Mr. John Danz's personal choice for that role.

I thank the Department of Zoology for its support during my entire time at the University of Washington. My graduate students have contributed immeasurably to my education. Results of my own research have been included in this book, work made possible only by a long succession of technical helpers and other professional associates. There have been far too many to list individually, but special mention must be made of those who made major commitments of time and effort. In order of first appearance those still present at the university are David E. Allison, Sally E. B. Abella, Arni H. Litt, Katie P. Frevert and Mardi I. Varela. Together these five people have contributed more than eighty years of excellent work on lakes in Washington state.

I am most grateful for the prolonged financial support of the agencies mentioned in the chapters and in published research reports, particularly the National Science Foundation and the

Department of Energy. The Andrew W. Mellon Foundation has generously given help essential for the completion of my work, including this book.

Finally, people who know me will recognize the special role filled by my wife, Yvette H. Edmondson, for nineteen years editor of the journal *Limnology and Oceanography*, who has edited this paragraph severely.

# The Uses of Ecology

*Lake Washington and Beyond*

# Part 1

## What Happened
## to Lake Washington

A disturbingly common environmental problem occurs when
a lake, formerly in satisfactory condition, begins to produce dense populations of certain kinds of algae. This change is
brought about by an increase in the nutrient supply of the lake,
known as eutrophication, that is often due to sewage effluent.
The unpleasant side effects can interfere with people's use of the
lake. Lake Washington started on such a course of deterioration
in the early 1950s, but was rescued by an unprecedented public
action. Our study at the University of Washington supplied new
data that helped us understand the response of lakes to eutrophication, that provided novel and unusual examples of established ecological principles, and that were helpful to the public
in making decisions about remedial action.

In the first chapter I will review the whole story and discuss
some aspects of the public action that have not been published
before. I will describe what happened with a minimum of scientific terminology and detail. Chapter 2 connects the Lake
Washington story to the rest of the book. In it I review some basic ecological principles that we need to know to compare the
Lake Washington experience with others.

In later chapters the Lake Washington experience is taken as
a central example to which other types of environmental problems can be compared. In some instances this will enhance understanding of those problems and perhaps help solve them. In
other instances the comparison will give insight into special features of the Lake Washington situation.

# Chapter 1

## The Eutrophication and Recovery of Lake Washington

Lake Washington is known throughout the world as the subject of a success story in lake restoration. Accounts of the diversion of sewage from the lake have been given in many publications with differing detail, emphasis, and viewpoint.

### Beginnings

Lake Washington took form at the end of the Ice Age nearly 12,000 years ago. Early in its history it was connected to Puget Sound, but within 1000 years of its origin it became separated and has been a freshwater lake ever since. The lake lies parallel to Puget Sound and is separated from it by hills (fig. 1.1). The settlement that became Seattle was founded in 1851 on Puget Sound at the present Alki Point. Before long the settled region was spreading, and within thirty or forty years much of the forested land along the west side of the lake had been cleared.

The lake had one major inlet, the Sammamish River at the north end, draining Lake Sammamish, and a few small inlet streams. The outlet at the south end was the short Black River, which flowed into the Cedar River, then via the Duwamish River into Elliot Bay on Puget Sound. During the summer of 1916 the level of Lake Washington was permanently lowered by about ten feet (3.3 m) as the result of a major engineering project, the construction of a locked ship canal connecting the lake with Puget Sound. The Cedar River was diverted through a new artificial channel into the lake to provide water for operating the locks, more than doubling the water inflow. The ship canal became the outlet (fig. 1.2). These changes greatly affected the character of Lake Washington and its use by people. As far as possible the level is now controlled to lie between 20 and 22 feet (about 7 m) above mean low low tide level in the sound. The lake is nearly 18 miles (28 kilometers) long and 214 feet (65 meters) deep.

Thomas Mercer, a Seattle pioneer, had proposed such a canal during a Fourth of July picnic in 1854. He suggested that the large lake should be named for the father of the country and the smaller one between that lake and Puget Sound should be called Lake Union because it would be part of the system that would unite Lake Washington with Puget Sound. It took a long time, but on the Fourth of July 1916, a large celebration with fireworks marked the completion of a major part of the project. Another celebration was held in 1917 when the whole thing was finished.

The motivation for building the ship canal is interesting in view of later events. The basic idea was to facilitate large industrial developments on Lake Washington, producing a sort of "Pittsburgh of the West." Coal was abundant south and east of the lake at Black Diamond and at Newcastle on Cougar Mountain. Iron ore was available nearby. Because financing was not forthcoming for such an expensive project with a limited goal, a case was made that a canal would convert Lake Washington into the safest harbor on the West Coast for the navy. Partly on that basis, a bill was passed by the United States Congress to build the canal at a cost of 5 million dollars. However a major economic depression in 1893–97 killed all the plans for industrialization, and a very different kind of development followed the opening of the canal.

Much later, in 1978, events caused me to think with some amusement about the original plan to industrialize Lake Washington. A naval air station had operated at Sand Point on the lake

*Fig. 1.1. Lake Washington from the southeast, 23 February 1990. Puget Sound and the Olympic mountains are beyond the city of Seattle. Two floating highway bridges that cross the lake are seen as straight white lines. Notice the extensive land development to the east of the lake (foreground). Photograph courtesy of Skynet Aviation.*

since 1926 but was being scaled down. The National Oceanographic and Atmospheric Administration (NOAA) proposed to
consolidate its western regional operations at Sand Point. The
plan included constructing large piers for its fleet of oceanographic research ships. This plan was strongly opposed by
homeowners who worried about pollution, increased traffic, and
especially interference with their views of the lake. A major point
used by the opposition to NOAA was that their plan would amount
to industrialization of the lake. I was puzzled to hear no mention in the public discussion that the Congress had financed the
ship canal for the express purposes of industrialization and of use
by the U.S. Navy! Another proposal was to convert the facility
to an airfield for private airplanes. It, too, failed. Eventually, the
pier plan was abandoned and much of the land was converted
to a public park.

Seattle and neighboring smaller communities began to develop sewage problems early. In 1865, Seattle organized a sewerage agency and, in 1883, started construction of a primitive
system of pipes. From 1891 to 1956, the system grew from about
15 miles (24 km) of pipe to 1060 miles (1705 km). At first, there
were no treatment facilities, so that sanitary sewage and street
gutter drainage ran down the same pipes, the conventional
practice at the time. Sewage was carried to about fifty outfalls
along Puget Sound. By 1922 there were thirty outfalls into Lake
Washington from Seattle, serving 50,000 people. A small system in Renton and individual outfalls elsewhere were also
pouring raw sewage into the lake.

Between 1889 and 1948 many reports were prepared by city and
county agencies with recommendations for control of pollution.
The condition of the lake was of great concern because it was still

*Fig. 1.2. The Lake Washington ship canal system seen across the lake
from the east, 30 May 1956 (before the Evergreen Point floating bridge
was built). Union Bay is in the center foreground with Puget Sound and
the Olympic mountains in the background. Lake Union is the large body
of water halfway between Union Bay and Puget Sound, Green Lake is
to the right of Lake Union, Ravenna Park is the elongate dark area east
of Green Lake. Photograph by Pacific Aerial Surveys.*

the source of drinking water for many people. In 1907 a serious outbreak of typhoid resulted in 570 cases in a population of about 200,000.

A major sewerage system was built to divert sewage from the Lake Washington side of the hills separating the lake from Puget Sound. This included trunk sewers that collected raw sewage from a large area of Seattle and delivered it to Puget Sound, much of it through an outfall at sea level near West Point. The system was completed in 1936, and by 1956, 70 million gallons per day (0.26 million $m^3$) of raw sewage were being delivered to Puget Sound at sea level along the Seattle waterfront. This situation lasted until 1966.

The diversion of sewage from the Seattle shore of Lake Washington was not a complete solution because the city was expanding beyond its former limits and other communities were developing around the lake. In 1941, two small plants with secondary treatment were built to serve the Sand Point Naval Air Station and adjacent homes. These were the first of what would eventually be eleven treatment plants affecting the lake (fig. 1.3). Major plants were built in Renton and Kirkland in the 1940s and in Bellevue and Lake City in the 1950s. (Lake City was soon incorporated into Seattle, but was still an independent political entity in 1954 when the plant was built.) All the new plants employed secondary treatment, which was regarded as advanced technology at the time. As will be explained further in chapter 2, secondary treatment is a method of purification that decomposes the organic materials, liberating inorganic nutrients that act as a chemical fertilizer.

Thus, Lake Washington went through two episodes of sewage pollution, the first ending in 1936. The second episode was brought under control as a result of a remarkable public action ratified by a vote in 1958.

## Eutrophication and Recovery

Lake Washington was presumably of low productivity when the first settlers from the east arrived. It was surrounded by dense coniferous forest and its inlets drained undisturbed land. The native soils had only moderate amounts of plant nutrients. The

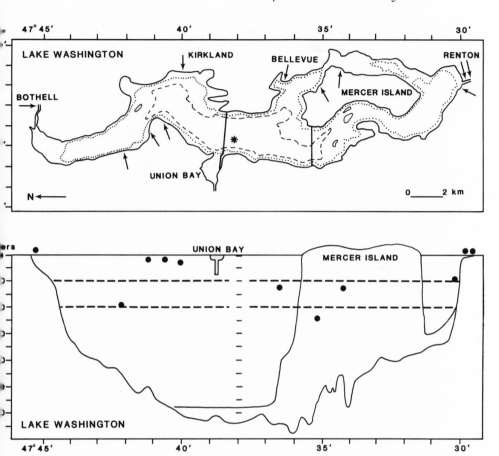

*Fig. 1.3.* Above. *Map of Lake Washington on its side showing location of outfalls from the secondary sewage treatment plants (short arrows). North is to the left. Contour lines are shown for 10 meters (dotted line) and 50 meters (dashed line). The star shows the main sampling station, visited on a regular schedule. Samples have been taken at more than twenty-five other locations around the lake at appropriate times.* Below. *Vertical section of Lake Washington along the deepest part and through Mercer Island, viewed from the west. Vertical exaggeration 166 times. Union Bay with the dredged ship canal is shown in profile. The large dots show the ends of the widely distributed sewage plant outfalls, several relatively deep. The thirteen short lines under the sampling station show the depths at which water samples were taken during stratification in the intensive study of the lake in recovery.*

early settlers described the lake as "clear." There is very little information about its early condition or the effect of the first episode of pollution. In 1933, Rex J. Robinson and Victor B. Scheffer made a detailed limnological study of Lake Washington. Robinson, a professor of chemistry, had done his Ph.D. work at the University of Wisconsin in analytical chemistry, and he enjoyed analyzing samples of lake water. Scheffer was a graduate student of Professor Kincaid in zoology doing a Ph.D. degree on the plankton of Lake Washington; he later changed fields and became one of the world's experts on marine mammals. Their coordinated chemical and biological study was very advanced for its time, and still stands as a baseline (Scheffer and Robinson 1939). (In 1983, the fiftieth anniversary of their study, we scheduled our own sampling dates as close as possible to theirs.) They found the lake in good condition, even though the diversion of sewage from the first episode had not quite been finished. Concentrations of nutrients were relatively low, abundance of organisms correspondingly low, and deep-water dissolved oxygen concentrations remained high all year. While neither light penetration nor transparency was measured, the lake must have been acceptably clear in 1933. In 1950, another study by two of my graduate students showed that the concentration of phosphate had doubled, and somewhat less dissolved oxygen remained in the deep water at the end of summer, although unusually high concentrations of algae were not seen. These changes indicated that Lake Washington was responding to the increase of nutrients in the sewage. Such eutrophication was known to produce unpleasant conditions in lakes, but in 1950 Lake Washington was still in acceptable condition.

On the basis of previous experiences we could have expected Lake Washington to deteriorate. For example, Lake Zürich in Switzerland was noted in the late nineteenth century for its clarity and valuable production of deep-water coregonid fish. With increasing input of sewage it started a series of changes that eliminated the deep-water fish community and had other displeasing effects. The first conspicuous change was the appearance in 1898 of a relatively dense population of a blue-green alga known as *Oscillatoria rubescens,* which made larger populations with increasing sewage input. Published descriptions of the consequences of eutrophication usually emphasize the phyto-plankton, the community of algae, microscopic photosynthetic organisms that are distributed through the open water of the entire lake. However, all types of photosynthetic organisms are affected, including the relatively massive algae (*Cladophora*) that form jungle-like growths attached to the bottom of some lakes. (See chapter 2 for a discussion of the kinds of organisms in lakes.)

Without secure projections of population growth in the area or information about future development of the sewerage system, there was little basis in the early 1950s for predicting a schedule for the deterioration of Lake Washington. Then, on 15 June 1955, the lake gave a clear signal that it was well on the way to serious deterioration, and the situation became much more predictable. It is worth knowing what that signal was and how it was delivered.

Dr. George C. Anderson had finished his Ph.D. degree in 1954 with a dissertation on the phytoplankton of several lakes, including Lake Washington. He then stayed here to work with me on a remarkable situation developing in Soap Lake that will be recounted in chapter 11. On a Sunday in June 1955, for recreation, he went sailing on Lake Washington and noticed that it looked strange. He brought a sample back to the laboratory in a beer bottle, saying, "That is not the lake I knew." We sent the sample to an expert on algae who identified the abundant organism as *Oscillatoria rubescens*.

This, of course, was wildly exciting to us. It was instantly obvious that we had a superb opportunity to turn the clock back fifty-seven years and see what must have happened to Lake Zürich, in a way that could not have been done in 1898. However, a research project of the magnitude required to define the condition of Lake Washington and the changes we expected would cost more than the small amount of state money available through the University of Washington. Fortunately the National Institutes of Health (Public Health Service) had recently developed a program in environmental health, and we obtained enough money for a boat, equipment, supplies and salaries for assistants to make a start for two years. Dr. Joseph Shapiro had just finished his doctoral degree at Yale and came to participate in the project. We initially regarded the project simply as an experiment in lake fertilization, basic research in limnology. We had no idea then that it would be useful for anything beyond advancing scientific knowledge.

The results were very interesting so we next applied to the National Science Foundation, which had been formed in 1950 for the express purpose of supporting basic research. The foundation has supplied most of the financial support for our work on Lake Washington ever since. We had some expectations of how Lake Washington would change, and we set out to make frequent measurements of selected properties so as to get a detailed description of its response to increased nutrition. We were especially concerned with the quantitative changes in properties related to nutrient input and the rates at which they changed, such as the increase in the phosphorus content of the water, and the decrease of dissolved oxygen concentration in the deep layer during summer. We expected further increases in the phytoplankton, and changes in the relative abundance of different types of algae. A particularly pertinent question that soon became important was how long it would take after the appearance of *Oscillatoria* for nuisance conditions to appear. Because Lake Washington had not yet seriously deteriorated, we were in on the ground floor of a study of the early stages of developing nuisance conditions.

Then, as the result of a public vote in 1958, sewage was diverted from the lake before any really serious deterioration had taken place. (See the following section on public action.) Thus, we were able to study in detail the processes involved in recovery. The experiment would have been better scientifically if deterioration had been permitted to go further before diversion, but it was good enough.

The lake responded promptly and sensitively to the changes in nutrient input. As sewage input was increasing, the concentration of nutrients in the water and the total nutrient content of the lake increased. There was a corresponding increase of phytoplankton in summer, with a consequent decrease in transparency (fig. 1.4).

The sewage effluent was diverted stepwise as pipes were built along the lake from south to north. In February 1963, about one-third of the effluent was diverted by connecting three plants at

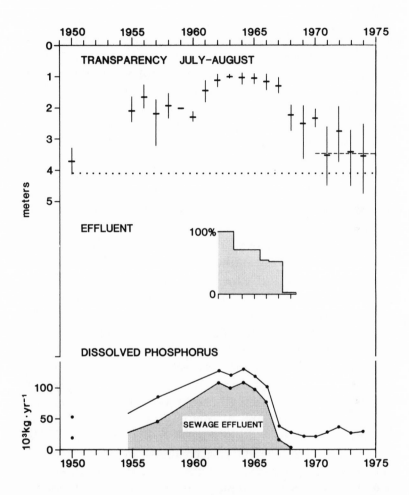

*Fig. 1.4. Pollution and recovery of Lake Washington.* Above. *Range and mean Secchi disc transparency during summer.* Middle. *Treated sewage effluent with maximum amount before diversion, 20 million gallons per day, taken as 100%.* Below. *Input (loading) of dissolved phosphate-P, metric tons per year. The amount contained in sewage effluent is shaded.*

the south end of the lake. By 1965 about half had been diverted and the final diversion was in February 1968, although 99% had been diverted by early 1967.

Limnologists are much interested in the relative importance of the different nutritive elements. The chemical changes before, during, and after diversion were very informative. One type of evidence is the relative decrease in concentrations of phosphate and nitrate during the growth of the phytoplankton during spring. Both phosphate and nitrate decreased in the water as the algae absorbed them (fig. 1.5). In 1933 when phosphate had become almost undetectable, there was still a significant amount of nitrate left in the water, indicating growth limitation by lack of phosphate. The situation had changed greatly by 1962. Wintertime concentrations of both nutrients were much higher than in 1933. Nitrate was 3.6 times as concentrated, phosphate 6.3 times. Phytoplankton absorbed the two substances in about the same proportion as before, so that at the end of the growth period there was still a large amount of phosphate left when nitrate had become undetectable, indicating a change to limitation by insufficient nitrate. By 1967 the winter concentrations were lower than previously, but still relatively high, with phosphate having decreased more than nitrate. The relation was almost the same as in 1933, with a slight excess of nitrate. In 1968 and in all subsequent years there has been a relatively large excess of nitrate in the water, indicating a return to phosphate limitation (fig. 1.6).

These changes are easily understood. In 1933 the input of sewage was minimal, and the natural water supply of the lake evidently had an excess of nitrate relative to phosphate. This is a common although not universal condition. By 1962, the lake had been enriched for many years with secondary sewage effluent. As will be explained in chapter 2, the secondary treatment process eliminates a greater percentage of the nitrogen and carbon than of phosphorus, leaving the effluent relatively richer in phosphorus content than lake water. Thus, the lake became relatively overloaded with phosphate. The ratio of nitrate-N to phosphate-P in sewage effluent during 1963-66 was 0.513 by weight.* This low ratio indicated relatively little nitrogen and

---

*Nitrate-N means the amount of the element nitrogen contained in the ion nitrate. Phosphate-P means the amount of the element phosphorus contained in the ion phosphate.

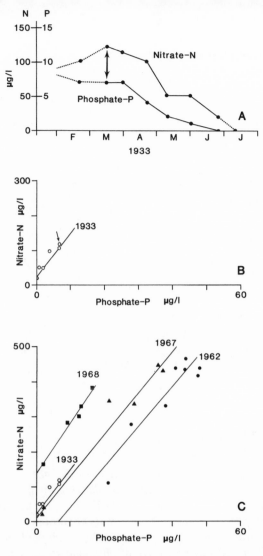

Fig. 1.5. *Changes in concentrations of phosphate and nitrate during spring in Lake Washington.* **Above.** *Concentration in 1933 as example. The concentrations are highest during late winter and decrease during spring when phytoplankton is growing. The double-headed arrow shows the date of maximum concentration for both nutrients. Note that since nitrate is more concentrated than phosphate, the scales are different. Data from Scheffer and Robinson.* **Middle.** *For each date the concentration of nitrate is plotted against that of phosphate. The point of maximum concentration marked by arrow in the top part is marked by an arrow here.* **Below.** *As in the middle panel but with data from later years added. Note that before (1933) and after (1967, 1968) eutrophication when the phosphate was exhausted, nitrate was in excess and remained in the water. During eutrophication with sewage rich in phosphate (1962), phosphate was in excess when nitrate was exhausted.*

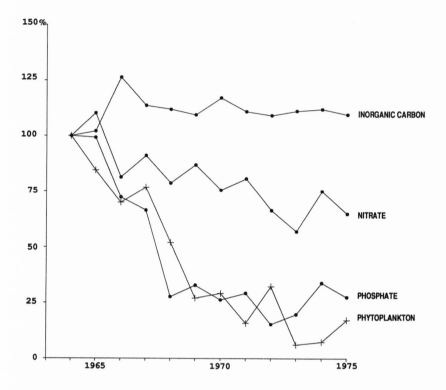

*Fig. 1.6. Change in the chemical content of the lake during recovery. Concentrations of three nutrients and the chlorophyll content of the phytoplankton are shown with the value in 1964, the year of maximum input, being taken as 100%. The nutrients are means of concentrations during January–March before the beginning of phytoplankton growth. Chlorophyll, an effective measure of phytoplankton, is the mean that developed during July–August of the following summer. The data for phosphorus are used in fig. 3.1.*

excess phosphorus. The ratio in the water of the tributary streams was 35.1, indicating a relative scarcity of phosphorus and much nitrate. The ratio in the lake is intermediate between that in the streams and in sewage. It reached a minimum of 8.0 in 1963, the year that diversion started. Between 1970 and 1978, after diversion, it increased and varied between 18.2 and 35.5. Thus, as diversion progressed, the relative input of phosphate decreased and Lake Washington was flushed through with low-phosphate water, restoring it to a condition of phosphate limitation.

We have not fully studied the reason for the increase after 1933 to such a large excess of nitrate after diversion, but an increase in nitrate entering the lake is an expected consequence of the extensive development in the drainage area. Nitrate, being more soluble, is more easily washed out of disturbed soil than is phosphate. Much of the cleared land in the watershed supports a dense growth of alder trees which can fix molecular nitrogen from the air, adding to the nitrogen already in the soil. The Cedar River in 1970 had a nitrate concentration more than twice as high as in 1957, while the phosphate concentration was only 10% higher.

Another way to show the relative effect of the sewage on the different nutrients is to examine the change over the years of the concentration in wintertime after decomposition of organic matter has returned nutrients to the water. During the post-diversion recovery, phosphate dropped steadily, while nitrate decreased much less and carbon dioxide even increased a little. The summer abundance of phytoplankton changed in closest coordination with phosphate (fig. 1.6).

The speed with which the changes occurred was of course influenced by the inflow of low-nutrient water from the inlets. The volume of water entering the lake annually during the period of recovery was 41% of the volume of the lake. This rate of replenishment and dilution is high but not unusual for lakes and it was a factor in the quick response of Lake Washington.

Visible changes were conspicuous. The transparency of a body of water is measured by the depth to which a standard white disc (Secchi disc) can be seen (Collier, Finlayyson, and Cake 1968). Transparency is decreased by an abundance of algae. Until 1963, the transparency had been decreasing each year (fig. 1.4). (See chapter 2 for an explanation.) With the first diversion it stopped decreasing and after that increased year by year. In the early 1970s the lake appeared to have come into equilibrium with its new reduced nutrient supply. The character of the phytoplankton continued to change during 1971–75 in that blue-greens, especially *Oscillatoria*, were progressively becoming scarcer and less obnoxious forms more prominent. The lake seemed to be running backwards in time.

The changes in Lake Washington described above were just what we expected and clearly could be attributed to the diversion of sewage effluent. In 1975 I wrote a paper (published in 1977) called "Trophic equilibrium of Lake Washington." "Equilibrium" does not mean that it is invariant. We could predict that the lake would vary from year to year with changes in weather, but with no long-term trend unless something new happened in the system. The idea was that we had reached or were approaching the end point of the experiment. I could look forward to preparing a series of papers describing the results and finding another interesting lake to study. As it happened, in 1976 the lake abruptly and unexpectedly changed its condition, becoming even more transparent than it had been in its supposedly equilibrium condition, more productive of fish, and it has maintained its interest for us ever since then. But before explaining the new situation, I will describe the public action that led to the recovery of Lake Washington from eutrophication.

## Public Action

One of the most remarkable things about the problem of the pollution of Lake Washington is that it was solved by public action and public vote. Further, the solution did not involve simply transferring the same problem somewhere else. (See chapter 4.) While the sequence of events has been described before, I can here add some information that has not yet been published about the public debates and private correspondence and conversations. I will do this in some detail because I think that the strange behavior of some of the participants typifies a kind of activity that occurs in many debates about environmental problems.

I have already described my ivory-tower research on Lake Washington that started in 1955. A current of public action had started a little earlier. For many years concern had been increasing about the pollution of the lake and of Puget Sound. State and city agencies commissioned a series of major reports by sanitary engineers and other professionals, the first in 1889, and conducted surveys to obtain new data. The Washington State Pollution Control Commission issued reports on two studies of Lake Washington, one of which involved repeated chemical determinations during 1952. It was becoming clear that both Puget Sound and Lake Washington were showing signs of deterioration related to pollution, and that this would increase. The opening of a floating highway bridge across the lake in 1940 facilitated the growth of suburbs. (The effect would have been magnified when a second floating bridge was opened in 1963, except that by then corrective action was being taken.) The concern crystallized into action in 1956 when Mayor Gordon Clinton of Seattle appointed a Metropolitan Problems Advisory Committee headed by James R. Ellis, a local attorney, to study all the different kinds of problems brought on by the urbanization of the Seattle metropolitan area. In July 1956, the city commissioned the engineering firm of Brown and Caldwell to review all previous studies, to study the existing sewerage systems and the condition of the receiving waters, and to make a series of recommendations of alternative plans to deal with sewage. A magnificent report, nearly 600 pages long, was issued in March 1958. It contained a wealth of historical information as well as an assessment of probable future needs, and proposed several alternative plans.

The two currents, basic research and public concern for the environment, merged on 16 December 1956 when a newspaper article appeared that implied that the committee was considering simply enlarging the existing secondary treatment plants. That bothered me, so I wrote a letter to Mr. Ellis expressing my views about the condition of and prospects for Lake Washington. That was the only time I took the initiative in the entire affair. He responded promptly, saying that the committee knew perfectly well that the sewage effluent would have to be diverted from the lake.

This led to an exchange of correspondence in which I wrote an eleven-page letter about the principles of limnology and laid out a series of questions about the lake that I imagined might be asked, and answers to them that could be used in discussion of the problem. That was the beginning of my participation in the action that led to the formation of the Municipality of Metropolitan Seattle (Metro). My function was to feed information to those who needed and wanted it. The letter to Mr. Ellis and an expanded version that I wrote later formed the basis for one of my review papers (1968).

It was clear that sewage could be diverted from Lake Washington to Puget Sound without creating the same kind of problems as in the lake (see chapter 4), but a political mechanism did not exist to allow that. The complicating factor was that several different governmental agencies at different levels were involved, and it would have been very difficult under existing state law for those agencies to finance something jointly. So the first step was to get the state legislature to pass enabling legislation for the formation of metropolitan agencies. The Metro Enabling Act was drafted by Mr. Ellis. It provided for a system in which a public vote could enable any group of communities to cooperate. There were to be two separate voting units, and for a proposal to pass, each unit would have to produce a majority. In the case of the Seattle Metro, one voting unit was the city of Seattle, the other was all the smaller cities and towns concerned. To get the legislation passed took some doing, for there were people who had political objections on the basis that this would be an undesirable form of super government. A young civil engineer, Daniel J. Evans, who had only recently been elected to the Washington House of Representatives, was in charge of the bill. Despite opposition, he was successful and the bill became law. (Later he was elected governor and became a U.S. senator upon the death of Henry M. Jackson.)

Next, the need for a public vote led to a public education campaign. People had to be shown that it was worth committing a great deal of money, in the form of a bond issue, to prevent deterioration of the lake and to make other improvements in the sewerage system. The campaign had several components. The Pollution Control Commission issued a number of informational leaflets. They had the virtue of being small, brief and clear, with each one focused on a single point or a few related points. There were newspaper articles, editorials, and advertisements (fig. 1.7). It was necessary to make reasonable predictions of the condition of the lake if sewage was diverted or if not; that is where

I came in. I gave a few public talks and spoke on radio and television. Mostly I talked to individuals on the telephone and wrote letters.

The aspect of the public campaign most interesting to me was a series of debates in community clubs and other civic organizations, and on television and radio. A very active and vocal opposition to the idea of Metro developed. Typically the pro- and anti-Metro people would present their cases, and sometimes there would be rebuttals. Many of the debates emphasized or even were limited to the Lake Washington problem. The opposition presented reasons against Metro which ranged from the political (it was creeping socialism and Big Brother government) to the scientific (sewage does not affect lakes that way, and if it does, it is too late to do anything about it).

Early in the campaign I began to get telephone calls from pro-Metro debaters who would quote some outrageous comment made by the anti-Metro opponent in a debate the day before and ask me what response he should have made. This led me to listen to one of the broadcasts, and I learned that there was a lot going on that I could not have imagined. On this occasion there was a fascinating exchange:

> Pro-Metro: Are you aware of the work they are doing out at the University of Washington?
> Anti-Metro: Oh, I am sorry you dragged Professor Edmondson's name into this. [He had not mentioned my name.] I don't want to get personal, but algae are plants, and Edmondson is a zoologist. Zoology is the study of animals confined in cages in zoos.

I am told that one of the anti-Metro people would show up at the debates with a textbook of zoology and show pictures of giraffes (maybe monkeys, too) to demonstrate that I could not know anything about "plants." The anti-Metro people did not seem to know that there were such sciences as biology or ecology.

I did not participate personally in the debates. The proposition for Seattle Metro involved several issues in addition to the problem of eutrophication. I did not feel qualified to make recommendations about the structure of governmental agencies or ways of handling public finance. I preferred simply to supply information about things I knew , realizing that it had to be factored in with everything else. In general I did not urge people to vote in a particular way. I intended only to present information that could be a basis for decision. I do not mean that scientists should not become educated in the way political and economic systems work nor that they should not participate in making decisions. My point is that decisions like the one on Metro cannot be based on only the "scientific facts." I would not propose that scientists and economists should merely feed information to some central authority who would make decisions without their further participation. Such decisions require feedback.

People could certainly use my predictions as support for Metro, however. Predictions are always made on the basis of some assumptions, and sometimes they are made in response to specific questions. As I reread some of my letters, I noticed that they could be interpreted as supporting a vote for Metro simply because I would answer a question without repeating all the assumptions. If I wrote "Sewage must be diverted from the lake soon to avoid trouble," somebody who wanted to avoid trouble would take that as an endorsement of a vote for Metro since that was the only mechanism being considered.

My first personal contact with the anti-Metro side was with a lawyer in Renton who telephoned on 10 January 1958 when the legislature was considering the Metro legislation. He had organized the King County Taxpayers' League Against Metro. He told me that he was opposed to Metro because it was a radical change in the form of government and would cost too much, although no cost estimates had yet been made. (I have since learned to be suspicious of any political organization that has "taxpayer" in its title.) He expressed some strange ideas about pollution and Lake

*Fig. 1.7. An example of anti-Metro propaganda published during the first Metro campaign in 1958. It illustrates the argument that the object of the proposition to form Metro was to make the suburbs pay to clean up Seattle's sewage. In fact, at the time the ad appeared, there were three sewage treatment plants discharging into the lake in Renton, one each in Bellevue and Kirkland, six in places outside Seattle not named in the ad, and one being planned for Bothell.*

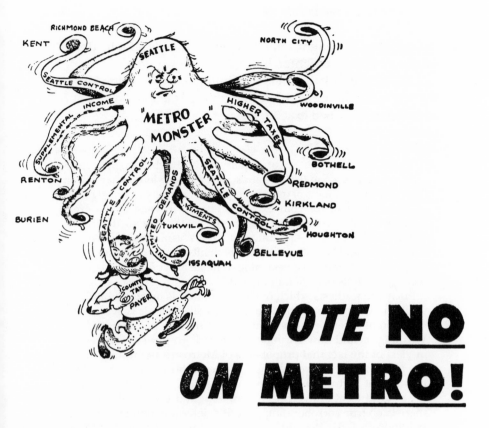

# VOTE NO ON METRO!

## METRO MEANS...

1. Seattle rule and domination.

2. Higher taxes.

3. Arbitrary property assessments, even if 100 per cent of property owners object.

4. Garbage collection, park purchasing and water installation can be added to sewers, planning and transportation without your vote.

5. Unlimited demands on the cities, towns and county for "supplemental income."

6. Tax-supported transportation system.

7. Granting unlimited authority to Seattle officials elected by and answerable only to Seattle.

8. Once Metro is voted in, there is no "getting out" or turning back. Seattle rules forevermore!

9. If Metro passes, the many constitutional and legal defects will result in years of expensive litigation, rather than any constructive action.

10. It is a grab for power by Seattle officials in the fields of transportation, planning, park purchasing, water and garbage collection in addition to sewers, clothed in the emotional appeal of "save Lake Washington now." Once this power is voted in the property owner is subject to unlimited taxes for any of the above purposes, at a time over which he has no further control or voice but solely at the pleasure of Arbitrary Seattle officials "who know what's best for their 'country cousins'." The second Lake bridge is a graphic example.

Washington. I thought something like "There's a lot he doesn't know; I'd better straighten him out."

So I wrote him two letters explaining eutrophication and the known condition of Lake Washington. His answer on 7 February 1958, transcribed exactly, was:

Dear Professor:

In reply to your letters of January 16 and February 5, respectively, I wish to state that the substance of these letters have been examined by members of our committee and we very definitely wish to commend you for your excellent efforts, in view of the great magnitude of the task that has been set for you to determine whether or not there is pollution in Lake Washington and the related waters and how it can best be eliminated. Indeed, we are rather surprised that you have been able to make a hypothesis to the effect that there is pollution in the Lake.

Such a hypothesis which of its very nature is most doubtful, no doubt, might be the starting point for a real scientific survey of the question of ascertaining whether or not there is pollution in Lake Washington and how it can be eliminated. To this end, therefore, in view of the fact that proponents of Metro are attempting to use the hypothesis you are making in order to bring about the establishment of Metro, which is an unwarranted, radical departure in the field of local municipal government, and principally because there is no true corroborating scientific determination that there is pollution in Lake Washington, King County Taxpayers' League Against Metro proposes that as soon as it is feasible there be made available funds by the Governmental Agencies involved here to bring to the City of Seattle a Board of three eminent scientists in the field of botany to study the pollution problem in the Lake and surrounding waters, and to make scientific findings establishing whether or not there is a pollution problem in the Lake and if so, how it can best be controlled.

Yours very truly,

(The man died in 1980 and I see no need to name him here.)

It was a new idea to me that there was doubt about the existence of pollution in Lake Washington. It was widely known that ten sewage treatment plants were contributing about twenty million gallons of sewage to the lake each day.

The Man from Renton telephoned from time to time. I never met him in person, but I spent many hours with him on the telephone and wrote several letters. It eventually became obvious that he was not really after information. He seemed to be looking either for support for his position or for statements from me that could be shown to be incorrect and therefore could be used against the Metro idea. Nevertheless, every time he called, I stayed with him as long as he wanted to talk and tried to correct his misunderstandings, in a nice way, of course. One time I explained about the problem of the depletion of oxygen in deep water by excess biological activity. A few days later he called back and said something like, "Professor, I have done some research on that oxygen problem and you are wrong. Water is $H_2O$ and O means oxygen, so if you have water you have oxygen." In this case I doubt it would have made any difference if I had said *dissolved* oxygen.

He had alternative solutions. One was to fill the lake in, or better, drain it because that would make farmland and eliminate the algae. One time he called to say he had a brilliant idea: use atomic energy. I asked him what we should use it to do and he said: "I don't know; that's for you scientists to decide." This kind of thing is very frustrating to someone who works for an educational institution.

In addition to discussions of scientific matters like the exchanges quoted above, two points occupied most of my time with the man. Much of the conversation was devoted to his desire to have an independent study made. In one conversation he said there should be a panel of twelve botanists brought in to see if Lake Washington had pollution. Later, in his letter of 7 February (quoted above), he moderated this to a panel of three. Their main qualification should be that they had not heard of me or read anything I had published; i.e., they should be ignorant.

The independent study idea seems to have been important to him. To get an actual independent study would have been difficult. No limnologist would have wanted to waste his time doing exactly what somebody else was doing. No granting agency would have wanted to support duplicate work except under extraordinary circumstances. Research grants are made only after intense scrutiny of an application that justifies the study, presents a good plan, and gives evidence of ability to do the work and thinking required. In fact, much relevant work was being done by various people. During 1957, Hollis M. Phillips of the

Seattle Engineering Department did an elaborate chemical study of the water of Lake Washington, of inlet streams, and of the effluent from the sewage treatment plants, among other things. The engineering firm of Brown and Caldwell hired a number of engineering professors from the University of Washington as consultants. Some other engineering firms also interested themselves in the Lake Washington problem. However, nobody was doing the same kind of full-scale limnological study that my associates and I were doing, sampling frequently at many depths in the lake and studying the plankton community in detail. I supplied data to Brown and Caldwell which they used in their report. Later I sent information to Metro on the continued improvement of the lake for their annual reports.

Anyway, after all this fuss about getting a panel of botanists to study the situation, it was a matter of some amusement when the International Botanical Congress met in Seattle in August 1969, attended by 4600 botanists from all over the world. In his opening address, the president of the congress, Professor Kenneth V. Thimann of the University of California at Santa Cruz, commented about the "remarkable achievement of clearing up Lake Washington as a tribute to what can be done when biologists and citizens collaborate." (*Seattle Times*, 25 August 1969, p. 7)

The other point made by the Man from Renton concerned my suspected collusion with Metro supporters. Repeatedly he pushed me to make some public declaration about my attitude toward the Metro legislation, as in a letter dated 29 May 1958, also quoted exactly:

Dear Professor Edmonds: [*sic*]

I wish to acknowledge receipt of your letter of May 23, 1958, wherein you set out again your position with reference to the pollution problem in Lake Washington.

First of all, may I state that it cannot be reasonably disputed that a scientific fact-finding determination by a board of independent scientists as to what the pollution problem in Lake Washington is and that the only manner of solution is by a central agency, should not be made. This determination is owed the people of King County, to set at rest and eliminate the controversy that has been engendered by the proponents of Metro by virtue of their insistence that

a Metro under S. B. 136 is the only solution to the pollution problem in Lake Washington. Therefore, this is a position which in good
conscience and equity our Metropolitan League of Voters cannot
recede from. There then remains the question of your relationship
to the controversy at hand that is the creation of the Metro under
S. B. 136. It would seem that the only reasonable course for you is
to define your existing relationship with reference to the formation of Metro under S. B. 136. Are you, or are you not a propo-
nent? If you are, then no doubt it must be assumed that you will
work for the passage of such an unwarranted and radical departure in the form of our local government and to this extent your
opinion in the scientific phase of the condition of the Lake is weak-
ened in the eyes of the electorate at large. This follows of necessity
from the practicalities and common sense of the situation.

I take it that further exchange of letters will not change your view
point.

Very truly yours,
(signed)

The Man from Renton never did get his independent investigation, but he evidently tried hard. In one of his radio talks he
said that he had obtained a statement from an outside, independent source. He then read very rapidly a statement that seemed
to contradict my position, something to the effect that properly
treated sewage should have no effect on lakes. Two things about
this were striking. One was that it sounded like one sentence out
of a longer statement. The other was, it could be true. One could
define properly treated sewage as that which would not have a
deleterious effect. The trouble was that, as far as I knew, no such
process of treatment was then available.

I wanted to find out more about the statement; what was the
rest of it? After all, if there was something I did not know, I
wanted to find out. So I telephoned the Man from Renton asking for a copy of the whole statement. He refused to give me a
copy or to tell me the name and address of his source. He said it
would be like giving away his case before going to court. This was
a fascinating insight into the difference between legal argumen-
tation and scientific disputes. In science, all the information is
supposed to be made freely available; nothing should be hidden. Apparently this is different in legal debates, although I am
told that there is a limit to the degree to which evidence can be

concealed. Further, scientists try to get all possible evidence before they form a conclusion. If they want to ignore some set of data, they have to present a good, objective reason. Otherwise, they can make fools of themselves.

The Man from Renton had already mentioned that the statement came from a particular research institute in the Southwest. Then, in another radio talk, he blundered and mentioned the name of the author. So, I wrote and eventually got a flippant, completely unhelpful reply from the author. Meantime, the Man from Renton was repeatedly citing the statement as authoritative. I became intensely curious to know what the statement actually said. After more unsatisfactory correspondence with the author, I got a copy of the statement and an explanation from the head of his department: A member of the staff had answered some vague questions from someone in Seattle. He sent me a copy of the questions and the answering letter. The letter to the institute had provided some misinformation about Lake Washington and asked several unintelligible questions. The sentence that had been quoted on the radio was near the end of the answering letter: "The effluent from properly treated sewage should have no effect when emptied into fresh streams or lakes."

A preceding paragraph had indicated ignorance and naivete on the part of the writer rather than any scientific ideas I had missed:

> As to the algal growth destroying the beauty of the lake, that is questionable. Increased algae growth also means improved fishing. Too often algae are considered to be obnoxious, when they really should be credited with the function they perform. Raw sewage will no doubt increase the algal growth. Properly treated sewage should produce an effluent with very low N & P and have little effect upon the aquatic life. No it is not feasible to treat effluent to remove N & P.

The contradiction between the last two sentences tells us something about the expertise of the writer. And of course the kind and quantity of algae will determine their effect, as will be shown in chapter 2. I learned a lot from this incident, and will return to it in the discussion of experts in chapter 15.

I tried to keep the conversations with the Man from Renton objective and focused on real problems, but sometimes he became rather personal. He was quite proud of the "research" he had done on the Lake Washington problem, and felt he had mastered all the concepts. When I objected mildly he said something like "I am equal to you in my profession; maybe I ought to enter your profession and crowd you out of it." I had no idea how he would do that, but did not ask. He then went on to say "I am a graduate of Harvard Law School; I am no fool." Later I regretted that I had not had the presence of mind to tell him the story about the Yale student who transferred to Harvard, thus raising the average IQ of both institutions. I have to be careful with that, for the story can be told in two ways. I have two degrees from Yale and my first teaching job was at Harvard. Both are pretty good places. But it is interesting that several of the people most prominent in the Metro campaign had studied at Yale, including Mr. Ellis, who drafted the Metro legislation.

Only once did I stop a conversation with the Man from Renton. He started by saying, "Professor Edmondson, you are a liar, a thief, and a coward." I was intrigued and asked what he meant. It turned out that I was a liar because what I said about Lake Washington was not true, I was a thief because my efforts had caused a lot of people to spend money unnecessarily, and I was a coward because I refused to debate him in public. After that, the path was downhill, and I hung up.

Later I learned that his behavior made a weird sort of sense. People who knew him told me that he wanted to run for election to the state legislature, and that each time his name was mentioned in the newspapers was worth a thousand dollars in publicity. Apparently he did not think it mattered how his name was mentioned. He did not make it into the legislature.

Finally, on 11 March 1958, Metro came to a vote. It was a glorious concept, covering a large part of the Lake Washington drainage area, and including sewage, transportation, and comprehensive planning. (These three had been selected for priority from a larger list that included solid waste disposal.) Apparently it was a bit too glorious, for while it got a majority of the total votes, it failed in the smaller communities. A stripped-down version, limited to sewage and a smaller area, was submitted to voters on 9 September 1958. This was much easier to accept because it focussed on the most immediate problem of the three and involved a more concerned voting population. The measure passed handily with 59% of a total of about 118,000 votes. While the success of the revised plan can be attributed to its difference from the first, passage was helped by some effective propaganda. A photograph of a group of children standing pathetically beside a sign—"Warning. Polluted Water. Unsafe for bathing."—was widely reprinted and drew new attention to the issue. They were the children of Robert and Dorothy Block, who were active in civic affairs, including the Metro campaign. Almost thirty years later in 1985, they reassembled for another photograph on the same beach, without the warning sign.

In the new plan, the effluent would be diverted from Lake Washington by large trunk sewers, part to a secondary treatment plant near the south end of the lake on the Duwamish River, which runs into Puget Sound, the rest through a primary treatment plant on Puget Sound. (The details will be given in chapter 4.) Lake Washington was not the only body of water to benefit. The seventy million gallons of raw sewage that had been entering Puget Sound along the Seattle waterfront were diverted to the primary treatment plant, making a large improvement in the inshore part of the sound.

When the results of the vote were in, the president of the League of Women Voters said, as I remember it, "If you explain it well enough, people will do the right thing." She does not remember saying it, but I know that somebody did.

The vote provided for a bond issue of $125 million. In a lecture, I once referred to the Metro sewerage system as a $125 million piece of limnological research equipment. A nuclear physicist friend commented that he was glad to know that there was a field of biology more costly than nuclear physics. (Remember, this was about thirty years ago!)

It is interesting that Metro was a completely local enterprise, including the financing. The project was financed by the sale of revenue bonds repaid from sewage service charges, initially $2.00 per month per household. No property taxes or assessments were required. By a remarkable stroke of foresight, the charges were collected from the start of the development program, before the treatment plants were built, so that Metro did not have to borrow to pay interest.

It is worth emphasizing that Metro was founded long before federal environmental programs had developed. The Environmental Protection Agency was created in 1970 by the Clean Water Act, the same year in which the State of Washington Department of Ecology was formed. During its first years Metro gained a reputation for completing projects under budget and in less time than predicted. Of course, Metro has since made use of federal support as it became available.

It is also important to realize that the Metro vote was taken before Lake Washington had deteriorated seriously. While its condition was beginning to be disturbing, it had come nowhere near producing the kind of nuisance that has been so bothersome in Europe and the Midwest of North America, and it never did get that bad. The voters' action made the lake experiment very much better, for we would be able to study the recovery of a large lake in a way that had not been done before, and has not been done very often since. However, the lake did continue to deteriorate during the five years after the vote in 1958, the time it took to assemble the money and staff, design the system, and get enough of it built so that the diversion could start in 1963. The change in the lake during that period was great enough to attract considerable public attention. The dense population of *Oscillatoria* present all summer was the basis of a headline in the *Seattle Post-Intelligencer* on 3 July 1962: "Lake Washington Brown—That's Algae, Not Mud and It'll Be There For The Next 10 Years." The next year, on 5 October the same newspaper had a headline about "Lake Stinko." This of course was highly satisfactory to me. The vote for Metro was based on the predicted condition of the lake, not its condition in 1958, and I liked to see the lake confirm the predicted deterioration. Also, some of my friends had started asking if I would leave town if the lake did not clear up, and so its rapid recovery as predicted was even more pleasing.

The proposition that the Metro project would be a general financial benefit to all property owners was tested in court in 1965, before diversion had a visible effect. Part of the system was a large pipeline laid in a trench dug in the bottom of the lake just offshore from a densely populated area. This involved temporarily dismantling a large number of private household docks. Metro offered a uniform scale of payment for the required easement and rebuilt the docks at no cost to the owners. With one exception the property owners agreed; one wanted a considerably larger payment for the easement. Metro sued to obtain a ruling that their uniform rate was adequate. I testified about the predicted condition of the lake. The judgment was in favor of Metro.

During all this time I lived in my ivory tower with its telephone and typewriter, finding out interesting things about Lake Washington. I felt that what I was doing was simply the normal work of a university professor: to find out things and tell people about them. That is known as research and teaching, and they come in that order because you cannot teach something that has not been found out. Thus, publishing a research paper is an act of teaching. Of course we do not teach only the results of our own work. Most of what we teach is learned by reading journals and books, but they too originate as products of research. I think it is a typical experience among university people to find their research or other original work and teaching to be mutually supportive. In my own case, I found it invaluable to have to review progress in the entire field of limnology every year for my course in the subject. It kept me aware of publications which I might otherwise have missed that helped me in the Lake Washington work. Conversely, the results of the work on Lake Washington produced excellent new examples to illustrate principles. The class had the advantage of learning about new advances in the field that did not get into formal publication until several years later. Further, research technicians paid with federal grant money and using specialized equipment bought from the same source were constantly bringing in freshly collected samples from the lake and I was able to present a much better laboratory course than if I had been totally dependent on state funds.

I enjoyed my contact with the outside world. Part of the professor's job is public service, but in this case it was really a public educational operation. It was not viewed that way by everybody, as I later found out. Dr. Charles Odegaard became president of the University of Washington in 1958. He had not been in that position long when he started getting strange telephone calls from a certain lawyer in Renton who complained that one of the professors was engaging in political activity and therefore should be fired. Dr. Odegaard did not mention it to me at the time, but he did tell me some years later when it was all over. Maybe one of the important functions of a university president is to protect the faculty against harassment.

### Public Response to the Lake Washington Cleanup

Because of widespread concern about pollution problems and the continued deterioration of lakes, the success of the Metro campaign and the response of Lake Washington to the diversion of effluent drew much favorable attention around the world. Metro, even though not a city, received the All-American City Award in 1960. Mr. Ellis's work as leader of the campaign to create Metro won much public recognition. Many articles appeared in newspapers and magazines.

Limnologists had a professional interest in the results, not only as an example of useful application of information but also for the scientific value of the study of the way Lake Washington responded. For one thing, there had been uncertainty among some limnologists about how rapidly such a lake might respond to a nutrient reduction on this scale. In 1965 I had made some optimistic predictions at a congress in Warsaw of the International Association for Theoretical and Applied Limnology (SIL) about the speed with which I expected lake Washington to recover. Some of the European limnologists were skeptical, and a Swiss bet me a bottle of liquor that it would take much longer to recover. One of the criteria for me to win was that the transparency in 1971 would have to exceed the maximum seen in the summer of 1950, 4.0 meters. We made measurements with increasing frequency during 1971. When one of the assistants came in from a trip on the lake announcing that the transparency was more than 4.0 m, I went out on the lake as soon as possible. I did not doubt her accuracy, I just wanted to see it myself: 4.5 m. The bet was paid off several years later at a meeting in Kiel.

In the meantime, another congress of SIL was about to take place in Leningrad in August 1971. I had been asked to give a report on the condition of Lake Washington. I was able to give them the fresh good news about the transparency, illustrated with a color slide of a celebratory cake decorated with an icing graph showing the seasonal change of transparency in 1950 and 1971. The newspaper, *Komsomolskaya Pravda* on 25 August 1971 carried an article about the congress; most of the space was given to an account of Lake Washington. To show the extent of interest in the lake at that early time, I include a translation here. The dramatic opening paragraph refers to the bet that had been made about the rate of recovery of the lake. People familiar with the Lake Washington situation will recognize that a certain amount of creative imagination has been applied by the journalist.

### HOW THEY SAVED THE LAKE

And then he made a bet. The wager, from his side, wasn't subject to value in dollars—Doctor Edmondson risked his good name as a scientist. His opponents (among them were Congressmen and even colleagues—specialists) forewarned him of failure. He himself knew that in the event of failure the owners of factories, which had been forced to cough up $20 million, would try to do everything so that Edmondson the scientist no longer existed.

Doctor Edmondson turned out to be right. At the plenary session of the XVIII International Limnological Congress his paper "The Present Condition of Lake Washington" brought forth enthusiastic applause, somewhat, if you please, unexpected in the restrained scientific auditorium. This stormy reaction, better than anything, said: Limnologists are extremely interested in the practical applications of their research and discoveries; they are sincerely glad about the successes of their colleagues who have averted the ruin of lakes, rivers and reservoirs.

About 30 years ago sewage and industrial wastes from surrounding enterprises began to be dumped into Lake Washington. The first signs of pollution caused alarm among scientists and local residents, but the managers and owners of the enterprises turned a deaf ear: they said the lake is big, there's a lot of water in it—we won't poison it all. In the 1950s, to put it plainly, a biological explosion developed in the lake: blue-green algae and plankton began to multiply catastrophically; the water became muddy. In 1962, after a thorough investigation, competent commissions pronounced the verdict: the lake had become poisonous.

Dr. Edmondson put forth more than a little effort to save the lake. He appealed to the state government, to the owners of the enterprises. When scientific reasoning didn't help, he and his supporters created commissions and societies to defend Lake Washington from final death. In the end, a special vote by the people of the state was needed to restrain the enterprises. After this, sewage treatment plants and diversions of sewage to other places began to be built.

Naturally, the scientific prognosis of Dr. Edmondson played an important role in this whole story. In part he stated: If we stop dumping wastes into the lake, it will return to its former condition in a very short time, literally in several years; water's ability to cleanse itself will perform a miracle. And thus he put to test his name as a scientist, maintaining that by 1971 the condition of the lake would be much better than it was in 1950.

The first stage of diversion of wastes from the lake was completed in 1963. In 1968 the dumping of wastes into Lake Washington had completely stopped.

Here before the participants of the Limnological Congress, a scientist has demonstrated the diagram of the process by which a lake was returned to its former condition. On the screen before us appeared graphs depicting the decrease in the lake of nitrogen and phosphorus, and changes in the acid content. In conclusion Dr. Edmondson employed a most "unscientific" argument: he showed a color photograph of a beach on Lake Washington crowded with bathers. The picture was taken during the swimming season of this year.

Naturally, it's understood that the scientific value of this work isn't contained wholly in the photograph or even in this story. The scientist succeeded for the first time in compiling a scientific prognosis for the recovery of a lake and make a "cardiogram" of this process.

The conclusions made by Dr. Edmondson as a result of his observations of the recovering lake allow us to hope that with rational management polluted bodies of water can be cured. More than that, upon receiving the prescription for curing a lake, scientists can now actively influence this process and can help nature to restore its strength.

At the meetings of sections and symposia which took place within the framework of the XVIII Limnological Congress, many Soviet and foreign scientists presented their papers which were dedicated to the rational use of the natural resources of rivers, lakes, and reservoirs. Contained in some of these presentations were valuable scientific conclusions and practical recommendations. Some limnologists are presently trying to make models of the processes which take place in bodies of water and are trying to find ways of increasing fish productivity of lakes. The papers of several Soviet scientists were dedicated to this topic.

A. Yurkov
(Special Correspondent)
[translation by Mary Cruger]

The Lake Washington situation produced information that has been useful in two ways. The sensitivity of the response of Lake Washington has increased our understanding of the factors that affect the ability of a lake to respond to restorative actions. The public action that established Metro can be used as a model for dealing with problems that require interaction of scientific knowledge and public values.

## The *Daphnia* Era

As previously stated, Lake Washington sprang a big surprise on us in 1976 by suddenly becoming more transparent than it had been at any time in recorded history (fig. 1.8). It was as if we had a new lake with the same name and in the same location. (Transparency is regarded as a favorable characteristic for lakes. An engineering study that included Lake Washington showed that there is a relation between property values and the perceived quality of nearby lakes [Dornbusch 1976].) There was no way to explain this abrupt change as part of the normal recovery process resulting from the diversion of sewage effluent. It appeared that the lake had switched to a different state. Some basic change must have taken place in addition to the reduction in nutrients.

It was not difficult to find the immediate cause of the change in transparency, but to explain how it happened took a bit more thought and work. Lake Washington not only had renewed its interest for us as an object of scientific research, but had given us a problem more challenging than the original eutrophication problem.

Actually, the lake had given subtle warning signals that something was happening during several years before the abrupt change. Although I did not realize it in 1950, one of the strange things about Lake Washington was that, although it had a lively population of planktonic animals, *Daphnia* was not one of them. *Daphnia* is a small crustacean about one-eighth inch (2 or 3 mm) long that can be very abundant in some lakes, but is not successful in all. Lake Sammamish contained a population of *Daphnia*. During the entire period of eutrophication when we were studying Lake Washington intensively, *Daphnia* would ap-

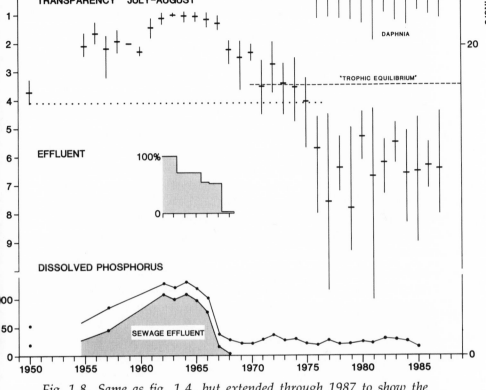

*Fig. 1.8. Same as fig. 1.4, but extended through 1987 to show the* Daphnia *era. The "trophic equilibrium" was not permanent. The summer abundance of* Daphnia, *June–August, is shown at the upper right.*

pear only rarely in the samples, and in very small numbers. Presumably they entered through the Sammamish River and other inlets but did not find conditions in Lake Washington to be suitable. In some years we would see no specimens at all. When a few appeared, they were the subject of considerable comment in the laboratory, but there were so many interesting things to think about that I did not pursue it as a problem.

In 1972, after an absence of two years, and again in 1973, a few *Daphnia* were collected on just one day of the year. In 1974, a more noticeable population developed and persisted for twenty-one weeks, with a maximum of nearly five animals per liter. This event was so impressive that, rather than ending the study, I requested renewed support from the National Science Foundation and intensified the sampling. The population in 1975 was smaller than in 1974, but in 1976 there was a population explosion with the numbers rising to about forty individuals per liter. *Daphnia* has been continuously present since then, persisting in very low numbers during the winter and becoming abundant every spring through the fall.

*Daphnia* is well known among limnologists for its ability to remove small particles, including algae, from the water by feeding. It does not eat large particles, so that the larger colonies of algae are left behind. The water may become very clear but look somewhat flaky with pinhead size colonies. Limnologists have been working to find ways to encourage the growth of *Daphnia* populations because of their ability to improve the appearance of lakes by grazing on small algae. This approach to protection and restoration of lakes has been called *biomanipulation;* one makes small changes that enable natural processes to help solve problems, rather than imposing large engineering projects. (See chapter 16.)

So there was no mystery about the increase in the transparency of Lake Washington, but what was not obvious at first was why *Daphnia* suddenly became so abundant. Here we have a situation that is common in ecological-environmental studies: something unexpected happens, how do we explain it? By the time the event has occurred, the opportunity is gone for doing special field experiments. What we can do when a detailed study has already been made is to use our knowledge of mechanisms of population control and search the records for relevant features that may have been involved in the observed change. Thus one develops a circumstantial account of what probably happened, and if there is enough information, the probability of being correct is high. The probability can be increased by special observations or experiments, and we did that with Lake Washington. Naturally, we had not limited our study of Lake Washington to chemistry and phytoplankton. We knew that the zooplankton could be affected by changes in the phytoplankton, so we had been making detailed censuses, and we had a good description of what the zooplankton had been doing all along. We also knew that changes were occurring in the watershed, and were aware of studies of fish.

The details of our explanation of the sudden success of *Daphnia* have been published. Here I will give only the highlights. The story is rather like that of the house that Jack built, because each successive answer led to another question. The question of why *Daphnia* succeeded so dramatically may be reversed to ask why the lake suddenly became hospitable to *Daphnia,* for that leads us to look for changes in the condition of the lake that might be responsible. There is good reason to think that between 1933 and 1976 *Daphnia* was suppressed by one or both of two conditions, one having to do with its own food and the other with *Daphnia* as food for other animals.

The *Daphnia* story includes in part a chain of predation (as did the house that Jack built). A field of ecology that has been drawing increasing attention since the time of Darwin is that of the interaction of species, specifically the effects of competition and predation in determining the success of species. There has been much fruitless argument about which of the two processes is more important, competition or predation. Whatever is the answer to that non-question, there can be no doubt that predation can be exceedingly important in determining the success of the prey species in many biological communities, and Lake Washington is no exception. The concept of the keystone predator, one whose feeding activity has an effect on community structure that is out of proportion to its abundance, has been well established. (See the papers by Paine 1969, 1980.)

From 1933 to the mid-1960s Lake Washington was inhabited by a significant population of a shrimp-like animal, *Neomysis mercedis.* Between 1962 and 1967, *Neomysis* decreased to about 10% of its former abundance, and its vertical distribution in the water changed. While little was known about the ecology of *Neomysis* at the time, its close relative *Mysis relicta* was well known to be a voracious predator specializing on *Daphnia. Mysis* had been introduced into a number of lakes with the hope of improving food conditions for certain fish. In every case that has been studied, large changes in zooplankton followed. For example, in 1963

*Mysis* and Kokanee salmon were introduced into Lake Tahoe; *Daphnia* essentially disappeared although the salmon made little use of it. With information like that and the background of predation ecology available, it seemed to me very probable that the decrease of *Neomysis* had permitted the population resurgence of *Daphnia*. This idea was explored intensively in a Ph.D. study by Paul Murtaugh. It received strong support from his experiments showing that the Lake Washington *Neomysis* was in fact a specialized selective predator, taking *Daphnia* over all other items of food when given a choice.

While the explanation was reasonable, there was a serious discrepancy: the timing was wrong. Why did it take about nine years for *Daphnia* to increase after *Neomysis* had decreased? I seriously considered the idea that it might simply take that long for a founding population of *Daphnia* to get into the lake after the predation pressure decreased, but the isolated occurrences that we had seen in several years showed that there were enough to get a continuing population started much earlier. Something else had to be going on. We scrutinized the record for changes in other features known to affect the success of *Daphnia*.

And here we came to consider the activity of grazing, the feeding of *Daphnia* on its phytoplankton foods. Food was an obvious feature to examine. On the basis of what we knew about *Daphnia's* requirements, we saw nothing in the phytoplankton record to suggest that it had been suppressed for lack of food before 1976. No major increase in edible species took place in 1976. Special experiments were done later with *Daphnia* from Lake Washington by two visiting scientists, Dr. Aida Infante of the University of Caracas, Venezuela and Dr. Annie Duncan of the University of London, England. They confirmed the early evaluation.

Conditions affecting the use of food were another possibility. One of the striking things to emerge from our scrutiny of the phytoplankton record was a progressive decrease in the abundance of *Oscillatoria* from its maximum in 1968 to 1976, when it occurred in very small numbers, to its disappearance in 1977. The blue-greens in general have a reputation of being less useful as food for planktonic invertebrates than other algae for both mechanical and chemical reasons. Specific information was becoming available in the literature that helped us to interpret the phytoplankton data. *Oscillatoria* interferes mechanically with the feeding apparatus of *Daphnia* in such a way as to prevent the *Daphnia* from making full use of a supply of good food organisms. *Oscillatoria* forms thin filaments, about 4–10 micrometers (0.0016–0.0040 inch) in diameter and about 500 micrometers long. (My hair is about 94 micrometers in diameter.) *Daphnia* creates a current in the water with its legs and then uses them to remove suitable particles from the water and transport them to its mouth. If a large organism gets into the filter chamber, the animal rejects the entire mass of food present by flexing its body, and starts filtering all over again. A mass of *Oscillatoria* makes a sort of log jam among the animal's legs and will be rejected along with whatever food is present in the feeding stream at that time. Further, the muscular effort involved in rejection takes much energy. It seems probable that after the removal of predation pressure in 1967, *Daphnia* was delayed in its success by the continued presence of *Oscillatoria* until 1976. This interpretation was strengthened by special experiments with *Daphnia* and *Oscillatoria* from Lake Washington. Reproduction and growth of young individuals were significantly decreased by concentrations of *Oscillatoria* even lower than those in the lake before 1976.

While the decrease of *Oscillatoria* could clearly be attributed to the diversion of sewage, the decrease of *Neomysis* could not be connected with diversion by any known limnological mechanism; so we tried to find something else, and realized that there had been another signal of change several years before the *Daphnia* era.

Few people in the Seattle area who read the newspapers or looked at television could be unaware that the sockeye salmon (*Onchorhynchus nerka*) suddenly became conspicuous in Lake Washington in the mid-1960s. This was of great local interest because of the potential of a multimillion dollar sport and commercial fishery. Young salmon had been planted in the Cedar River in 1935, but apparently maintained only a small population, and the salmon attracted little public interest before 1960. Estimates made of the fish returning to the spawning area (escapement) during 1960–66 showed relatively small, but increasing numbers, from 2100 to 68,500. Regular annual counts started in 1967 when the number was 189,400. In 1970 commercial fishing was permitted in the lake.

Adult fish returning from the ocean enter Lake Washington in summer through the ship canal and in autumn swim up the Cedar River, which is their principal spawning area. In the spring the fingerlings come down into the lake, and stay for one year before going to sea, where they feed and grow for three years.

There is no way that the abrupt increase of returning salmon in 1967 can be attributed to the cleanup of the lake. Most of the fish returning in 1967 had developed from eggs that had been laid in the Cedar River in 1963. They had spent their first year of life in Lake Washington at the height of eutrophication, and the conditions in the lake in 1963 were not responsible for the number of fish returning in 1963. Their parents had developed from eggs laid in 1957, near the beginning of pronounced eutrophication. In 1957, there had been no major increase in the zooplankton food used by the young salmon entering the lake from the river. However, the large increase of salmon returning in 1967 signaled that something in the Lake Washington system must have changed earlier. This impression was confirmed when we learned that another species of fish that spawns in the Cedar River, the longfin smelt (*Spirinchus thaleichthys*), had increased in 1960. This fact suggested that some change might have taken place in the river that improved spawning conditions or survival of both species. If so, it must have been a widespread change since the two fish spawn in different parts of the river at somewhat different times of year. The smelt is another keystone predator, specializing in *Neomysis,* and could have accounted for the decrease of *Neomysis.* Here is another potential link in the chain of predation that led to the success of *Daphnia.*

Again, we searched relevant records to find out whether there had been any change that could have improved conditions for both salmon and smelt. In fact, there had been a major change.

Heavy snowmelt in the mountains had been causing the Cedar River to flood, rise over its banks and erode cliffs of glacial deposits. Slides and slope failures made the cliffs collapse into the river, covering much of the downstream river bed with clay. With the increase in development along the river this became a problem because the flood waters eroded large areas of cleared land and damaged the houses built on them. To reduce property loss, local agencies started a program of dredging during the summer to deepen the lower section of the river (the artificial channel that was dug in 1916 to divert the Cedar River into the lake). This permitted faster flow and reduced the rise of water during the following winter. The dredged gravel was thrown up on the banks. It seems obvious that this program was no way to treat somebody's spawning bed. However, this disturbance ceased in 1947 when the dredge broke down and was not replaced. In 1959 there was an especially severe flood, and the agencies then started a new program of building revetments in the upper part of the river. These are piles of large boulders ("riprap") laid along the shoreline. They confine the water to the river bed and prevent erosion of the higher banks. Between 1960 and 1965, about 30% of the length of the banks became protected by revetments, mostly in the locations of most rapid erosion. The spawning beds were no longer stirred up every summer by dredging nor were they smothered by clay during the winter.

So, on the basis of information available to me as I write this summary, I think that the probable explanation of the success of *Daphnia* involved a chain of circumstances. Between 1933 (the first detailed study of the lake) and about 1967 *Daphnia* was suppressed by predation by *Neomysis*. Between about 1955 and 1976 *Daphnia* was suppressed by interference with its feeding by *Oscillatoria*. Between 1955 and 1967 it was suppressed by both. *Oscillatoria* decreased between 1964 and 1967 as a predicted result of the diversion of sewage. After 1967 *Neomysis* was reduced by predation by an increased population of long-fin smelt. Both the smelt and the salmon were able to increase after spawning conditions in the Cedar River were improved.

Some uncertainties exist, however. Possibly still another predator might have been involved. Indirect evidence suggests that the northern squawfish (*Ptychocheilus oregonensis*) decreased in abundance during the early 1960s. To-day it is a significant predator on salmon and smelt in the lake. However, data on its actual abundance in the early years do not exist, and it is not known if the squawfish could have been part of the control of the smelt and salmon. I am still trying to locate all sources of additional information about changes in the Cedar River. It is of course possible that my explanation will have to be modified, but at present I am reasonably satisfied with it.

It would be well worth while to find out as much as possible about the conditions that led to the success of the sockeye salmon, for it has a large potential commercial and recreational value, but has not been as productive as was hoped at first. Nevertheless, in 1988 the salmon returned in unusually large numbers: "Sockeye run called biggest in 11 years," according to the *Seattle Times* for 12 July 1988. The lake had been closed to salmon fishing for the three previous years. Survival of the salmon during their first year, spent in the lake before migrating, has been unexpectedly low. Also, survival at sea is less than expected. The matter is being studied and debated by the two state agencies involved, the Department of Fisheries (in charge of the salmon) and the Department of Wildlife (in charge of the other fish, including rainbow trout which they are stocking in Lake Washington.) Fisheries suspects that predation by trout accounts for the low survival of the salmon in the lake. Trout do indeed eat small salmon, but Wildlife thinks the number is insignificant.

If my explanation for the success of the salmon is correct, the cost of the revetment program in relation to the financial value of the salmon is of considerable interest. So we made a preliminary analysis of what data we could get on the cost of the revetments and the value of the salmon. Since the data extend from 1964 to 1985, I have adjusted the values for each year to the 1985 level of the U.S. dollar, using U.S. government figures.

An estimate of the cost of the revetment program was obtained from files of the King County Public Works Department. The initial construction costs were the equivalent of $2,536,000 during 1961–73, supplemented by $1,014,000 for reconstruction following a major flood in December 1975, totalling $3,550,000. Only recorded governmental expenditures are included; this figure does not include costs of privately built revetments.

The benefits were calculated as the value of the sockeye salmon fishery originating in Lake Washington. The data, supplied by the Washington Department of Fisheries, consisted of the amounts paid to commercial fishermen during 1970–85 and the weight of fish caught by sportsmen in Lake Washington during 1964–85. We did not subtract the costs to the fishermen for their catch. The total value was $6,037,000. This figure also is an underestimate, since the records for the considerable commercial catch between 1964 and 1970 were inadvertently destroyed.

Despite the deficiencies in the data, it is clear that the revetment program produced a benefit considerably more than its total cost. Since the revetments were not built for the purpose of producing a fishery, but to protect property against damage by floods, the benefit of the salmon fishery really accrued as an unforeseen side effect at no cost at all. Moreover, the benefits will continue to accrue as long as the salmon continue to return in adequate numbers, as they did in 1988. Of course, a more appropriate measure of the benefit would be the potential repair costs incurred by flood damage and reduced property values that would have resulted had the revetments not been built. I am not prepared to attempt this rather speculative calculation, which would be more appropriately made through the collaboration of a hydrologist, a real estate agent, and a flood insurance adjuster.

## Milfoil

*Daphnia* was not the only organism to become prominent suddenly in Lake Washington in 1976. The new invader, the Eurasian water milfoil (*Myriophyllum spicatum*) attracted much more public attention than did *Daphnia,* although not as favorable.

Milfoil is a graceful, submerged plant consisting of a long, flexible, loosely rooted stem with many finely divided feathery leaves. It grows rapidly and forms dense underwater jungles reaching up close to the surface. Unlike many other aquatic plants it can break loose from the bottom easily and form floating mats of intertangled stems. When it is abundant in a lake it is regarded as a nuisance because it entangles boat propellers, water skis, sailboat keels and swimmers. However, stands of milfoil have the same beneficial effects as many other aquatic plants in providing cover for fish and food for fish and birds.

*Myriophyllum spicatum* was introduced into the eastern part of North America near the end of the nineteenth century and spread westward. It reached Michigan by 1962 and Minnesota by 1970. The time of introduction into Lake Washington is not known, but it was first widely noticed in Union Bay of Lake Washington in 1973, and by 1976 it was becoming a nuisance reported in the press: "Bird-born aquatic weed has moved to Union Bay" (headline in *Seattle Times*, 25 July 1976). A year later it was worse: "Milfoil takes over lake" (headline in *University of Washington Daily*, 26 September 1977).

Union Bay has received more attention than other bays in the lake because of its many users and its greater size. Actually, Union Bay is more like a big pond nearly separated from the lake (fig. 1.3). It is only 6–10 feet deep, aside from the twenty-eight foot deep dredged ship channel that bisects it. Part of the bay is bordered by extensive marshes that attract many species of birds. Such wetlands are a most unusual amenity for a densely populated city area (Higman and Larrison 1951). At first there was confusion about the cause of the outbreak of milfoil. Many people thought that the floating masses of milfoil were mats of algae. With the eutrophication experience fresh in mind, some people thought that the outbreak must have something to do with pollution. One of my telephone callers was sure that Metro was surreptitiously pouring sewage into Union Bay. Knowledge that the lake was much more transparent than before generated a different hypothesis, that the increased transparency permitted light to strike deeper into the water and support increased plant growth. I entertained this idea briefly myself until I remembered my first trips through Union Bay in 1949 when I saw stands of aquatic plants growing in the deepest places, fully as dense as the beds of milfoil are now. They were mostly pond weeds (*Potamogeton*). So we were not seeing increased plant growth, but a change in the dominant species of the plant community. We were experiencing just one more example of the way an introduced species can spread into a new region and outcompete the existing species. Hundreds of lakes across the country had had the same experience with milfoil before Lake Washington. Many other lakes in Washington and British Columbia now have nuisance growths of milfoil; obviously the diversion of sewage from Lake Washington is not responsible for their milfoil.

There has been a great deal of discussion about how to control the milfoil in Union Bay. Several techniques have been developed, especially in the Midwest of the United States. There are two major types of control. One is mechanical, usually by harvesting with large floating machines that cut and collect the weeds for use as compost outside the lake. The other is chemical; many different aquatic herbicides have been developed. A more recent technique involves laying down strips of plastic screen that prevent the plants from growing up into the water.

Many of the boat-owning residents were eager for immediate control with herbicides. Others who were uneasy about spreading poisonous materials around a swimming and fishing area preferred mechanical means. Union Bay has long been a favorite place for bird watchers because of the rich fauna, and those who value having such a facility in the middle of a city were not eager for any control at all. In any case, much of Union Bay has been designated as a nature preserve and the amount of disturbance permitted is limited.

Metro and some other agencies opposed chemical control, so exploratory studies of other methods were made cooperatively between Metro and the University of Washington Civil Engineering Department. One problem about the use of harvesting machines is that milfoil breaks easily and the small pieces can take root. One of the experiments was to study the effectiveness of the bottom-covering method. It obviously would be impractical to cover the whole bottom of the bay, 360 acres (146 hectares), but it was thought that lanes could be made so that boats could get from docks to deep water without being fouled by the milfoil.

The study program led to a most unfortunate incident, an example of a kind of arrogance that is too common. The investigators had spent a great deal of time studying conditions in Union Bay and scuba divers had staked out a suitable place for the study plots, naturally the best area they could find in the bay. Before the experiments could be made the plants over a large part of the study plots died. The evidence is clear that somebody had illegally used herbicides. Signs had to be put up to warn against swimming and fishing in the area, and new study plots found. Eventually tests were made and showed that the plastic screen could be used effectively.

The milfoil problem is an excellent illustration of a conflict among groups of people with widely different priorities and interests. What is the best function of Union Bay—a swimming pool, a race course for water skiers, or a unique city nature preserve?

### The Case of the Starving Salmon

Soon after salmon became prominent in Lake Washington in 1967, questions were raised about the possible deleterious effect of the cleanup of the lake on these fish because of reduced amounts of food organisms. In fact, the juvenile salmon did grow to a somewhat larger size in 1968 than in the following three years. They were, however, still considerably larger when they migrated after one year than those in some of the important salmon-producing lakes in Alaska that migrate after two years in a lake. Of course fish populations are affected by the productivity of the lakes in which they live, but Lake Washington in its present state still has a higher basic productivity than the important salmon-producing lakes in Alaska. Among fisheries biologists Lake Washington has the reputation of being the world's champion lake for the size of its juvenile sockeyes.

I had an amusing but also rather disturbing experience with the problem of the allegedly starving fish in Lake Washington. In 1971 *Water in the News*, a publication of the Soap and Detergent Association, quoted an interview in *Nation's Business* with the late Dr. Philip Handler, then president of the National Academy of Sciences. Part of the report read:

> Lake Washington, near Seattle, was called a dying body of water a few years ago. By dint of enormous political effort the situation was turned around; that is, the amount of untreated [sic] sewage going into the lake was markedly reduced.
>
> Since this has happened, I am told, the lake has difficulty in supporting salmon, the game fish that was at the top of the food ladder. Smaller fish have taken over, much as in Lake Erie, but for quite different reasons.
>
> Please understand that no one in his right mind would favor going back to polluting Lake Washington. My point is that ecosystems are very complex; some are very fragile, others self-sustaining. Any steps that the government takes in the public interest must first be carefully weighed for all possible consequences.

This was surprising news to me, so I wrote to Dr. Handler to ask the source of his information. His response included:

My 'information" concerning the state of Lake Washington was second-hand but came to me from an extremely reputable scientist who in turn informed me that it came from one of the scientists in the Seattle region who had been among the leaders in stimulating the social and political action required to reverse what had been happening to the lake.

With a little more correspondence I tracked the rumor down to what I had thought was a friendly, bantering conversation that I had had the year before with the "reputable scientist," who turned out to be a mutual acquaintance. He and I stood on the deck of my house looking over Lake Washington. Somehow the question of the condition of the salmon came up. I suggested that if it turned out that the growth of salmon were adversely affected by the cleanup, it might be nice if we could trickle in just the right amount of sewage to maximize fish food production without making algal nuisances. When this conversation was reported to Handler later it somehow got scrambled and turned into a positive statement that the salmon were in trouble. I did not find out where the idea about the lake being taken over by small fish came from. I do not know why Dr. Handler thought that the sewage was untreated, but I have my suspicions; this bit of misinformation was being widely circulated by the soap and detergent people, whose tactics will be discussed in chapter 3.

I was once asked by a local fisheries biologist early in the eutrophication of Lake Washington why I was worried about the sewage when at the same time I was involved in deliberately fertilizing another lake. (See Bare Lake, chapter 12.) The idea of titrating Lake Washington with sewage effluent at a controlled rate is based on a valid concept of lake productivity (discussed in chapter 2), although it is impracticable. The idea as applied to Lake Washington was impractical for several reasons. It would require considerable research to determine the limits within which the sewage would have to be controlled. It would require an expensive program of continuously monitoring the lake to adjust the dosage to weather conditions that would affect the phytoplankton. It would also require construction and maintenance of facilities to deliver effluent to the lake. This would not substitute for the diversion system that was built, for much of the effluent would still have to be detoured from the lake. The cost would surely exceed the commercial value of the salmon produced. Further, although I had great respect for the intelligence of the voting public in this area after the Metro campaign, it would have been exceedingly difficult to persuade them that it would be all right to turn around and build an expensive system to return part of the effluent to the lake.

Finally, there is a Universal Lesson in the episode of Handler's interview. It is common for information to be scrambled by successive transmissions, especially by vocal communication. So, check your sources, the sources of your sources, and if possible get it in writing.

### The Present Condition of Lake Washington

At present, in 1990, Lake Washington is in excellent condition for a lake in an urban area. The transparency is rarely less than 17 feet (5 meters) and is usually much more. The lake still produces algae, including a small portion of blue-greens, but the algae are not a nuisance. While it is well used for all types of recreation, including fishing, the lake also continues to be a fascinating object of scientific research. In 1988, after being in a fairly steady state since 1976, it gave a signal of entering a new phase. There was an abrupt increase in a chemical property called alkalinity (acid neutralizing capacity). There were also changes in the small concentrations of phosphate and nitrate in the water. We are exploring the idea that the new condition is a response to accelerating land development in the drainage area. When a forested area is bulldozed, exposing subsoil, and is replaced by a housing development with concrete streets and storm drains, the chemical content of the streams draining the area is likely to be changed. This kind of activity has been going on at an increasing rate for many years along the east side of Lake Washington.

Changes in the chemical environment as large as those observed can be expected to affect the character of the phytoplankton, with consequences for the zooplankton. The lake with its present supply of phosphate is unable to support massive blooms, but the kinds of algae produced by that supply can be controlled partly by the alkalinity. High alkalinity encourages blue-greens, other things being equal.

Although the blue-greens tend to form colonies, or clumps of cells, and may be noticed more readily than other types of algae, I do not expect Lake Washington to start producing nuisance blooms. Nevertheless, we need to keep aware of any changes. For example, in recent months, for reasons that are not understood, toxic and potentially toxic populations of the blue-green *Anabaena* have appeared in American Lake and in Clear Lake, each about 25 miles away, which had not been reported to produce such blooms previously. (For additional information about toxic algae, see chapters 2 and 10.) *Anabaena* has been present in Lake Washington in small quantities for many years, but has been scarce recently. We are working to find out exactly what is going on and why. Stay tuned.

## Conclusions

The preceding description of the Lake Washington experience is more than just an account of historical events. It can also provide a guide for thinking about other environmental problems. The two components described, scientific research and public action, are intermixed in all current environmental problems. The key to the successful solution of a problem is to identify the kind of scientific knowledge required to assess it and the kinds of corrective actions available.

An unusual aspect of the Lake Washington situation was the extent and character of the scientific background. The studies of 1933 and 1950 showed what the lake was like before pollution was far advanced, and the accidental sighting of *Oscillatoria* in 1955 assured that the early stages of deterioration would be studied in detail. While many of the deteriorated lakes in Europe had been studied early by pioneer limnologists for their scientific interest or by fish biologists because of their important fisheries, not many lakes had been studied in adequate detail during the process of deterioration. Also, it has not been clearly recognized that some nuisance lakes are productive of algae for natural reasons having nothing to do with human activities.

There were other unusual things about the Lake Washington situation. The problem was localized to the lake and the part of Puget Sound immediately adjacent to Seattle so that public awareness was clearly focused on local conditions. It could be solved by immediately available technology. And, despite the report in *Komsomolskaya Pravda*, there were no large industrial interests whose financial success was threatened. Of course, it was understood that there would be a cost, expressed as an increase in utility bills for all individuals and businesses in the area served by Metro. A few companies threatened to leave Seattle if the charges were too high, but the rates were adjusted and there were no defections. The Metro sewage system was built under budget and completed sooner than scheduled, and the initial sewer charge was less than first announced.

The public action about Lake Washington is a useful guide for future public actions, for the public education campaign preceding the vote was unusual. In general the pro-Metro propaganda was accurate. The leaflets issued by state agencies presented clear, concise descriptions of the problems, and were objective, even when urging a vote for Metro. The debates gave a good chance for arguments against Metro to be presented to a wide audience. The newspapers printed letters to the editor and carried paid advertising on both sides of the issue. The important thing is that the voters were provided with information as well as informed opinion to use in making their decision. They were not deciding simply on the basis of emotional statements about Big Brother or Dead Lake. Indeed, there was some emotional involvement; people properly got excited about the issues and threw themselves into the campaign. It is possible that some of the pro-Metro debaters overstated the potential damage to the lake, but the anti-Metro people were not completely innocent of exaggeration.

Among many unusual features, perhaps the most unusual was the public action that led to the formation of Metro. The work was done by dozens of citizens who volunteered their time and effort to the educational and planning activities. No group, however talented, can function without strong, intelligent leadership. While we recognize the special efforts of those people involved in planning and those who did the actual day-to-day committee work, debating, and everything else needed, if any one person is to be considered responsible for the success of Metro it is James R. Ellis, who seems to have had a knack for organization and persuasion. He is sometimes called the "Father of Metro" which is quite appropriate because he both wrote the enabling legislation, and, by chairing the Advisory Committee, guided it through birth to maturity. The lesson to learn here is, I think, that without strong guidance from someone with the character of Mr. Ellis, a project of the scope, complexity and imagination of Metro will fail.

Of course not all environmental decisions are made by public vote; some are made by elected governmental officials or by people delegated by them. But in all cases, there has to be the same kind of evaluation of information and conflicting interests and attention to public support. Otherwise, the results can be disastrous, as they were with the Washington Public Power Supply System (WPPSS, better known as WHOOPS for its dismal failure). The Supply System was created in 1957 in the same legislative session that passed the Metro legislation, but in a separate act that did not require a public vote. Contrary to the way Metro functioned, electrical rates were not to be increased until the plants were producing power. As a result of this and some other planning errors, coupled with unforeseen inflation, WPPSS completed only one of the five nuclear plants started and accomplished the largest default on its construction bonds in municipal history.

Finally, of all aspects of the Lake Washington situation, possibly the least expected was the apparent effect on the lake of the revetment program in the Cedar River. After all, the clear-cut response of the phytoplankton to the diversion of sewage was to be expected, and the condition of the lake between 1971 and 1976 was acceptable in terms of its public appearance. If my interpretation is correct, after 1976 the lake was improved in three distinct ways that can be cataloged as unforeseen, beneficial, indirect side effects of the program to reduce flood damage in the Cedar River, done with no consideration of effects on the lake:

1. The increase in transparency of Lake Washington in 1976 was over and above what could have been expected from the diversion of sewage alone. It required the help of *Daphnia*.
2. A second effect of *Daphnia* has been to provide an increase in the food supply of the rainbow trout which has been stocked in the lake since 1977 by the Department of Wildlife. Several other species of fish eat large numbers of *Daphnia* as well.
3. The development of a multimillion-dollar fishery for sockeye salmon was a major economic benefit.

It is interesting that these benefits derive from improved conditions for two different species of fish. The first two effects listed can be attributed to the long-fin smelt, not the salmon. Projects affecting streams often have unexpected side effects that are deleterious, but they do not always have to be that way. A relatively recent development in the practice of lake management and lake restoration involves manipulations to facilitate biological interactions which will result in improved conditions. This "biomanipulation" approach has usually been applied within lakes. Finding ways to extend it into the watershed is well worth further efforts.

Remember that, while many people will think of the successful public action and the response of the lake as the main lesson from Lake Washington, my own motivation was the scientific opportunity. In effect the Metro population did a series of gigantic experiments for us. First there was the lake fertilization experiment in which we could measure the response of the lake to large changes in nutrient supply. Then there was the experiment in predation pressure that led to the population explosion of *Daphnia*. Part of this was an experiment with the success of salmon spawning in the Cedar River. Finally, we are just now seeing an experiment on the effect of terrestrial conditions on the chemical content of a lake with consequent effects on the flora and fauna. I will say more about the nature of whole-lake experiments in chapters 12 and 16.

# Chapter 2

## Lake Washington in Context: How Aquatic Communities Work

As demonstrated in chapter 1, it is possible to recount the Lake Washington story with a minimum of technical terms. Nevertheless, to relate the story to the rest of the book requires more familiarity with a number of basic ecological concepts. Many of these are widely known and well presented in textbooks of biology, ecology, and environmental science, but often they are stated in a way that is not easily applicable to the problems discussed here. Therefore, I will review a selection of the ideas that are most relevant to this book, with special reference to lakes. Many of the ideas can be generalized to other kinds of systems, especially marine ones like Puget Sound, although the specific conditions may be very different. (Incidentally the word *marine* should be restricted to seas and oceans. Lakes do not have marine life or seaweeds.)

This review should give readers immediate access to the concepts and to the essential terminology. It should be equally useful to make professional limnologists aware of my personal viewpoints. Much of the material covered in this section is included because there is considerable misunderstanding or disagreement in both the popular and professional literature. (See chapter 3 for outstanding examples.) In particular, the way I approach concepts of limiting nutrients, recycling and, above all, eutrophication is rather different from that of some of my colleagues. Readers with extensive background will find this chapter a convenient preview of the material emphasized in later chapters.

In the following sections I describe relevant physical conditions, the nature of biological communities, the chemical support system for the community and related topics. Some of the topics will be expanded in later chapters in connection with specific problems. I will continue to minimize the use of technical terms, but the few that I do use will make reading easier; without them, I would have to repeat many long-winded phrases. In a society that can speak freely of rhododendrons and chrysanthemums, I should be permitted to mention algae and phytoplankton. The index will help the reader locate definitions or explanations of terms. To some degree I may oversimplify by failing to make fine distinctions that would be important in a more rigorous treatment. Those who know enough to recognize those places can use their knowledge. Those who do not will not be seriously misled.

### Ecosystems

Probably the ecological concept most familiar to laymen, next to the food chain, is that of the ecosystem. Early during the development of the science of ecology from natural history, a common approach was to focus attention on a species and study the environmental conditions in which it thrived. In time it became evident that the environment consisted of two quite different components, other organisms (biotic factors) and physical factors, including chemical properties (abiotic factors). A species could no longer be treated in isolation, but had to be considered as part of a system of interacting species, a community, in a physical environment. With increasing knowledge of the interaction of communities with the environment by way of nutrition and recycling, it then became productive to think of community and environment together as a more effective unit of study comprising all the component parts and interacting processes, the ecosystem. This is well described by a word invented by a student in my ecology course during an examination: "These things are all intertwingled."

The ecosystem concept has provided an effective basis for organizing many kinds of ecological data and concepts. It has dominated the thinking of many ecologists, sometimes almost to the exclusion of other aspects of ecology, and not always to the benefit of ecology. In my view, the best use of the term ecosystem is to identify a concept that organizes and generalizes observations of nature. It is not a thing to be studied. I once read a description of a project that included something like: "The investigator entered the ecosystem and secured samples." Close reading showed that what he had done was to wade into a pond and scoop up some water.

### External Influences on Lakes

The biological character of a lake is affected by a set of interconnected physical and chemical influences from outside. Those that impinge most directly on the lake are properties such as solar radiation, and the inflow of water and its chemical content. These are related to the lake's geographic location which determines the seasonal changes in radiation, winds, and rainfall, the chemical nature of the geological substrate, human influence and many other features. The way the lake uses its supply of water and nutrients is affected by its size and shape.

Water is moved around in lakes by currents powered by the wind. This turbulent motion tends to stir the water from top to bottom, keeping the temperature and concentrations of dissolved materials uniform at all depths. In the spring, with longer days and increasing amounts of sunshine pouring into the lake, the surface layer becomes heated during the day and the warmed water is mixed downward by the wind so that the entire lake gains heat. However, warm water is less dense than cold and thus tends to float. If the lake is deep enough, a situation arises in which the force of the wind is no longer strong enough to mix the warm water all the way down, and the lake becomes stratified, with a layer of warm water (*epilimnion*) floating on top of the colder bottom layer (*hypolimnion*). This is important because in summer the epilimnion isolates the rest of the lake from contact with air. Also the energy of the sun now feeds into a smaller volume of water so that the surface layer heats more rapidly and becomes warmer than if that heat were distributed through the whole lake. The hypolimnion receives little or no light except in very clear lakes. Between the epilimnion and hypolimnion there is a transitional layer, the *metalimnion* within which there are steep gradients of temperature and chemical properties.

During autumn, with shorter days and less sunshine, the epilimnion progressively loses heat. The temperature decreases, and the top layer becomes progressively thicker as cool water is mixed in. Eventually the whole mass of water circulates fully, creating nearly uniform conditions from top to bottom once more. In mild climates, where the lakes do not freeze, the water circulates throughout winter. If a lake freezes, the layer of ice isolates the lake from contact with the air and circulation is again limited.

Because of special circumstances some lakes never mix completely. They have a layer of water in the bottom made dense by higher concentrations of dissolved material than in the upper part. Such a lake is called *meromictic*, which means that only part of it mixes. It consists of two parts, the deep layer called the *monimolimnion* and the upper, mixing part called the *mixolimnion*. The mixolimnion may go through normal mixing and stratification, forming an epilimnion, metalimnion and hypolimnion, while all the time floating on top of the monimolimnion. Diffusion of material from the monimolimnion is so slow that it retains its identity for decades, or centuries in a deep lake if the difference in density is large. The monimolimnion is very different chemically and biologically from a hypolimnion, and thus should not be called a hypolimnion. An understanding of meromixis is needed to understand the remarkable behavior of Lake Nyos, the killer lake discussed in chapter 14.

Most meromictic lakes are in semi-arid regions where the high evaporation associated with aridity can establish meromixis. Some are near seacoasts where unusually high tides and winds can throw a charge of seawater into a freshwater lake. Others are in places where protection from wind by hills can prevent mixing even without a large difference in density.

The depth of penetration of sunlight is affected by small particles that scatter it and dissolved materials that absorb it, thus altering in turn the distribution of heat to the lower depths. Transparency can be measured by lowering a standard white disc into the water under controlled sighting conditions; the depth of disappearance is called the Secchi disc transparency because the method was invented by an Italian oceanographer named Secchi.

When properly done, the method gives reproducible, meaningful results. It is not the same as an actual measurement of light intensity with a photometer, but it has its own application. Because of the effect of small particles on this measurement, it can in many lakes be used as an index of the abundance of small organisms such as algae, when other kinds of particles, such as clay, are not present. Thus Secchi disc transparency is useful for conveying information to people in discussions of the effects of pollution. (See fig. 1.4 for such a use.)

## Biological Communities

Each of the two major regions in a lake, the open water and the bottom, is inhabited by a community of organisms necessarily adapted in structure, life history and behavior to the special conditions there.

The community of the open water is called the *plankton*. This is sometimes defined as those organisms that float, but actually some of the animals work very hard to stay up in the water. A more functional definition is that the plankton is the community of organisms which do not depend on the bottom of the lake to complete their life history (except for resting stages which lie on the bottom). Planktonic animals have relatively little control over their horizontal location in the lake, but many can control their vertical position and may make large daily migrations up and down.

The *benthos* is the community of organisms on or in the bottom of the lake which require a relationship with the bottom to live or to complete their life histories. A few species lead a double life, scampering around on or burrowing in the mud at some times, swimming up into the water at others.

The organization of communities can be described in terms of the food chain, or more precisely, food web, concept. The different species can be grouped into three major categories according to their main function: *primary producers, consumers* and *decomposers*. There are two main physiological groups, *autotrophs* and *heterotrophs*. The categories are based on the physiology of nutrition. Autotrophs can make use of inorganic compounds of carbon—carbon dioxide or bicarbonate ions. Primary producers are autotrophic; they absorb dissolved inorganic materials from the water and synthesize organic molecules, using the energy of solar radiation to drive the process of photosynthesis or using energy derived from special chemical reactions in chemosynthesis. Heterotrophs must be supplied with organic carbon compounds such as carbohydrates as a source of carbon; they include animals, most bacteria and certain other groups of microorganisms. Consumers eat other organisms, ingesting solid material. Decomposers are microorganisms that break organic molecules into their inorganic components. Finer divisions can be made: animals that eat primary producers are *herbivores;* those that eat other animals are *carnivores* or *predators; scavengers* are animals that specialize in eating corpses or wastes of other animals.

The primary producers in the plankton are called *phytoplankton,* a name coined in the days when one could still think of living things as being classifiable into only two kingdoms, plants and animals. Phytoplankton is composed of several rather diverse groups of microorganisms collectively called *algae.*

There is a complication of modern classification that I must mention to avoid confusion for those who want to read in this field. Since the early 1960s it has been known that the organisms called blue-green algae are structurally different in a basic way from all other groups of algae, in fact are identical with bacteria in cellular organization. The modern practice, established in 1974, is to call them blue-green bacteria (Cyanobacteria). To avoid confusion, I shall call them simply *blue-greens.* This is not just a trivial matter of names. The main thing that they have in common with algae is that they are autotrophic and liberate oxygen as a by-product of photosynthesis. Major differences are that some of the blue-greens can use molecular nitrogen gas as a source of nitrogen and some have gas vacuoles that permit them to float.

The blue-greens will be prominent in this book because of their relation to pollution. Characteristically they dominate the plankton of highly productive lakes, and can become very abundant, as *Oscillatoria rubescens* did in Lake Washington. Many float to the surface in calm weather, forming dense scums of decaying material that move downwind with unpleasant consequences. It is important to realize that blue-greens are a normal part of the flora of unpolluted lakes. They thrive under some kinds of pollution and outgrow the algae. (See the later section on eutrophication.) Most phytoplankters occur as single cells or relatively small groups or colonies, while the blue-greens tend to make larger colonies and are therefore more visible.

The animal consumers of phytoplankton, *zooplankton*, are small crustaceans, rotifers, and certain kinds of protozoa. The planktonic decomposers are mostly bacteria that use corpses, feces, and dissolved organic material as their source of nutrients. Bacteria are ubiquitous in plankton, existing as cells or groups of cells moving freely in the water or attached to the surfaces of particles including algae. Many of the zooplankton eat bacteria as well as algae.

The food web concept and its categories have been useful in organizing data and thoughts about community structure, but it should not be taken too seriously for lake communities because so many fresh water animals are omnivorous and will eat any particles of a size that can be handled by the feeding apparatus. Many zooplankters regularly eat large phytoplankton and small zooplankton, thus functioning both as herbivores and carnivores. Some algae can use organic sources of carbon. Even the division between primary producers and consumers is blurred by the fact that many flagellated algae can ingest organisms like bacteria and smaller algae.

The benthic community is made up of organisms that fill all the functions described for the plankton, but their character is very different. Most of the primary producers are plants with roots and many get a significant part of their nutrition from the mud. Consumers are mostly insects, crustaceans and fish. Bacteria are very abundant at the interface between mud and water, and much of the dead material that was produced in the upper layers or imported into the lake from the terrestrial community is decomposed and recycled there, although a considerable part escapes destruction and is permanently buried.

Dense growths of plants in shallow water have attracted public attention because they interfere with water sports and other

activities involving contact with the water. However, the conditions leading to an abundance of water weeds are different from
those controlling the phytoplankton.

Large swimming organisms such as fish and insects have full
control over their location and are called *nekton*.

## The Chemical Support System

Lake water can be thought of as a culture medium providing
dissolved materials for nutritional and osmotic needs. About
twenty elements have been identified as essential for organisms
in general, but some species have additional special requirements. The concentrations and proportions of the major elements are determined largely by the chemical composition of the
geological substrate in the drainage area, modified by the vegetation on the land and the flow of water. An excellent example
of the dependence of the chemical content of a lake on the nature of the substrate is given by Cedar Pond in Connecticut.
Quarrying operations cut into the drainage area of two of the inlets into Cedar Pond, exposing them to a relatively soluble trap
rock. Between 1937 and 1975, the concentration of several elements in the lakes increased, sodium by a factor of twenty (Norvell 1977). Lakes in regions with calcareous sedimentary rocks
have higher concentrations of dissolved material than those in
regions with less soluble granitic rock. Since geological forma-
tions tend to be extensive, the water in lake districts tends to show
a certain degree of chemical uniformity. The total amount of
dissolved inorganic material, TDS (total dissolved solids), is also
called *salinity*, even though the proportions of the chemical elements are different from those in the ocean.

The major inorganic ions are present in concentrations much
larger than the amount needed and absorbed by the phytoplankton, and their concentrations are affected little, if at all, by
biological activity. In most districts there is relatively little seasonal change of calcium, magnesium, sodium, potassium, chloride, or sulfate caused by direct absorption by the plankton. In
freshwater lakes their concentrations are measured as milligrams per liter or parts per million (ppm).

Most of the nutrients are present in much smaller concentrations, measured in micrograms per liter or parts per billion (ppb). Substances like phosphate and nitrate show large seasonal variations as they are absorbed by phytoplankton. Understanding the conditions of nutrition of phytoplankton is essential for understanding the changes in Lake Washington and the controversy about detergents discussed in chapter 3. The element carbon is obtained by algae from carbon dioxide or one of its combinations with water, bicarbonate. The element nitrogen is usually obtained from nitrate, but nitrite and ammonia are used when present. A few specialized organisms can use elemental molecular nitrogen. The element phosphorus is obtained by absorbing phosphate ions, and phosphate is the form used by the algal cells. Strict primary producers can synthesize all the organic compounds they need from inorganic sources. Others need to be provided with certain organic molecules which they cannot synthesize, vitamins. Some primary producers are able to obtain carbon from organic molecules like glucose.

Lakes that are part of drainage systems get most of their nutrients from the inlet streams, although carbon dioxide and molecular nitrogen are provided by the atmosphere as well. Lakes without surface inlets are dependent on nutrients contained in seepage water or springs. In many lakes, input of leaves and other material from the terrestrial community contributes much nutrition. Normally a lake receives nutrients continuously, but at a rate that varies widely with the seasons. During the productive seasons, nutrients are withdrawn from the water by primary producers as described above.

To understand the control of productivity of lakes, we must consider the rate of supply of both water and nutrients. A given amount of nutrient will have different effects depending upon the volume of water that carries it. The annual income, or loading, of a nutrient is calculated by multiplying its concentration by the amount of water entering the lake during the year; in practice, one measures the concentration and the rate of flow of water at intervals during the year.

The flushing rate is calculated as the ratio of the total inflow to the volume of the lake: if the inflow during the year is half the volume, then the flushing rate is 0.5 times per year. The retention time is the inverse, the ratio of volume to inflow; in this case, two years. The retention time can be thought of as the time it would take the annual flow to fill up the lake. The word flushing may be misleading: the water coming in mixes gradually with the water already there, so that the water flowing out of the lake is a mixture of both.

An element that limits production because of its scarcity is called a limiting factor. During the spring growth of phytoplankton, nutrients are removed from the water and incorporated into the cells. The elements are rarely present in the water in the same proportions in which they are used, so usually one is reduced to a low, limiting concentration before the others. A subsequent section on bioassay has more information on this point. (For an example see fig. 1.5.)

An important part of the control of primary producers is the fact that part of the nutrient supply to the lake is recycled. Processes of excretion, respiration and decomposition result in the partial breakdown of the organic material and its liberation in inorganic form such as carbon dioxide or phosphate. Part of this material makes repeated trips through the community. Regeneration can take place as corpses or feces sink toward the bottom. Bacteria attach to such objects and start breaking them down, liberating carbon dioxide into the water. Some compounds are resistant. Most of their decomposition takes place after they have reached the bottom, but decomposition is incomplete and organic material can be found at all depths within the sediment. A large part of the nutrients that enter a lake is permanently buried in the mud, out of contact with the water.

Phosphate and other substances accumulate in the hypolimnion during summer. When the lake mixes, these substances are distributed throughout the lake and added to that which has been delivered to the epilimnion during summer. Some limnologists refer to the amount of phosphate regenerated as internal loading, and add it to the external loading to get a total loading. I prefer to think of it in a different way. Because the extra phosphate has already been measured when it first entered the lake as external loading, I prefer to use the external loading as the basic figure and to consider that some lakes use their phosphate supply more efficiently than others by recycling more. This puts emphasis on developing clear concepts of the processes that control productivity and the circulation of elements.

Oxygen is freely available from the atmosphere and is liberated into the water by photosynthetic organisms where there is adequate light. However, when the hypolimnion is cut off from contact with the atmosphere, ordinarily not enough light reaches it to support oxygen production. During summer the amount of oxygen dissolved in the hypolimnion steadily decreases as it is used up for respiration by fish, invertebrates, bacteria and other organisms. The respiratory activity of the deep-water benthos is related to the supply of decomposable or edible material that falls from the productive layer above. In a highly productive lake the concentration of oxygen may go to low values, even to zero, rendering the deep water uninhabitable by fish and other organisms that require abundant oxygen. Fully as important for the biological character of the lake is the fact that, when the water is devoid of oxygen, biological changes occur that cause chemical reactions which multiply the rate of release of such materials as phosphate from the sediment. This effect on recycling and internal loading can increase significantly the total productivity of the lake over time. Nevertheless, dense blooms of algae cannot be explained by rapid recycling of nutrients alone. There must be a large amount of nutrients present at one time. A ten-gram bloom cannot be made by recycling one gram ten times.

The relative magnitude of recycling varies with the size and shape of lakes. In unstratified, shallow lakes the entire volume of water is continuously exposed to sediment, instead of being partly isolated from it during summer as it is in deep, stratified lakes with steeply sloping bottoms. A larger proportion of the bottom of a shallow lake can be inhabited by rooted plants, which can be effective in bringing nutrients up from the mud and in producing decomposable material when they die back in winter.

## Productivity, Population Density, and Nutrients

The abundance of organisms is the most easily noticed feature of the biological activity of lakes. The abundance or popu-

lation density at a given moment is the result of a balance between production and consumption, or birth and death, during
the time leading up to the moment of observation. The production of organisms in a lake is based on the supply of nutrients,
but the way in which that basic nutrient supply is converted into
a community of organisms is affected by environmental factors
and by biological interactions within the community. Especially
important factors are input of solar radiation, temperature, and
mixing by wind. The depth and shape of the lake determine the
area that can be occupied by rooted plants.

As mentioned above, for geological and climatic reasons, lake
waters in some regions have relatively low concentrations of
dissolved material including nutrient elements. These lakes
produce relatively small populations of phytoplankton and remain clear all year. In regions where the waters have higher
concentrations of nutrients, the lakes produce larger populations of algae and become cloudy or turbid during spring and
summer. Commonly the densest populations in especially rich
lakes are dominated by the blue-greens.

Terminology was developed early in this century to describe
the nutrient (trophic) basis for production. The concentration of
nutrients in the water is the primary criterion of richness. Lakes
rich in nutrients were called *eutrophic* (well fed), those poor in
nutrients were called *oligotrophic* (poorly fed). An intermediate
condition, *mesotrophic*, has been established more recently.

There was a time when limnologists gave much attention to the
concept of lake types, trying to define them with some precision, as if they were clearly separated categories. We now realize that such typological thinking is inappropriate; there is a
graded condition from eutrophic to oligotrophic. Also, it has become important to distinguish between the concentration of nutrients observed in a lake and the rate of supply to the lake, or
loading, although the two are usually closely connected. Failure
to make this distinction can lead to false conclusions.

Unfortunately confusion developed early in the literature. Since
the nutrient supply was hard to measure, limnologists sought
another property that could be used as an index, and diagnoses
of trophy were based on measurements of some secondary effect or symptom of nutrition. The basic fallacy is the use of "eu-

trophic" as a synonym of "highly productive" and then the use of the abundance of organisms as a direct index of productivity. A lake that produces dense populations of algae is likely to be eutrophic, but sometimes floating algae can be concentrated by wind in a bay of a mesotrophic lake and give a false appearance of an algal bloom. A clear, deeply mixed eutrophic lake may not make algal nuisances although it may support a high rate of production. The population produced is distributed through a large volume of water and therefore does not become as dense as in a lake with a thin epilimnion. A eutrophic lake will not be able to make algal nuisances if it has some inhibiting condition. (See Long Lake, chapter 10.) These relations are shown in fig. 2.1.

People are sometimes confused by the sight of a dense growth of rooted plants in shallow places, thinking they are seeing an algal bloom. Such a growth may have taken all summer to develop slowly, taking nutrients from the mud, and by itself is not evidence of high productivity, much less eutrophy.

Even worse, some early investigators tabulated the characteristics of oligotrophic and eutrophic lakes known at the time to see what they had in common. It is clear from the literature that by

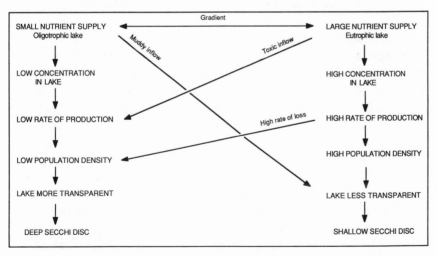

*Fig. 2.1. Relations among nutrient loading (trophic state), productivity and abundance of phytoplankton, and some complicating factors.*

coincidence, some of the best known oligotrophic lakes were large, deep ones in the mountains of Scandinavia and Central Europe, and the best known eutrophic ones were smaller, shallower lakes in rich lowland farming areas. Thus, correlated conditions of abundance and kind of phytoplankton, oxygen, temperature, and even depth sometimes were used to diagnose trophic conditions even though the correlation was based on coincidence, not causation. But a deep lake full of nutrient-rich water is eutrophic according to the original concept of the word. A shallow pond in a granitic basin is likely to be oligotrophic. It is important also to realize that a lake can be eutrophic and produce dense populations of blue-greens for natural reasons, without any human influence, as in the case of Lake Lenore (chapter 11).

The seasonal changes in phytoplankton and nutrients give insight into the processes that control the growth and size of populations. In temperate regions lakes commonly have small populations of phytoplankton during winter. As spring comes on, the supply of light increases with longer days and higher sun angle, which leads to increases in the rates of photosynthesis, growth, and reproduction, and results in larger populations. What we see at any moment is the result of conditions during the preceding several weeks. Since the use of nutrients is at a minimum during the dark winter months, they accumulate in the water; their concentration tends to be largest at the beginning of the spring growth period. Commonly during spring the algae absorb the nutrients faster than they are delivered to the lake, and the concentration in the water decreases. By the time a dense bloom has developed, some essential nutrient may even have disappeared from the water, but it is still present inside the cells.

The activity of the community can affect the concentration of oxygen as well as that of the nutrients. Primary producers release oxygen into the water during daylight hours as a by-product of photosynthesis. During dark they continue respiring and absorb oxygen. When a population of algae or plants gets very large, its respiration at night may be enough to use up all the oxygen, resulting in death of fish and other animals that depend on the water for their oxygen supply.

To interpret some of the arguments about phosphorus to be

discussed in chapter 3 we need to realize just how dynamic these systems are. In some seasons one can sample a lake repeatedly over a period of time and find about the same concentrations of nutrients and organisms. But during that time there has been a steady turnover of material so that the molecules of phosphate and cells of algae present in March are different from those in January. The static number representing the concentration of phosphate is maintained by a balance between the rate of uptake by the algae and the rate of input. Both rates can be high or low, giving the same concentration, despite different rates of recycling. (The rates are difficult to measure and are not part of conventional limnological studies.) When spring phytoplankton growth starts, the uptake of phosphate increases and the concentration in the water decreases.

## Eutrophication

I presented Lake Washington as an example of eutrophication, that is, enrichment with nutrients. Understanding the general problem of eutrophication requires additional information. Many large lakes in Europe and North America, once valued for their clarity, deep-water fish, and aesthetic appeal, have lost all three as a result of the annual development of dense populations of blue-greens. Now, blue-greens individually seen are very handsome; so are dandelions. But whenever either of these grows in a place where it is not wanted, it makes trouble and people try to remove it and to prevent its continued growth. Excessive phosphate in lakes may cause trouble, but nobody objects to it in rocks. (See the general discussion of pollution in chapter 14.) The results of excessive blue-green growth can be spectacular and cause serious deterioration. Here is a statement by Dr. Clair Sawyer based on experience with Lake Monona in Wisconsin:

The most obnoxious conditions produced by algae are those which result from concentration of floating forms under the impetus of a gentle breeze with deposition on the leeward shoreline. Such accumulations, often several inches thick and extending several feet from shore, in the heat of a warm summer sun die, decay, and emit odors that will dampen the spirits of the most ardent recreationist in the area. [See also the vivid description in chapter 3.]

Such a condition is known as an algal nuisance or a nuisance bloom. The word "nuisance" may be appropriate when the greatest effect is on recreational use of a lake. It is a weak word when a commercial fishery for deep water species is eliminated. Normally the condition is not dangerous for people, although some develop skin rashes. Some blue-greens are capable of producing toxins, however, and under some conditions the water becomes dangerous to vertebrate animals that drink it. Toxic blooms have been responsible for deaths of many cattle and dogs that drink from eutrophic lakes. (See chapter 10.) There is at least one case of a child drowning in shallow water close to shore because blue-greens were so abundant that he could not be seen.

Blue-greens are not the only organisms that produce nuisance conditions in lakes. Some lakes have dense populations of insect larvae. Many species have highly coordinated life histories by which enormous swarms of the flying adult midges emerge from lakes at the same time. Seen from a distance they look like rising columns of smoke. They can cover the windshields of automobiles, completely obscuring the view, and give trouble with air filters and hamburgers.

In most cases of repeated nuisance blooms in lakes that formerly had not produced them, the changes have been preceded by the construction of a sewerage system that discharges effluent into the lake. Because even treated sewage contains high concentrations of nutrients, an oligotrophic lake receiving large amounts of such effluent becomes eutrophic. The productivity usually increases correspondingly, with consequent maintenance of large populations of algae. One might suppose that that would be good because it increases the food supply of fish. If the enrichment could be controlled well enough, it could be beneficial to fish, but this has not happened, at least not often. Two things have usually prevented heavy nutrient enrichment with effluent from being useful. The first is that there is a change in community structure: the blue-greens increase more than the algal groups. Not only do they make nuisances as described above, but they are relatively poor food for the kinds of animals that are important links in the food web that supports the fish. (An example of this is the effect of *Oscillatoria* on *Daphnia* discussed in chapter 1.) Thus the food base for fish is not increased in proportion to the increase in productivity and may even be diminished. The second thing is that much of the increased production is funnelled to the decomposers in the deep water, leading to exhaustion of the oxygen supply and elimination of a large volume of the lake as habitat for fish.

Many examples of deterioration of formerly acceptable lakes were seen in Switzerland and Germany toward the end of the nineteenth century. Characteristically in many of these lakes *Oscillatoria rubescens* appeared early in the period of enrichment, and nuisance conditions developed later. Thus the sudden appearance of this species serves as an early warning of approaching deterioration, as it did for us in Lake Washington. Lake Zürich began receiving increasing amounts of raw sewage in the late 1800s. A dense population of *Oscillatoria rubescens* appeared in 1898. By 1930, the deep-water oxygen was low, and desirable coregonid fish had disappeared. The production of shallow-water cyprinid fish increased. The nearly separate upper basin of the lake remained undisturbed and did not change until urbanization with its accompanying sewage spread there; *Oscillatoria rubescens* appeared in 1947. This was the first example of a situation that we could regard as a fertilization experiment on a whole lake, with a valid experimental control basin. From this and other experiences we can generalize that the impression a lake makes on people will be related to its input of nutrients (fig. 2.2).

At this point I must clarify an unfortunate matter of terminology. The public understanding of some important environmental issues has been clouded by the application of the term *eutrophication* to four quite different concepts of the function of nutrients in control of productivity. I emphasize this point because understanding it is essential for effective management of lakes. Also, it illustrates a general problem about scientific terminology. Words are supposed to mean something, but as knowledge increases, concepts for which the words stand become refined. New processes, formerly associated with a given

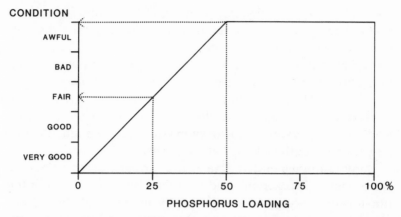

*Fig. 2.2. Idealized diagram showing relation between nutrient input and condition of lake as expressed as a reaction by people associated with the lake. Starting with an oligotrophic condition judged as "very good," increasing additions of phosphate are matched by proportional changes in the condition of the lake up to a point at which the lake has as much phosphate as it can use, and further additions have no perceptible effect. Another element has become limiting. A fifty percent decrease in loading from a heavily overloaded condition will not affect the condition of the lake (100–50%), but a 50% decrease from that point (50–25%) will make a great improvement in the lake.*

phenomenon, are discovered, and it is confusing when people continue using the same word label for both. That is what happened to the word eutrophication.

It seems clear to me that the word eutrophication implies a process of becoming eutrophic, and that means changing from a state of lesser nutrient input to one of greater nutrient input. Such a change will ordinarily be followed by changes in a group of conditions that are affected by the nutrients, for example productivity and consequent population density. Confusion about terminology can arise when a definition of eutrophication includes a description of such consequences and readers assume that those conditions are part of the definition of the term. An example is Vollenweider (1989). Then, since the associated conditions caused by nutrient increase are easier to measure than the nutrient input, they are used as the criteria of eutrophication and become identified with eutrophication. I have been trying to promote among my colleagues a use of the word that is meaningful in terms of our modern knowledge of the control of lake productivity. Please note that in the following account I am going to discuss the *meanings* that have been attributed to the word eutrophication, not to create *definitions*.

*Meaning 1.* This meaning is the one implied by the form of the word eutrophication, the process of becoming eutrophic. Therefore I use eutrophication to mean an increase in the nutrient supply, or loading, over and above the basic supply from the undisturbed surroundings or from its previous condition. Thus the introduction of sewage into a lake is an act of eutrophication. Since most cases of eutrophication that we know were caused by human activity (sewage, agriculture, or lumbering) the term artificial eutrophication has been used. This implies that there can be natural eutrophication. This would be an increase in the nutrient supply by some process not under human control, such as a landslide diverting a nutrient-rich river into a lake or exposing a soluble rock formation that was not available before.

*Meaning 2.* The increase in production and consequent increase in abundance of organisms resulting from an increase in nutrient supply has itself been called eutrophication, as for example:

"The term eutrophication describes the biological reaction of aquatic systems to nutrient enrichment, the eventual consequence of which is the development of primary production to nuisance proportions" (Marsden 1989). In my view, this is applying the term eutrophication to a symptom or result of eutrophication. A variation of this meaning states that eutrophication is the increase in *organic* matter produced both within the lake and brought in from outside. (See the discussion by Rodhe [1969].)

A difficulty with this concept is that organisms may increase in abundance for reasons having nothing to do with nutrition, such as a decrease in consumers or in toxicity. (See chapter 10.)

*Meaning 3.* A third meaning is subtly different from Meaning 1, the one which I favor. The difference is subtle in that both meanings may be expressed in the same words: eutrophication is the nutrient enrichment of waters. In the sense I prefer, this would mean an *increase* in the amount of nutrient that enters the lake during a given time. In the sense of Meaning 3, it means merely the *amount* of nutrient entering the lake during a given time. The difference can be great.

In its Meaning 3 version, enrichment means simply that all lakes have an income of nutrients; the process of delivering that income, even at a steady rate, is called eutrophication. When that rate of income is increased, as by sewage, eutrophication by Meaning 3 is said to be "accelerated" (Bartsch 1970). Now it seems to me illogical to say that a mountain lake receiving water with barely detectable concentrations of phosphorus is being eutrophied. It is not becoming eutrophic. The lake may hold steady at an oligotrophic and unproductive level for millennia in an undisturbed watershed. If it were necessary to invent a word to say that a lake has a nutrient income, that word might be *trophication* (feeding). The word in common use is *loading*.

This third use is sometimes justified by saying that lakes accumulate nutrients continuously over time as a result of the loading, and therefore are continually increasing in total nutrient content. The rationale seems to come from considering the lake to consist of its water and all of its mud, and represents a serious misunderstanding of the availability of nutrients from sediments. Much of the nutrient material that enters a lake is deposited on the bottom, contained in dead organisms. Only a fraction of that material is returned to the water and recycled through the community; the rest is permanently buried. This is an important point and I will discuss it further with examples in chapter 3.

*Meaning 4.* A fourth meaning, closely related to the third, has been very confusing to the public and has actually interfered with rational protection of lakes. That is the assumption that lakes originate in an oligotrophic condition and progressively become more eutrophic as they age and fill in with accumulated sediment containing nutrients. Many lakes formed by glacial processes at the end of the last ice age, about 12,000 years ago, went through a brief period during which nutrients were leached rapidly from the bare surroundings and increased the chemical content of the lakes. However, as soon as a cover of vegetation was established on the land, perhaps in one or two thousand years, leaching was reduced and a relatively steady nutrient input from the drainage area followed, lasting for many thousands of years. This type of lake, spread across North America and Europe, has been intensively studied by limnologists and has provided the most experience with the development of nuisance conditions when the nutrient input was increased. The prolonged steady state led to the concept of trophic equilibrium; the lake is in balance with its nutrient income.

Now there is good reason to think that the total productivity of a lake will increase as it fills in, since more of the bottom becomes occupied by rooted plants, and the hypolimnion becomes smaller. On an areal basis, the production by rooted plants is generally higher than that by phytoplankton. But as pointed out earlier, this kind of increase in production does not require any increase in nutrient input. It is a consequence of the change in depth and volume with age. In other words, eutrophication is not the same thing as aging, or ecological succession, which is a change in community structure over time brought about by the interaction of community and environment. There is no known geological or ecological process that will assure a consistently increasing rate of nutrient input during the existence of lakes in general. The use of eutrophication as an increase in abundance seemed to draw support from early paleolimnological studies that showed an increase in the content of organic matter in sediment as the lake aged. This could be interpreted as an increase in production, but not necessarily nutrient input.

A good example of this confusing but widely held fourth concept of eutrophication was given by Russell E. Train, then Chairman of the Council on Environmental Quality, in 1971 testimony before a U.S. House of Representatives committee:

> Eutrophication is the natural aging process that takes place in standing bodies of water. All lakes go through a natural cycle of eutrophication, which normally takes thousands of years. Over time, nutrients and sediments are added; the lake becomes biologically productive and shallower. As nutrients continue to be added, large algal blooms grow and fish populations change. Over time, the lake becomes a swamp and finally a land area. These nutrients are available from natural sources such as weathering of rocks, de-

cay of natural vegetation, and, in some areas, phosphorous deposits. The problem with which we are concerned is the rapid acceleration of this natural process by man's activities. Man can accelerate the eutrophication process by adding nutrients, particularly nitrogen and phosphorus. These added nutrients come from a number of sources including human wastes, phosphate detergents, industrial effluents, and agricultural runoff. Accelerated eutrophication depletes the oxygen supply in the water, creates esthetic problems, affects recreation use, results in adverse changes in the fish population, and causes taste and odor problems in drinking water supply.

I quote this discussion not to berate Mr. Train but to illustrate my point about the prevalence of confusion generated by use of a single term for quite different ideas. This fourth meaning is often presented in the textbooks and popular literature. It is sometimes combined with the third, apparently on the assumption that all of the nutrients that enter a lake accumulate and continue to be available. This fallacy will be dismissed in chapter 3.

How did this idea get established so firmly in the professional and popular literature? It can be traced very clearly back to a review by K. Munster Strøm of recent advances in limnology, published in 1928. After reviewing a descriptive concept of two lake types, "eutroph" and "oligotroph," he wrote "The natural process of the maturing of a lake is that of eutrophication. The original state of all lakes *must be assumed to be oligotroph* [my emphasis] but during the course of time there will always be a surplus of organic sediments accruing from the life processes of a lake, and the originally *oligotroph* lake is changed to a *eutroph*."

Although Strøm and the sources he mentions clearly indicated that they regarded oligotrophic lakes as having little nutrition and eutrophic lakes as having more, they did not make a distinction between productivity and abundance of organisms. Strøm's idea planted in 1928 spread rapidly.

P. S. Welch, in the first American textbook on limnology, published in 1932, quoted extensively from Strøm's paper, thus giving wide circulation to a misconception that is still widely held. I think we ought to do better now, over sixty years after Strøm's unfortunate assumption.

In addition to the confusion described above, concepts of eutrophication really got mixed up in the popular literature during the 1960s when eutrophication was dramatically redefined as "the death of a lake." A lake dies when it finally fills in and is replaced by a meadow. A lake choked with blue-greens may smell bad but it is no corpse.

Now if, through some unfortunate consensus, the word eutrophication, which is logically defined by Meaning 1, were to be appropriated for Meaning 2 (increased production and abundance) or Meaning 3 (loading) or Meaning 4 (succession), we would have to invent a new term for Meaning 1. That would create additional confusion. The only candidate for substitution I can think of is the ambiguous *nutrient enrichment*, which has been used, but not commonly. If we could agree to use nutrient enrichment for Meaning 1, which of the other three would become eutrophication? And why? Certainly it could not be Meaning 4 which is simply wrong if applied to nutrients. Meaning 3 is not useful; the rate of delivery of nutrients is usually called "loading" or "nutrient income" and an *increase* in loading can be called just that which is the same as eutrophication by Meaning 1. To designate Meaning 2, the consequences of enrichment, as eutrophication would be illogical and confusing since production or population density can be increased by changes having nothing to do with nutrition, such as a decrease in consumers or of toxic conditions, as mentioned above.

Some readers of this book may think the preceding discussion to be unnecessarily picky, but the fact is that failure to make these distinctions has unnecessarily confused public discussion and awareness of the consequences of some types of pollution. (Chapter 3 presents examples.) A body of technical terminology is essential for discussion of technical matters as long as it is clearly defined and not allowed to deteriorate into jargon. (Please notice that I have not traced the historical development of the concepts except for Strøm's contribution.)

## Sewage and Eutrophication

To understand Lake Washington and the many other examples of eutrophication, we need to know something about the technique of treating or purifying sewage. The invention of the flush toilet facilitated the delivery of raw sewage to lakes and streams wherever towns and cities were growing. Several problems were magnified by this process. In addition to the obvious visible deterioration of waters used for swimming or boating, the spread of diseases was increased. A less obvious effect had serious consequences for freshwater lake fisheries. Raw sewage has a very high biological oxygen demand (BOD) because of its large content of organic matter. In a polluted lake or stream, the normal recycling process is taken on by the bacteria at a rate much higher than that normally supported by production within the water and its immediate surroundings. Since these bacteria use oxygen, large volumes of water may become devoid of dissolved oxygen. Not only does this eliminate much of the volume of a lake for use by fish, but hydrogen sulfide produced in anoxic conditions leads to unpleasant odors. It should be emphasized that no new process has been generated by the disposal of raw sewage in the lake; normal, already existing processes of recycling have simply been magnified.

Primary treatment is accomplished by leading the sewage through screens into large settling tanks so that floatable and sinkable solids are partly removed. The easily settled material, sludge, is removed to a disposal site. In some cases it is put through a biological digestion with bacteria to reduce its organic content and bulk. The rest of the material still contains large quantities of dissolved organic material and minute suspended particles which bacteria can break down, so that the effluent from primary treatment has nearly as much effect on the dissolved oxygen in the receiving water as does raw sewage.

To overcome the oxygen problem, secondary treatment was invented. After primary treatment the material is put through additional purification. There are variations in the procedure, but always there is a final stage in large tanks where air or oxygen is bubbled through. This extra supply of oxygen permits rapid microbial destruction of organic molecules in the tank, so that the effluent does not have the high demand by bacteria for oxygen and can be put into a lake with little direct effect on the oxygen supply. More sludge is produced during the secondary stage. During the treatment process, the sewage is also deprived of some of its carbon and nitrogen content since carbon dioxide, methane, and ammonia are washed out in the bubbled air. Elements that do not have a gaseous form under treatment conditions are not affected as much, although some are carried down in the additional sludge that forms.

Of particular interest to lakes is the phosphorus content; normal secondary effluent is very rich in phosphorus relative to natural concentrations and also has a high proportion of phosphorus to nitrogen and carbon. Because phosphorus has special importance in eutrophication, much attention has been given to reducing the phosphorus content of sewage effluent. Sewerage systems were invented primarily to take care of human wastes and there is little likelihood of eliminating that source. Other materials containing phosphorus are introduced into household waste water and they are more controllable. (See chapter 3.) Another option is to modify the treatment process. The simplest type of modification is to add iron salts to the primary or secondary stage to enhance the removal of phosphorus. A more complete treatment is made by introducing a third stage of chemical precipitation (tertiary treatment) that carries down other substances as well.

Although the sludge produced by both primary and secondary treatment, like wet mud, is bulky and must be disposed of, ways of using it productively have been developed. (See chapter 4.) Tertiary treatment removes more material than secondary, so the amount of sludge produced is larger, magnifying the disposal problem. Furthermore, this sludge may contain higher concentrations of such toxic metals as zinc, lead, and cadmium. This limits the possibilities of using it. Many tertiary, or Advanced Waste Treatment, plants, have been built, but have not been universally successful.

Whatever the degree of treatment, it is important to recognize that processes for removing substances from sewage do not get rid of them, but merely transfer them from one place to another. The difficulty of sewage disposal is so great that proposals have been made to abandon piped sewerage systems, and alternatives are being tried. The resolution will be a long time coming.

## Cause and Effect

The logical fallacy of "post hoc, ergo propter hoc" (after this, therefore because of this) is common thinking. It is easy to observe that some particular condition follows a certain event and therefore to attribute the condition to the event without knowing enough about the system. (An extreme example of this is Long Lake, which will be described in chapter 10.) The general correlation that has been found between phytoplankton abundance and chemical conditions cannot be attributed certainly to cause and effect without considerable physiological knowledge and without experiments on the part that nutrients play in determining the growth of algae. A correlation that was given a probably erroneous causal explanation was that certain lakes that produced the most blue-greens had relatively high concentrations of organically combined nitrogen. That is true, but the lakes were also receiving untreated sewage, not only a good source of organic nitrogen, but with a higher inorganic nutrient content as well. All the major nuisance blue-greens have been grown successfully in purely inorganic media. Therefore, the prevalence of blue-greens cannot be attributed simply to organic matter. (This point arises again in chapter 3.) In general, establishing correlations in field data is a good way to start a study, but experimental studies in which conditions are deliberately manipulated in the lake, in a portion of the lake, or in the laboratory are required to establish an actual sequence of cause and effect. (See also chapter 12.) One of the experimental techniques used to identify limiting factors is known as bioassay.

## Bioassays

Operationally, we can define a limiting element by adding it to a system. If the addition is followed by an increase in the activity or abundance of some organism, we would say that the lack of that element had been limiting to such an increase. Experiments have been done with whole lakes by adding fertilizer and measuring the increase in abundance of algae. Since a number of processes are affected by such an addition, more precise experiments to identify the specific processes by which limiting elements limit are done by bioassay techniques.

Samples of lake water are enriched with different amounts of various elements and the changes compared with an unenriched control sample (fig. 2.3). The response can be measured either in bottles suspended in the lake or in flasks in the laboratory held under uniform light and at uniform temperature. There are two common ways of conducting the bioassays. In one,

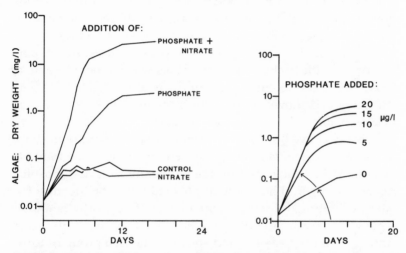

*Fig. 2.3. Bioassay. Curves show the increase over time of abundance of algae inoculated into flasks with different amounts of nutrients added. The scale is logarithmic. Left: Water from the Snake River. Note that nitrate added by itself had no effect, but phosphate had a large effect. Right: Different amounts of phosphate added to water from Lake Michigan. There is a relation between the maximum amount of algae produced and the amount of phosphate put in at the start. The increase with no added phosphate was supported by surplus phosphate in the cells inoculated at the beginning of the experiment. During the growth phase, the rate of growth, shown by the slopes of the lines, was greater with more phosphate at low concentrations (0–5). With higher concentrations, the algae were growing as fast as they could, and the slopes were the same for 10, 15 and 20. Redrawn from Maloney and Miller (1975). Copyright ASTM. Published with permission.*

samples containing their natural phytoplankton are enriched; in the other, all the natural phytoplankton is filtered out and replaced with an inoculum from a pure culture of a single test species of an alga with well-known physiological properties.

A complication arises when the natural population is used for bioassay, because the species that grow best under confined conditions are usually not the ones that dominate in the freely circulating water of the lake. While the use of the natural population gives information about the relative significance of different nutrients to the species that will grow in a lake at a given time, it complicates the comparison of different lakes or of the condition of one lake at different times. To permit such comparisons, the Environmental Protection Agency developed a highly standardized systematic procedure using pure cultures. Actual population densities achieved in the flasks will not be the same as those to be expected in a lake, but the relative effect of different enrichments is shown clearly. This is the method in common use in lake management situations (fig. 2.3).

Bioassays have been widely used to assess the nutrient status of lakes. As a generalization, the elements most often found to be limiting in sizable lakes in the temperate zone are phosphorus and nitrogen. Phosphate has turned out to be the most frequently limiting nutrient in a broad area of the north temperate regions of North America and Europe. One study in North America with the EPA method showed that in a group of forty-nine widely distributed lakes, thirty-five were limited by phosphorus, eight by nitrogen, and six by something else, not identified. Phosphate is not limiting in such places as the parts of Florida where phosphate is mined and in some alkaline saline lakes. It is also not limiting in many polluted lakes that have been overloaded with sewage because that supplies more phosphate than the lake can use. Many coastal marine waters are limited by nitrogen rather than by phosphorus. As chapter 3 will show, carbon dioxide is rarely limiting in lakes, although it can be in shallow, enriched ponds.

There are also two different ways of measuring the response in bioassays. One is to count organisms repeatedly over a period of days, or to use some other measure of the population size such as dry weight, optical density, or chlorophyll content. From this information we can calculate algal population growth and the maximum population size achieved. The other way is to add a small amount of radioactive carbon dioxide and, after a few hours, to determine how much has been taken up by the algae. This is a direct measure of the rate of photosynthesis. These two methods measure different things and naturally give somewhat different results.

The rate of uptake of radioactive carbon dioxide has been widely used with natural populations because the experiments need last only a few hours so that the population responding is that initially present. The interpretation is different from that based on population size. The maximum population size that can be achieved in the lake cannot be predicted from the initial rate at which the algae photosynthesize because that rate cannot be maintained when one of the nutrients becomes exhausted. Thus, adding trace metals may stimulate a higher rate of photosynthesis, but this will not result in sustained growth of the population because such growth will usually be determined by the concentration of phosphorus or of some other nutrient. This fact has confused the discussion of detergents. For example, in one case carbon dioxide uptake was increased by additions of any one of several elements, molybdenum, zinc, cobalt, manganese or iron. This does not mean that massive blooms would be made by large additions of any of those elements. Too much zinc is toxic to algae and too much iron or manganese would precipitate most of the phosphate. In chapter 3 I will develop this discussion in detail.

## Paleolimnology

It is often desirable to know what the condition of a lake was before the advent of limnologists. Fortunately, remains of many kinds of organisms are preserved in lake sediment and can be identified in cores of mud. Because dead organisms and other materials are continuously falling to the bottom, the depth in the core below the surface of the mud is an appropriate time scale. It can be calibrated with dating methods that use the isotopes carbon 14 and lead 210. In some sediments seasonal changes in the material falling result in annual layers called varves.

The best fossils are the shells of diatoms that permit exact identification so that one can draw up a list of species inhabiting the lake for the past tens, hundreds or thousands of years. Many species occur only in either acid or alkaline water, so a crude but usable estimate of past pH can be made from counts of diatom species. Such data have been widely used in studying the development and distribution of acid precipitation (chapter 7). An episode of pollution with copper waste in Lago d'Orta in northern Italy is recorded by characteristically distorted diatoms in the mud. Some green algae with thick cellulose walls preserve well also. Many of the pigments contained in algae are undecomposed or only partly broken down, including some of those produced by blue-greens. Thus we have a way to determine changes in the phytoplankton that occurred even in the distant past. The onset of dominance by blue-greens in Lake Zürich is well shown by pigments, and the episode of occupation of Lake Washington by *Oscillatoria* is preserved in the form of a section of mud containing oscillaxanthin, a carotenoid pigment produced by no other abundant planktonic blue-green. Hard chitinous parts of insects and crustaceans preserve very well. Appearance or disappearance of certain kinds can result from changes in the occurrence of predators, such as the introduction of planktivorous fish.

The ideas and examples in this chapter were selected from a large body of knowledge for their special relevance to the problems discussed in the rest of the book.

# Part 2

## Lessons from Lake Washington

The Lake Washington study was made for its basic scientific interest, and the results improved our understanding of the role of nutrients in controlling populations. That information has been useful in developing programs for the protection and restoration of lakes. But the application of scientific knowledge about Lake Washington is not the only lesson to be learned. The character of the public education campaign and other aspects of public action can be used as guides for working with other situations or, failing that, for helping to understand what went wrong with them. Conversely, a study of other problems may help us to evaluate the Lake Washington experience.

In this section I will review several current environmental problems and show in what ways they resemble or differ from the Lake Washington case. Some of the problems are gigantic in scope, encompassing the entire earth. Others, like Lake Washington, affect a single body of water. The topics included are similar in several ways. Each involves a scientific evaluation of an environmental problem. Each involves political action, based on an understanding of the scientific background and combined with a system of community goals and priorities. Each involves a major effect on the financial interests of large industries willing to protect their own special interests by liberal spending. In all cases, a solution of the problem requires that choices be made among actions, each of which has disadvantages for somebody. One can hope that the choice will be made on the basis of an objective evaluation of the balance between all the advantages and all the disadvantages, but often there are too many subjective matters and special interests to permit clear decisions. To fail to act on a problem is, in effect, a decision in which a judgment is made that the environmental benefit to be gained is not worth any of the necessary costs or disadvantages.

Chapters 3 and 4 are closely connected with the chapters in part 1, the former because it concerns the chemical control of production, the latter because Puget Sound is physically connected with Lake Washington and is affected by Metro. Chapters 5, 6 and 7 describe different kinds of environmental problems in which we can see parallels with the way the Lake Washington situation was evaluated and handled.

# Chapter 3

## The Detergent Problem

In the early 1970s a fantastic controversy developed over the use of detergents—cleaning agents—that contain phosphate. It spread through North America and Europe and gave rise to stiff diplomatic exchanges between Canada and the United States, foreshadowing an even more acerbic confrontation about acid precipitation. (See chapter 7.) I will review the detergent controversy in considerable detail for several reasons. It is an especially clear case of an environmental problem for which a genuine understanding of ecological principles is essential. It illustrates the conflict between environmental protection and strong economic interests. And it provides a pattern against which to compare other controversies, by helping to identify the different components. Another reason for giving the detergent problem so much attention is that more than fifteen years later it is still going on and nonsense is still being published and presented in public actions and court hearings. So this chapter is not just a historical review—it deals with a contemporary problem. There are many examples here of misunderstanding, misuse, and misrepresentation of scientific data and concepts. We see similar arguments being made currently about acid precipitation, the ozone layer in the atmosphere, and the environmental effects of smoking tobacco, among others. Since this is my principal example, I include more technical information about it than about the others. I am indebted to Dr. David W. Schindler for much background information used in this chapter.

The basis of the controversy is that at a particular time it became important to some members of the soap and detergent industry that people believe that eutrophication of lakes was caused by the content of organic carbon compounds in sewage, and that phosphate had little to do with the process. They maintained that phosphorus is present in excess in most lakes and that eutrophication is based on the production of carbon dioxide by the bacterial decomposition of organic matter. To come to this conclusion required great ingenuity.

The kind of concern about eutrophication that led to the formation of the Seattle Metro in 1958 was spreading in North America during the 1960s. The eutrophication of Lake Washington was readily reversed by diverting the effluent from the lake in such a way as not to cause the same problem elsewhere. (How this was possible is explained in chapter 4, which concerns Puget Sound.) Because most communities do not have such an option, there was motivation to search for techniques that, singly or together, could improve the condition of lakes that had deteriorated under the influence of sewage effluent, or could at least prevent further deterioration. These techniques emphasized modification of the effluent to reduce its effects, although modification of the lakes themselves was also being considered.

The growing concern about the deterioration of lakes led to a series of symposia and governmental hearings to define the problems and find solutions. Starting in 1963 an elaborate study with hearings was conducted by the Natural Resources and Power Subcommittee of the House of Representatives Committee on Government Operations, culminating in a report in 1968 (U.S. House of Representatives 1968). The report, *On saving America's small lakes,* surveyed the views of governors of the states. The main worry expressed was about pollution, with emphasis on eutrophication. By that time Daniel J. Evans, who as a Washington state legislator had been so effective in the creation of the Seattle Metro, had been elected governor. He mentioned eutrophication and expressed concern about lack of adequate funding.

In 1965 the National Academy of Sciences appointed an advisory committee to organize an international symposium on eutrophication. It was held in June 1967, with about 600 people attending from twelve countries, and a proceedings volume was published containing thirty-four contributions (National Academy of Sciences 1969). Although the scope of the book was very general, several of the papers discussed the special significance of phosphorus. By then I had reported that Lake Washington was responding satisfactorily to the protective action that had been started four years earlier. Eugen Thomas of Zürich had made an elaborate bioassay study of forty-six Swiss lakes, finding that phosphorus was the predominant limiting element. At the NAS symposium he reported a further study of fifty-five European lakes and concluded, "Harmful algae are best controlled by limiting inflow of phosphates." He also reported a new program of reducing the phosphate content of effluent entering Lake Zürich by adding ferric (iron) chloride to the aeration stage of secondary treatment plants.

Since it was clear that phosphorus was a dominating element in large areas of the world with major lakes, and deterioration of many of those lakes in historical times was coordinated with increased input of sewage, it seemed reasonable to concentrate on improving ways or finding new ways to reduce the phosphorus content of sewage effluent.

There are two possible approaches to this. One is to modify the treatment process to increase the removal of phosphorus. Most methods for removal have disadvantages, such as increased production of sludge with associated problems of disposal, as well as the additional cost of chemicals and, in many cases, expensive structural modification of the treatment plants. At the time of the Lake Washington diversion, there had been little experience with advanced treatment, and some methods widely used at present had not been invented, much less perfected. At about the same time as the Metro vote, the officials in Zürich had decided that diversion under their conditions would be too expensive, so they started the precipitation program mentioned above.

The other approach is to reduce the amount of phosphorus that is put into the sewage in the first place. An irreducible minimum amount is produced physiologically by the human population. (See chapter 2.) Various other activities add phosphorus, and some can be stopped or reduced. For example sink garbage grinders (popularly known as garbage disposals) make a purée of unused vegetable material, a convenient but wasteful way of disposing of it. It puts an added burden on the sewage treatment plants and discards material that could be composted productively. For that reason, some communities have banned the use of such garbage grinders in order to encourage composting. Other communities make their use mandatory because it reduces the problem of disposing of solid waste. This kind of decision is strongly influenced by local conditions and customs.

A more significant component of the material added to sewage is the detergent used for washing dishes and clothes. Most soaps were made from animal fat, and the supply was potentially limited by the rate of slaughter by the meat industry. Synthetic detergents were introduced soon after World War II and came into wide use as a substitute for soap. Two problems developed almost immediately. The earlier versions contained agents to produce a reassuring foam, but that was overdone and made problems in sewage plants. Many photographs were published in newspapers and magazines showing mountains of foam in streams and lakes that received effluent containing such agents. This problem was handled by changing the formulation so that the foaming agents were decomposable or "biodegradable."

The other problem was brought on by the fact that, for chemical reasons having to do with their ability to combine with dirt, the best detergents then known contained large amounts of phosphorus. In the 1960s concern was increasing about the deterioration of lakes, especially that brought about by sewage disposal. Attention became focussed on phosphorus in detergents because the compounds used break down into phosphate ions, the form most available to algae. The percentage of the phosphorus in sewage that originates in detergents varies considerably depending on the other material added, but it can exceed that contributed by human waste. A representative figure appears to be about 50%; that is, detergents doubled the previous concentration of phosphorus in sewage. Therefore about half the phosphorus introduced into lakes in sewage effluent could be eliminated simply by not using detergents that contain phosphorus. The suggestion was made that such a change could reduce the phosphate loading on some lakes by a significant amount, and could be one of a number of techniques to protect lakes against eutrophication. Of course, no one could expect the change to be a cure for all eutrophied lakes everywhere, but a reduction in the loading of phosphate by 50% could be expected to improve the condition of lakes that were not already above the critical level of loading (fig. 2.2). By itself this would not be enough to improve overloaded lakes, but it could be combined with other procedures to limit the amount of phosphate in effluent or its effect in the lake. (Remember we are talking about lakes that were observed to deteriorate under the influence of phosphate-rich input generated by human activities, not lakes that are naturally productive for geological reasons.)

Getting detergents changed was not easy. In 1967, Secretary of the Interior Stewart L. Udall urged the detergent industry to produce detergents free of phosphate. Some companies tried to comply. Procter & Gamble, according to W. C. Krumrei, its technical director of government relations, in a Senate hearing in 1970, was "working all-out to achieve a steady reduction in the phosphate content of all its heavy-duty laundry detergents. We are, in fact, working to achieve complete elimination of phosphates." It was the hope of the industry to substitute nitriloacetic acid (NTA), and at the time of Mr. Krumrei's statement, Procter & Gamble had ordered $167 million worth. Meantime, in 1969 a House of Representatives subcommittee chaired by Henry Reuss of Wisconsin had been holding hearings about the significance of phosphorus in eutrophication and was about to issue a very aggressive report (U.S. House of Representatives 1970b). In May, the Department of the Interior "demanded" that the detergent manufacturers reduce their use of phosphate, and some did that, increasing their use of NTA. In December 1970, as a result of preliminary experiments at the National Institute of Environmental Health Sciences, NTA became suspected of causing birth defects and perhaps cancer when present in high enough concentrations. There was considerable doubt about the validity of the claim, but the mere suspicion of that kind of damage was enough to end the use of NTA and change the attitude of the soap and detergent industry toward phosphorus. In September 1971, the use of NTA was formally banned, and governmental officials advised continued use of phosphate detergents until something better could be found. (As it happened, later work failed to confirm the initial conclusions, and NTA is now being used in some detergents for commercial use.)

The sudden reversal caused considerable confusion and led to a fantastic controversy about limiting elements. Mr. Krumrei had expressed doubt about the importance of phosphorus. Now it had suddenly become important to the industry to believe that phosphorus had nothing to do with eutrophication, or rather, to persuade governmental officials to believe that. A more moderate view, expressed occasionally by some members of the industry, was that phosphorus had some importance, but controlling detergents would have little or no benefit. Jesse L. Steinfeld, then surgeon general, wrote for the *Reader's Digest* an insider's view of the governmental actions that illustrates the developing confusion within the government about detergents. (It is quoted later in this chapter.)

Increasing awareness of the phosphorus problem had already led to international concern; the International Joint Commission had been appointed to study the relation of American and Canadian activities to the Great Lakes. Its report in 1969 emphasized the role of phosphorus in eutrophication and called for action by both governments. Its recommendation to reduce the input of phosphorus to the Great Lakes brought forth a violent reaction in a technical magazine, *Canadian Research & Development*, in 1970. In a series of articles the editor, Douglas Dingeldein, and Robert F. Legge, a free-lance writer, tried to show that carbon was the element responsible for trouble in eutrophied lakes and that phosphorus was of little importance. The scene was set by the cover of the magazine: a dramatic photograph of a rope noose encircling the words: "We hung phosphates without a fair trial," set on a black background with a red border. The first article began, "Has the International Joint Commission . . . been a party to what may prove to have been the most incredible scientific/political hoax in the history of Canadian and American relations? What hoax? Do you believe phosphates are the key nutrient in the process of eutrophication? You are wrong. *You have hung phosphates without a fair trial.*" This approach brought a vigorous rebuttal by Dr. J. R. Vallentyne, chief scientist on the Eutrophication Section of the Freshwater Institute at Winnipeg. In the next issue of the magazine, he presented an excellent, clear discussion of the problem and pointed out some of the serious flaws in the carbon argument. The following issue carried further comments by Legge and six letters to the editor including one from me.

This exchange was a forerunner of prolonged public debates about the phosphorus problem. All of them involved a strenuous promotion of the untenable ideas that eutrophication depended on pollution with organic materials supplying carbon dioxide which supported increased production, and that phosphorus was of no concern because there was so much of it.

In February 1971, a major symposium on the topic was sponsored by ASLO, the American Society of Limnology and Oceanography (Likens 1972). The meeting was attended by 109 participants representing universities, governmental agencies and industries of Canada and the United States. I gave a talk on Lake Washington specifically designed to be relevant to the controversy. The scientists and the soap and detergent people had different opinions about the meeting, well expressed in two published reviews. (Compare Legge 1971 and Likens et al. 1971. Also see the section on Lake Washington later in this chapter.)

Meantime, the matter had been attracting official U.S. governmental attention. Congressional subcommittees held hearings on the problems of pollution and phosphates in detergents (U.S. House of Representatives 1970a, 1972; U.S. Senate 1970). Many scientists, engineers, and other persons testified at these lengthy hearings on all possible sides of the issues. The soap and detergent industry was represented by officials of several companies, most prominently Procter & Gamble and FMC Corporation. Not all manufacturers of cleaning material opposed phosphorus control, however. Advertisements by Lever Brothers and Sears and others made it clear that products were already available that were not based on phosphorus, that is, the ones provided by their own companies.

It was a matter of considerable anxiety to companies that made phosphate detergents and suppliers of phosphate to them when the Federal Trade Commission entertained the idea of requiring that a warning label be put on boxes containing phosphate detergents and called for public hearings that were held in April 1971. The proposed label was:

WARNING: EACH RECOMMENDED USE LEVEL
OF THIS PRODUCT CONTAINS _____ GRAMS
OF PHOSPHORUS, WHICH CONTRIBUTES TO WATER
POLLUTION. DO NOT USE IN EXCESS. IN SOFT WATER
AREAS, USE OF PHOSPHATES IS NOT NECESSARY.

The statement would have to be included in advertisements. In addition, all ingredients would have to be listed on the box.

This threat elicited a vast outpouring of testimony covering 928 pages of stenographic transcript plus several long prepared statements submitted in advance. Some of the documents were apparently widely distributed by Procter & Gamble and FMC Corporation along with reproductions of news articles, speeches by industry officials and the like. The testimony has not been published, but I obtained a copy from the U.S. Federal Trade Commission under the Freedom of Information Act. The testimony by representatives of the industry attacked any restriction on the use of phosphorus on all conceivable grounds and some that are difficult to conceive. Their argument was that no satisfactory substitutes for phosphorus existed and that phosphorus was not important anyway.

There were in fact definite disadvantages to some of the substitutes that were available at the time. Some were very caustic and corroded metal parts and pitted the porcelain finish of washing machines, resulting in costly repairs or replacements. Considerable attention in the testimony was given to the danger of having such materials around the house with small children present. There had been unfortunate accidents in which children had tasted the material they found in a box under the sink and received serious, even fatal burns. Further, the substitutes were said not to clean as well as those with phosphate. In hard water a precipitate formed that remained on the clothes, making the colors dull. The cloth itself was damaged by the stronger materials. Possibly there were some economic reasons having to do with costs of various components and profit margins, but the industry's testimony tended to downplay or even deny that financial matters were of any concern to them. All they wanted was a Clean, Healthy America. Nevertheless, H. J. Morgens, president of Procter & Gamble, testified that a major reason for objecting to the labelling proposal was that they frequently changed the composition of the mixture of components. When the price of one ingredient increased, they would substitute something else to fill the same function. An official of another company said that he did not want to provide information to his competitors. Another said his company knew the composition of competitive brands because they analyzed samples. (See Rodgers 1973 for a summary of the economics of the industry.)

## The Nature of the Problem

The basic problem originates in the observation that many large lakes have changed in historical times from being clear and pleasant to a condition in which they produce prolonged dense algal nuisances with unpleasant side effects, as described in chapters 1 and 2. Why did they change and what can be done about it? It is important to recognize the causes of algal nuisance blooms and to correct them. To study this problem we will return to several of the ideas discussed in chapter 2.

Many of the presentations by the S & D industry emphasized a perceived false complexity, as stated, for example, by L. E. Kuentzel (1970), a research associate of Wyandotte Chemicals Corporation: "Technical facts tending to discredit the ban phosphates approach are complicated and difficult to understand and so, for the most part, are ignored." I agree; I find their reasoning very difficult to understand because it does not make sense.

Paul F. Derr, assistant director of research and development of the FMC Corporation, gave an example of the exaggerated view of the complexity of the algal nuisance problem in his testimony before the Federal Trade Commission. After congratulating the members of the committee for their record of sincerity, interest and attendance at meetings, he told them that "The problem of man-caused eutrophication is the most complex subject in our world. It truly encompasses the 'mystery of life on earth.' Thus we are attempting to understand and answer the questions: Why do plants grow? How can we retard or stop their growth?"

This of course is nonsense. We are faced with many much more complex problems than eutrophication, which is actually very simple in concept and is not dangerous in the same way as some of our other problems are. If you add fertilizer to a lawn you can expect the grass to grow faster and taller as long as you water it and the temperature is warm enough. The chances are it will become overgrown with weeds if you do not make special efforts.

Some people fell into the trap of thinking that before they could evaluate the problem and possible solutions, they would have to understand every detail of algal nutrition or physiology. No. What is important is the *change*, and what we must do is to match it against *changes* in conditions that are known to affect algae. Where records exist, almost always they show that there has been a large, clear-cut change in the drainage into the lake, and most often that has been an increase in sewage. Sometimes, under special conditions, large changes in agricultural practices may have an effect. For example, farmers in the drainage area of Lake Mendota in Wisconsin used to spread manure on the snow cover of their fields during late winter. When the snow melted, much of the material drained into the lake instead of staying on the fields and thus became part of the support of the blue-greens. Correcting such wasteful practices can benefit both the economic condition of the farms and the condition of the lakes.

In this discussion, I will contrast two views of the importance of phosphorus. In general, the view of members of the soap and detergent industry favored retaining phosphate detergents, and tended to downplay or deny the importance of phosphorus in generating algal nuisances, although this was not true of all companies nor of all individuals. I will refer to supporters of the retention of phosphorus detergents as "pro-detergent people" or "S & D" people. They opposed the idea of a warning label. People who favored the labelling proposition or some control of phosphorus cannot be so easily identified with an affiliation since they were a diverse group; many were university scientists, including limnologists and a few sanitary engineers. A very large number of sanitary engineers affiliated with universities, however, gave support to the S & D viewpoint. To simplify, I have taken most examples from only a few of many sources. FMC Corporation issued a pamphlet *Eutrophication* that included subsections on "The eutrophication problem: a review and critical analysis (The *Non*-role of detergent phosphates in eutrophication)" and "Lack of correlation between phosphorus and algal growth." It was entered into the record of the Senate hearings of 1970.

The presentations to the Federal Trade Commission (FTC) by Paul F. Derr, William C. Krumrei, and F. A. Gilbert, a vice-president of the FMC Corporation, are rich sources of examples. The examples are of several different kinds. Some can be classified as either true or false. Most of the true ones are irrelevant red herrings, having nothing to do with the case. The most clearly false ones are simply misstatements in contradiction to well-demonstrated facts, or are misquotations. In between the true and the false are vast numbers of misunderstandings, misinterpretations of facts, misapplications of concepts, simple mistakes, and much fuzzy thinking.

In this discussion, I am not making a personal attack on anybody. I have met only a few of the industry S & D people whose writing I quote, most of them casually. I know little of their intellectual qualities or professional qualifications beyond what shines through in the written words. What I attack are those written statements with which I disagree. I will name people and companies only to identify sources so that readers can see the context of the selections I make, check what I say about them, and pursue any of the points further. One has to be careful when quoting excerpts not to change the meaning of the whole statement, but reading the excerpts quoted below in their full context only makes them seem worse.

### Relative Amounts of Carbon and Phosphorus in Algae

A common fallacy is to make a judgment of the relative importance of elements on the basis of their amounts in algae. The amounts vary in different kinds of algae, but in general, carbon is about 50% and phosphorus about 1% of the dry material. On this basis F. A. Gilbert explained during the Senate hearing in 1970: "It is obvious that the major element required for growth of algae is carbon." No. It is obvious that this is a poor criterion for importance. What matters is how the composition of the algae relates to the availability or rate of supply of the components. The atmosphere and the carbon dioxide system in the water normally provide an abundant source of carbon, but phosphate is very much less available.

Try an analogy: the weight of the nails in a conventional wooden house is a very small percentage of the weight of the wood, but you cannot build a conventional wooden house without them. If the supplier delivered an ounce of nails with every ton of wood, the rate of building the house would be limited by the nails, not the wood. Extra wood would accumulate.

The percentages of carbon and phosphorus given above are based on the weight of the solids left after drying the algae. Fresh algae contain about 90% water, so on the basis of the reasoning by the S & D people, the best thing would be to reduce the water supply of the algae; i.e., dry the lake up. If that idea sounds weird, just keep reading.

### Upside-Down Thinking

Many of the pro-detergent people used a strange approach that I think of as upside-down thinking. For example, W. J. Oswald, professor of sanitary engineering at the University of California, testified:

> In the pristine environment phosphate is quite often a limiting factor for aquatic growth but, in the case of bodies of water into which nutrients of sewage origin are introduced, phosphorus is usually in vast excess. In these and many other cases phosphorus contributes less to algal growth than do carbon, nitrogen, iron, and perhaps other crucial elements, all of which must be present in minimum concentrations if algae growth is to approach phosphate limitation. Thus, in bodies of water receiving sewage effluents phosphates are rarely the limiting factor and methods other than detergent phosphate limitation must be sought for their control. (U.S. House of Representatives 1972).

This seems to say that if you load up a nice clear lake with so much sewage that it is no longer limited by phosphate, you cannot help the problem by reducing the input of phosphate back to what it was before, an astonishing conclusion. If a lake is limited by phosphate, its production of algae would increase if you added more phosphate and decrease if the input of phosphate were reduced. If it is overloaded with phosphate you would have to reduce the input of phosphate to bring it down to the level where further reductions would have an effect. (See fig. 2.2.)

### Response of Lakes to Changes in Phosphate Alone

A direct approach to identify the relative importance of phosphate and carbon would be to fertilize an unpolluted oligotrophic lake with phosphate, not accompanied by an organic source of carbon. If the production of algae increased, you would know that carbon had not been limiting. Many such tests have been made. Outstanding examples are the whole-lake fertilizations by D. W. Schindler and associates in the Canadian Experimental Lakes Area. (See chapter 12.) One lake was fertilized with different additions for six years. Sugar was used as an easily available usable source of organic carbon. Additions of phosphate, nitrate and sugar combined produced algal blooms. When phosphate was omitted and only nitrate and sugar were added, blooms were not formed. When the phosphate addition was stopped, the lake recovered promptly. Those lakes are representative of many in the drainage area of the Great Lakes.

Many other studies have been made of the effect of added phosphate alone or phosphate added with nitrate but not carbon. The first detailed study was done by W. Einsele in Germany in 1937 and 1938 with superphosphate agricultural fertilizer. Organic carbon and nitrate were not added. The plankton rapidly took up phosphate and, after some delay, increased in abundance. Unexpectedly, the nitrogen content of the lake increased. Later, C. N. Sawyer, then at the University of Wisconsin, showed experimentally that the addition of phosphate could support the growth of nitrogen-fixing blue-greens that converted molecular nitrogen gas, which constitutes 80% of the air, into organic combination in the cells, thus using molecular nitrogen rather than nitrate as a source (Sawyer 1965). The first year after Einsele's fertilization stopped, the lake returned to its original condition. Part of the added phosphate was firmly bound in the sediment, the rest had gone out the outlet.

The papers by Einsele and Sawyer were widely ignored by the

S & D people, although both were available. In 1957 Hutchinson gave a concise summary in English of Einsele's paper and referred to the discovery of the return to original state after the disturbance of the phosphorus cycles as "one of the most important that have ever been made in limnology." Sawyer's paper was published in a well-known journal devoted to sewage science.

Little Otter Lake in Ontario is another clear-cut example of response to phosphate alone. A manufacturing company discharged a large quantity of a polyphosphate cleaning compound for two months in 1971. The lake promptly developed a bloom of blue-greens not seen there previously. The discharge was stopped and by the next summer the lake was back to normal (Michalski and Conroy 1973). This response showed that the lake was limited by phosphate, that the natural carbon dioxide system was enough to support a dense crop of blue-greens, and that the algae needed a continuing supply of phosphate to keep producing blooms.

Kootenay Lake in British Columbia received significant amounts of inorganic phosphate from a fertilizer plant and developed blooms of blue-greens. After the enrichment from the fertilizer plant stopped, the phytoplankton decreased somewhat and its composition changed greatly, no longer including significant quantities of blue-greens. The lake continued to receive agricultural drainage. The interpretation of the abundance of plankton is complicated by the fact that there was a change in grazing zooplankton at the same time. *Mysis* had been introduced and *Daphnia* was eliminated (R. A. Parker 1976).

Many studies have been made of ponds and lakes fertilized with a mixture of elements not containing organic carbon. Long experience in successful fertilization of fish ponds in the southeastern United States with a commercial N-P-K fertilizer showed that phosphorus alone gave about the same production of fish (Swingle et al. 1963). Oligotrophic Bare Lake in Alaska was fertilized with phosphate and nitrate without a source of carbon in a study of sockeye salmon production. Fertilization was followed by large increases in the rate of photosynthesis, abundance of phytoplankton, and the rate of growth of the individual fish. (See chapter 12.)

As long ago as 1954 C. H. Mortimer, then of the Freshwater Biological Association (U.K.), surveyed the literature on fish pond fertilization in detail. He concluded that "Phosphatic fertilizers, often combined with lime and potassium fertilizers, have produced by far the greatest increase in fish crops in ponds, and are therefore most commonly recommended and employed." Further, about organic fertilizers, "in general, mixtures of phosphate and organic manures produced crops no larger than those produced by the application of phosphates alone." This evidence is contrary to the S & D position.

More examples could be cited to show that the addition of organic carbon is not ordinarily required to generate algal blooms. This is only half the story, because all the examples so far cited were of additions of phosphate. Converse experiments have been done by removing phosphate. As shown in chapter 1, the secondary sewage effluent entering Lake Washington was a poor source of organic carbon, and the diversion had a much greater effect on phosphorus than on nitrate or carbon. The program of adding ferric chloride to the secondary treatment plants emptying into Lake Zürich reduced the phosphate income of the lake considerably without a corresponding reduction in carbon, and the condition of the lake improved.

The effect of removal of phosphate was studied experimentally by precipitating phosphate from Potomac River water with ferric sulfate in flasks (Shapiro and Ribiero 1965). The supernatant water, deprived of phosphate and trace metals, supported much less growth of algae. When the concentration of phosphate was restored by adding pure phosphate without metals, the ability to support algae was equally restored. This showed that even though other elements had been precipitated, they were not controlling the production of algae. Despite the clarity of this experiment and of the presentation of the results in the original publication, F. A. Gilbert objected before a Senate Committee in 1970 that the report: ". . . incorrectly assumed this 'proves' phosphates are the cause, because the other 14 to 19 essential elements are ignored. These are removed to some undefined degree in the chemical precipitation step, whereas phosphate is almost completely removed. All agree 'complete' removal of any one essential nutrient, including phosphate, will limit algae growth." Obviously Gilbert totally missed the point, as did so many of the S & D people. After all this it is fascinating to read Derr's evaluation for the FTC:

> I wish to emphasize that no one—no government, no scientist, no one anywhere—has ever demonstrated that a reduction in the phosphate added to a lake will have any effect whatsoever on the growth of algae in the lake. . . . No one has ever demonstrated that restriction of the input of phosphates to a lake will have any effect whatsoever on the growth of algae in that lake. In fact every time scientists have attempted to show a correlation between phosphate added to a lake and algae growth they have obtained the opposite answer—there is no correlation!

I wonder what he had in mind. So, apparently, did Commissioner Mary Gardiner Jones who said to Derr unbelievingly, "I have never heard anybody say what you said before." Remember that the information summarized in figs. 1.4 and 1.5, and much more, was available to Mr. Derr when he made his statement.

In using the S & D evaluations of the literature one must be careful to check against the original. Sometimes relevant material is omitted, and some of the material given is simply wrong. For example, Gilbert, in his 1970 Senate testimony (U.S. Federal Trade Commission 1971), misreports a study by Sylvester and Anderson (1964) of Green Lake in Seattle: "A study of Green Lake in Washington showed offensive algal blooms even though the phosphorus content was seldom above 0.01 ppm [=10 micrograms/liter] the reported limiting level." In fact, the published graph for soluble phosphorus (essentially the same as phosphate) has a scale to 60 micrograms/liter, and the values are more than 10 most of the time. (Note: 60 micrograms/liter = 0.060 ppm or parts per million.) A table shows the median value for the outlet water as 26, meaning that half the values for soluble phosphorus were more than 26. The total phosphorus values were much higher, almost always more than 40, with a median of 64. Anyway, the reference to 0.01 ppm is a misuse of Sawyer's limit, which is discussed later in this chapter.

A striking thing about the S & D testimony is the way they ignored relevant papers, especially those published before 1960.

The FMC testimony in the 1970 Senate hearings lists no paper earlier than 1964 (FMC Corporation 1970 and the corporation's four undated pamphlets). In a rare stroke of candor, the bibliography is divided into two parts, one of which is identified as "Additional pertinent references (not specifically cited in this report)." Significantly, that list contains one of my Lake Washington papers, but not the one most applicable to the phosphorus problem.

E. J. Griffith of Monsanto Company actually wrote in an "Environmental Phosphorus Handbook": "Until the early 1960s, the concentration of phosphorus in the freshwaters of the earth was considered by most investigators to be too insignificant to be worthy of analysis." I commented extensively about the many mistakes in that article in a 1974 review of the book in which it appeared.

### Apparent Lack of Response of Lakes to Reduction in Phosphate Loading

Not all lakes are expected to respond to changes in phosphate loading. There are several reasons why a lake might not respond to a reduction in phosphate loading from sewage. One reason would be if the change is not large enough to bring the loading down into the responsive zone. (See fig. 2.2.) Another reason would be special circumstances of depth and water income. A combination of shallowness and small inflow can permit a formerly polluted lake to retain the effects of pollution for many years. An extreme example of these conditions appears to be shown by Stone Lake in Illinois, cited by Gilbert (U.S. Federal Trade Commission 1971). This very heavily polluted lake is shallow, has no outlet and is maintained by seepage water, so that it is not diluted and flushed out.

A more interesting example is Lake Sammamish near Lake Washington, which has had prolonged study by E. B. Welch and associates at the University of Washington in connection with a sewage diversion project. Superficially, Lake Sammamish looks like a small Lake Washington, but had not been as productive as Lake Washington and had not had the blue-green *Oscillatoria*. It is different in an important way. The hypolimnion is a relatively small part of the volume of the lake and becomes devoid of oxygen (anoxic) early each summer. This condition increases the amount of phosphorus released from the sediment. In 1968 sewage was diverted from Lake Sammamish, reducing the phosphorus loading by about half. At first the lake seemed unaffected. During the first seven years after diversion the phosphorus content and total abundance of phytoplankton of the lake changed very little; however, the relative abundance of blue-greens decreased by 50% within two years. It took until 1984, fourteen years, for the phosphorus content to be reduced to half the original value (Welch et al. 1986). The relative sensitivity of the blue-greens is an important point which will be developed later in this chapter.

### The Myth about Organic Carbon

Briefly stated, the thesis pushed by Legge and Dingeldein and taken up enthusiastically by the S & D people is that waste rich in organic matter that enters a lake is decomposed by bacteria, liberating carbon dioxide that is then used by algae, producing a bloom. They appear to have been introduced to this obvious idea largely by papers by W. Lange (1969) and L. E. Kuentzel (1969, 1970, 1971). Lange, an employee of Tanner's Council Laboratory, University of Cincinnati, used the term *symbiotic* in his title. Kuentzel, who did no experimental work himself, headed the introduction of a review paper "Bacteria and Blue-Green Algae—A Mutualistic Symbiosis?" Now it turns out that all they are talking about is simply the normal community function of bacteria as decomposers, organisms that live by breaking down organic molecules as a source of building material and energy for their own growth. In so doing they liberate $CO_2$. Bacteria are always associated with blue-greens just as they are associated with diatoms and all other planktonic organisms. Lake water is not sterile. Bacteria are ubiquitous in lakes; one cannot dip up a sample of lake water anywhere without getting bacteria. Some of them move freely in the water, others attach to solid surfaces including the cell walls or gelatinous coatings of all kinds of algae. In fact, one of the major technical difficulties experienced by algal physiologists is that it is very difficult to get cultures of algae that are not contaminated with bacteria. Special techniques are needed to free algal cells of bacteria.

Somehow, the naive misuses of the terms mutualism and symbiosis caught the imagination of people who did not know any ecology and gave an air of special importance to the simple idea that if you dump a lot of organic material into a lake it will be decomposed there by the resident bacteria. In fact this is the basis for one style of fish pond fertilization, in which the bacteria, by decomposing organic fertilizer, support a food chain involving protozoa, small crustaceans and other invertebrates that can eat bacteria.

This is not the place for a detailed discussion of terminology. Let us just note that while "symbiosis" translates from the Greek as "living together," in biology it is used as a technical term with a special meaning. It does not mean simply living in the same place or near each other. As widely used by ecologists, it refers to a special kind of association between two species that is beneficial to one or both and harmful to neither. This misuse of the word symbiosis is a common type of error; one cannot define technical terms simply by making a literal translation of the term from its Greek or Latin origin. Mutualism is a special type of symbiosis in which both species benefit from the association. The association may be close or not. For example, certain species of bacteria capable of fixing molecular nitrogen live in special structures, nodules, on the roots of legumes and some other plants. The bacteria live in a protected place supplied with organic carbon by the plant, while the nitrogen supply of the plants is increased by the bacteria: obviously *mutual* benefits. Another, more visible, example is a lichen, an organism that consists of two species, a fungus that makes a mat of filaments and a species of alga living in the mat. Each has special structures on its cell walls that permit exchange of materials. The photosynthetic algae produce organic materials and pass the excess to the heterotrophic fungus that provides protection. The relation between bees and pollen-producing plants is a more spectacular example of the mutual adaptation of form and function of species without involving continuous contact.

Lange states "Planktonic Cyanophyta [blue-greens] are always associated with bacteria, and I have found that abundant algal growth results from a symbiotic relationship within their systems." Nothing in the rest of the paper gives evidence of a reciprocal relation between the bacteria and algae that could properly be described as a symbiosis. To validate Kuentzel's idea of mutualism, it would be necessary to show that the bacteria receive some special benefit from the blue-greens rather than from other kinds of algae. Kuentzel, in response to a question about this point, mentioned two features: that the bacteria could benefit from oxygen liberated by the blue-greens; and that blue-greens exude a gelatinous sheath to which the bacteria attach. Now, all algae liberate oxygen and many produce gelatinous sheaths. Bacteria can attach to the cell walls of those without a sheath. Thus the argument for a *special* relation with the blue-greens collapses. He could have mentioned that many algae secrete organic materials that can be used by bacteria, but this is not limited to blue-greens. In any case, I doubt that these very generalized effects qualify for the concept of mutualism. There are relations between the groups that may turn out to be mutualistic, but Lange's experiments were not designed to identify them. For example, one of the nitrogen-fixing blue-greens increases its secretion of nitrogen-containing organic compounds when a source of carbon is scarce, thus potentially benefitting bacteria by enhancing their nitrogen supply (Paerl 1984). If this turns out to be general, it might qualify as mutualism, but it applies only to the nitrogen-fixing species of blue-greens and depends on scarcity of carbon dioxide, just the opposite of Lange's proposition.

The concept of a special relationship was magnified and became dignified as the "Lange-Kuentzel-Kerr thesis." P. C. Kerr, of the Southeast Water Laboratory of the U.S. Department of Interior, got into the act by participating in a study of carbon and phosphorus in some small bodies of water in Georgia. Few things are clear about that study. Almost no information about the lakes is given in her report, but from internal evidence it appears that they were shallow and overloaded with phosphate. The experimental design is inscrutable; this is the only governmental publication I have ever seen published with a foreword that reads like a disclaimer by the administrator of the agency. A later publication was devoted to what was described as a "small Georgia fish pond." It appears that the results from these studies are not easily extrapolated to large, stratified, genuine lakes of the kind that cause the main concern about eutrophication.

To give full credit for supporting algal growth to carbon dioxide produced by decomposing sewage implies that everything else the algae need was present. The proponents of the carbon dioxide "thesis" have never presented a case in which added carbon dioxide had a large effect when it was known that phosphorus was scarce. In fact, Lange himself gave phosphorus credit as a primary element: "bacteria-assimilable carbon compounds may be one of the factors leading to algal blooms in lakes and ponds, especially when growth is not limited by the supply of phosphorus or other inorganic elements."

### "Bottom Muds—an Inexhaustible Source of Phosphorus"

"All *lakes* contain huge amounts of excess phosphates—always have and always will since this is the balance of nature. Most of these phosphates are found in the bottom sediments of the lake rather than in the water." (Derr 1971) Yes, but how much of the sediment phosphorus is available for recycling? Not much, as will be shown in detail below.

"If one could completely stop the input of all phosphates to a lake (an obvious impossibility), the phosphates in the bottom sediments would simply re-dissolve to maintain essentially a constant concentration of phosphate in the lake *waters* for hundreds of years." (Derr 1971) No. This is a gross misapplication by a physical chemist of a principle of physical chemistry— mass action.

To demonstrate a mass action reaction, one could shake up a relatively insoluble substance in water. A small amount would dissolve, saturating the water and establishing an equilibrium. There may be a continuous interchange of molecules between the solid and dissolved phases, but the concentration in the water remains the same. If one removes some of the dissolved material, more will dissolve to bring the concentration back to saturation. The implication of Derr's statement is that the mud of a lake behaves like an inert physico-chemical system when in reality the chemistry of the system is dominated by the activity of a dense population of bacteria with enzymatic systems providing energy to drive reactions that do not occur in sterile systems.

Other considerations invalidate the idea of redissolving. Only a fraction of the phosphorus is biologically available, even if shaken up in water. Some of the phosphorus becomes incorporated into the atomic lattice of crystalline compounds and is very tightly bound. One of these is the mineral apatite, a form of calcium phosphate that forms the hard part of vertebrate bones. Apatite is highly insoluble. While it can be attacked by bacterial action in some environments, once it is buried in sediments it is likely to stay there, as witnessed by the abundance of fossilized dinosaur bones, for instance. A fish bone 10 meters deep in mud will not contribute to the phosphorus dissolved in the water above the mud.

Some of the material is tightly bound to clay or other substrates, and only a small fraction can return to the water. Mud consists of closely packed particles with water in the tiny interstices between. Diffusion of dissolved material is very slow in such conditions, and you cannot expect much of even fairly soluble things to drain up out of the mud. All lake sediments that have been examined for phosphorus have measurable amounts at all depths in the mud down to the origin of the lake, about 12,000 years ago in glaciated regions, longer elsewhere. Undecomposed organic matter can be demonstrated by chemical analysis. Microscopic examination shows visible remains of organisms including even soft parts, such as some of the components of algal cells. Even very ancient sediments, now rocks millions of years old, contain organic components such as amino acids.

The FMC presentation by Gilbert to the Senate quoted snippets from a variety of publications. Some were irrelevant, some misleading. For example, one of them quoted from an informal report in 1969 by Dr. George P. Fitzgerald of the University of Wisconsin, a paragraph ending "Will the bottom water supply such nutrients?" It did not give his answer (No) provided in a paper in a professional journal; the last sentence of the abstract of that paper reads "These findings suggest that the sorption of phosphorus by lake muds under aerobic conditions can be used to *remove* phosphorus from lake water." [emphasis added]

Phosphate does recycle to some extent in lakes, and some returns to the water after being in the sediment, but the amount is relatively small as long as the water remains oxygenated. When oxygen is depleted, more phosphate can return, sometimes enough to affect the production of the lake, but it still is limited, and in no way can the store of phosphate in the entire mass of sediment be regarded as available to organisms. Some simple calculations can make this point. The amount of phosphate that accumulated in the hypolimnion of Lake Washington during summer at the height of eutrophication was equal to only 10 percent of the content of the top half inch (centimeter) of mud exposed to the water. Even in lakes that develop anoxia, the amount of phosphorus released is small relative to the amount in the mud. In Lake Sammamish the rate of phosphate release from the mud decreased after sewage diversion, showing that the release depends on continued input to the lake.

Finally, some definitive experiments have been made with radioactive phosphate. In a very direct approach, dissolved radioactive phosphate was added to oxygenated water over a core of sediment in a tube. After two weeks the sediment was cut horizontally in very thin slices. Almost all of the radioactivity was in the top tenth of an inch (3 millimeters), and of that, 96% was in the top millimeter, indicating a very thin layer of exchange (Hayes 1955).

In a converse experiment radioactive superphosphate fertilizer was placed on top of a core. The material is slightly soluble, and after 15 days 1.2% had escaped into the water. In similar cores, superphosphate was placed at different depths below the surface. In 15 days half the amount that dissolved from the surface, 0.6%, emerged into the water from a depth of a quarter inch (6 millimeters), 0.08% from one half inch (12 mm), and the amount from one inch (25 mm) was undetectable. This shows directly that the amount of phosphorus available from mud is limited (Zicker et al. 1956).

It is worth mentioning once more that these reports were available long before the detergent argument started, but they were absent from the discussion by the S & D people. Another bit of information ignored by them is that there is much more carbon than phosphorus in the mud.

## Vitamins

Some of the S & D people have emphasized the need for vitamins, materials that some organisms need but cannot synthesize themselves. Krumrei (1971) summarized an elaborate study by Professor L. Provasoli of Yale University, as "[it was] found from comprehensive assay studies that vitamin $B_{12}$, thiamine and biotin have general importance to algae" (FTC 1969). No. Provasoli showed that of 204 species tested, 57 did not need any of the three vitamins that are required by some species. Of the blue-greens, 9 out of 16 did not need any vitamins at all. The major nuisance species of blue-greens have been grown in pure mineral media without vitamins or any other organic matter. Thus, vitamins affect which species can be present, but not the quantity produced of those species that do not need them. A chemical and bioassay study of vitamin $B_{12}$ in Lake Washington during 1966–68 showed that the vitamin was present in excess relative to the needs of the species present (M. Parker 1977).

## Trace Metals

Some of the S & D literature suggests that eutrophication can be caused by the addition of certain metals that are so scarce in normal freshwater that they are commonly called trace metals, such as iron, manganese and copper. Algal physiologists who want to work on trace metals have trouble because it is hard to purify chemicals to the point where trace contaminants do not have an effect. For example, a typical analysis of reagent grade (highly purified) cobalt chloride shows 0.001% each of lead, copper and iron, 0.05% nickel and 0.01% zinc. For use of this material in nutritional studies it would have to be purified further. Water that has washed through forest soil on a rich geological substrate is likely to have plenty of the normally required trace elements except under unusual conditions. (In some parts of the world zinc and selenium are so scarce as to limit certain kinds of organisms.) Some metals are parts of enzyme systems and their availability affects the quantity of enzymes present, and therefore the rate at which some physiological reaction can take place. But while the rate of cell and population growth may be increased temporarily by the addition of trace metals, growth cannot continue at all once the supply of an essential structural element such as phosphorus has been exhausted.

Nobody has yet shown that a nuisance bloom can be caused by the addition of trace metals. Added molybdenum increased the productivity of Castle Lake in California but it did not cause a nuisance (Goldman 1960, 1967; Cordone and Nicola 1970). Iron can remove phosphate from water by precipitation and reduce production. For this reason, the addition of a waste product from steel mills, "pickling liquor," rich in iron, was used effectively to reduce the phosphate content of secondary sewage effluent in Michigan and Wisconsin. Ferric chloride was added to precipitate phosphorus in sewage from the city of Zürich, Switzerland and adjacent suburbs. Manganese in traces is required by algae. After the addition of manganese to a stream system in Pennsylvania the proportions of algae attaching to solid surfaces changed; blue-greens decreased and diatoms increased (Patrick et al. 1969). This fact was seized on by the S & D people as an example of good results from adding something to the water. However, the effect, if any, on the planktonic algae in a lake has never been tested. Because metals are toxic to algae if too concentrated, there is a limit on the degree to which metal enrichment can be used. In fact, copper sulfate formerly was widely used to control algal nuisances in small lakes by killing the algae.

### Sawyer's Limit

Repeatedly during the various hearings, references were made to the importance of the concentration of 0.01 ppm (milligrams per liter) of phosphorus, sometimes given as 10 micrograms per liter or ppb, based on work by C. N. Sawyer at the Massachusetts Institute of Technology. He had a good grasp of both engineering and limnology long before the controversy began and was in charge of the first determination of nutrient budgets that included phosphorus and nitrogen in lakes at Madison, Wisconsin. He understood well the significance of phosphorus, but the S & D literature emphasizes a misinterpretation of his results and does not mention the sound advice he gave about limiting phosphorus. Sawyer's limit continues to plague discussions of eutrophication today.

Sawyer was interested in developing criteria by which to use the nutrient condition of lakes as an indicator of their potential to produce nuisance blooms. He developed his ideas over time, reporting them in a series of three papers. These were widely misquoted and misinterpreted, in some cases evidently by people who had not checked the original publications but had simply relied upon secondary sources.

Sawyer tabulated data on inorganic phosphorus and nitrogen from seventeen lakes in southeastern Wisconsin, including the five at Madison. Seven of the lakes were said to produce nuisance blooms regularly. In his first paper (1947), he concluded that "nuisance conditions can be expected when the concentration of inorganic phosphorus exceeds or equals 0.01 ppm." He explained a bit more in the second paper (1952): ". . . any lake showing concentrations in excess of 0.01 ppm of inorganic phosphorus and 0.30 ppm of inorganic nitrogen *at the time of spring overturn* could be expected to produce algal blooms of such density as to cause nuisance." [emphasis added] Now in fact, the values tabulated in his earlier paper do not support this conclusion; three of the non-bloom lakes have values in excess of the so-called critical values. Various authors duplicated Sawyer's table without comment about this discrepancy. In the third paper (1954), Sawyer moderated his interpretation even further:

> The author at one time . . . suggested that if the 'cash in bank' assets of inorganic nitrogen and phosphorus exceeded 0.30 and 0.01 ppm, respectively, at the start of the active growing season (time of spring overturn in northern climates), a season with nuisance blooms would follow. This suggestion was made following two years of study on 17 lakes in southeastern Wisconsin and, undoubtedly, does not apply in strict manner to all lakes. At least it has served the purpose of stimulating investigations along the lines of obtaining better information.

I added emphasis to the middle quotation to indicate that we are dealing with a dynamic system in which nutrients are simultaneously being added and subtracted by a variety of processes, not a static system in which the growth resulting from a limited, definite initial supply can be measured. A phosphate ion in the water is on its way from one place to another. Thus, a lake that is able to accumulate a high concentration of phosphate by the beginning of the growing season can be expected to build up a larger population of algae during the season than one that was able to store only a lesser amount. The critical level at the start of the season will vary among lakes, depending on a number of factors involved in determining the concentration and the way the lake is able to use the phosphate supply. Sawyer gave a concise, effective discussion of these factors in his third paper.

Not all lakes behave like Sawyer's seventeen. For example, Lake Washington in 1950 had about 0.015 ppm (15 micrograms per liter) of phosphorus at the beginning of spring growth but did not produce a nuisance bloom. Even after sewage diversion, nutrients exceeded Sawyer's "limit." In 1974 before spring plankton growth started, phosphorus varied between 0.018 and 0.020 ppm and nitrogen between 320 and 390 ppm. There was no algal nuisance in the summer.

Despite all this, many people have seized on the 0.01 ppm figure as an absolute value and have based predictions not on conditions observed in a lake, but on calculations of concentration that would be made if some amount of phosphate were dumped in all at once. Obviously this leads to false conclusions. This can be seen by comparing 0.01 ppm with the amount contained in planktonic populations. The maximum phosphorus contained in the plankton, i.e. organisms, in Lake Washington at the height of eutrophication was about 0.06 ppm. Populations containing only 0.01 ppm were not large enough to be nuisances. In other words, a nuisance population develops by absorbing phosphate from a continuing supply, not by making a fixed, limited amount of phosphate into algae. In Lake Washington there was a proportionality between the concentration of phosphate at the beginning of the growing season and the maximum amount of algae during the summer, but the phosphorus content of that population was less than the earlier phosphorus content of the water. As the phytoplankton population grew, there was constant attrition by grazing and other losses.

To use the concentration of phosphate at the beginning of the growing season to predict blooms, one must know something about the personal characteristics of the lake by studying it empirically, as Sawyer did with his group of lakes. Much more effective predictions can be made by measuring the input of phosphorus and water, and taking account of the size and shape of the lake and the thickness of the epilimnion. This is a field in which good advances have been made during the past fifteen years, some of which I mentioned in chapter 2.

Furthermore, while taking the questionable figure of 0.01 from Sawyer, the S & D people ignored his conclusions about the significance of phosphorus. After showing that phosphate added alone to experimental vessels stimulated the production of blue-greens which were able to fix molecular nitrogen, Sawyer wrote, "it may be concluded that phosphorus is a key element in the fertilization of natural bodies of water and that any deficiency of nitrogen can be obtained from the atmosphere. Therefore the control of the amount of phosphorus entering lakes becomes of considerable concern." He continued by writing in a section on detergents: "Thus it seems likely that the phosphorus content of domestic sewage in the U.S. today is about twice what it was before the advent of modern syndets." He rather optimistically concluded: "Thus the importance of phosphorus as a key element in the fertilization of algal forms is becoming generally recognized."

## Irrelevancies

Because many of the arguments of the S & D people did not focus on the main problem—algal nuisances—their writing brings in many points that, even when correct, have nothing to do with the problem and therefore do not help us to understand it. Several examples have been given in the previous sections, and I wrote at length about this in my 1974 book review. Such obfuscation may be an effective technique in a debate where the aim is to win an argument. It is inappropriate in a discussion among scientists about a scientific problem. It seems clear to me that in much of the presentation of testimony and in public talks, some people with scientific training were not functioning as scientists. They were debating, not making an objective, thoughtful evaluation of information.

In all the environmental problems discussed in this book there has been disagreement that in part involved the introduction of irrelevant material. In this section I will mention a few more examples from the detergent debate, hoping to identify by analogy similar kinds of confusion with other problems.

A rich source of examples is the appendix to testimony by F. A. Gilbert (U.S. Senate 1970). "Complexity illustrated by fact there are over 18,000 species of algae (15 classes: >2500 in just one class)." So? What does this have to do with the problem? Is the implication that each will respond differently? Actually they all have many features in common. There is a unity in biochemistry. All organisms need phosphorus, nitrogen, carbon, etc. All diatoms need silica but the blue-greens do not. In another place we find some confusion about how many algae there are and also a non-sequitur: "There are tens of thousands of different algae, which contributes greatly to the complexity of any plan for control." Actually, the number of species of blue-greens that make most nuisance blooms is probably no more than a dozen.

Even stranger is the testimony to the Federal Trade Commission by William C. Krumrei. This contains a long list of quotations from the literature, some of which are irrelevant, others misinterpreted. For example, references are given to three papers with the evaluation that "All concluded that silicon was the key to increased growth." In fact, two of the papers reported laboratory *experimental* studies of diatoms, algae that require silicon. The other was a field study of five lakes with special reference to phosphorus. Some of the lakes were dominated by diatoms, and naturally silicon would be important as well as phosphorus. In any case, diatoms do not normally produce nuisance conditions in lakes.

Krumrei quotes the distinguished British algal physiologist G. E. Fogg: "Blue-green algae are of frequent occurrence in environments rich in organic matter and in freshwater lakes a distinct correlation exists between their abundance and the concentration of dissolved organic substances." Krumrei implies that the organic matter causes the growth of blue-greens. But is he correct about which is the cause and which is the effect? The question is partly answered by reading a following sentence of Fogg's paper: "However, such observations must not be taken

as definite evidence that the species concerned have requirements for exogenous supplies of organic metabolites since some
of them have been grown in pure culture in purely inorganic
media. . . . "

Further, limnologists know that Fogg himself has demonstrated that healthy growing populations of many different species of algae exude a variety of organic compounds. Automatically, a dense population of these algae will be accompanied by
dissolved organic matter that they created. Other conditions can
lead to an abundance of blue-greens and organic matter at the
same time: when a dense bloom of blue-greens is dying and decaying, cells break open and liberate their contents into the water,
increasing the content of dissolved organic matter in the water.

Some of the testimonies refer to studies of fish ponds or un-
specified waters as showing no correlation between phosphorus and algae, without saying what properties were being studied. A frequent mistake is to notice that there is little phosphate
in the water when algae are abundant and not to realize that the
phosphate is still there but has moved inside the algal cells.

Several people at the FTC hearing introduced confusion by
quoting competent oceanographers who had pointed out that in
general, coastal marine waters, for natural reasons, have excess
phosphate relative to nitrate. Sewage discharged into seawater
loses its nitrate to phytoplankton, leaving excess phosphate in
the water. Naturally, a change in detergents would not improve
such waters, and neither would removal of phosphate in treatment plants (Ryther et al. 1971).

Finally, several people emphasized that only about 15% of the
U.S. population contributed their sewage to lakes, and it was not
reasonable to impose a burden on the remaining 85%. The basis
of this evaluation is that many major centers of population such
as New York City, Boston, San Francisco and Chicago deliver
sewage to the ocean or to rivers. However, if you turn the basis
of evaluation around, the emphasis is different; a very large
fraction of the volume of freshwater in the U.S. is affected by
sewage and therefore by detergents. For example, the Laurentian Great Lakes have about one-fifth of the standing freshwater
in the world, and they have been strongly affected. Further, lakes

have been created by series of dams on many rivers across the country, and they too can be affected.

## Emotion

A striking thing about the detergent literature is the frequency of the word emotional to describe the mental state of the opponents of phosphate detergents. Another word frequently used is hysteria. The implication seems to be that the opposition to detergents is based on brainless emotion. The massive response of the industry to the labelling proposal could equally well be described as hysterical, a word they used to describe the reaction of environmentally concerned people to the deterioration of lakes. One of the funniest things in the detergent literature is the emotionally charged writing by the S & D people when they encounter the concept of phosphorus as a pollutant.

## Phosphorus as a Pollutant

The emotional strength of the abhorrence of the word *pollution* expressed by the S & D people comes through on the printed page; just try reading the following passage aloud with appropriate declamatory style:

> Specifically, the proposed wording of the detergent phosphate warning label misapplies the word 'pollution.' By definition, 'pollute' means 'to make foul or unclean; dirty.' [*Random House Unabridged Dictionary*]. Stating that phosphates *contribute* to water pollution clearly implies that phosphates are unclean, dirty substances. That is erroneous.

Hint: Any time somebody refers to a standard dictionary during an argument about technical matters, beware; you probably have trouble. We have already noted misuse of the terms *symbiosis* and *mutualism*. Some common words have taken on specialized meanings as technical terms over the years, and a nineteenth-century definition may be irrelevant now. Nevertheless, let us play along and look at the *Random House College Dictionary*, Revised Edition (1973). It defines pollutant, in a definition not included in the unabridged version, as "1. Something that pollutes. 2. Any chemical or waste product, as automobile exhaust or sewage, that contributes to the air or water pollution."

Nobody says phosphates are unclean, dirty substances. What they object to is the consequences of enrichment with phosphorus as described, for example, in Lake Monona, Wisconsin, in an engineering report:

> The prevailing winds at Madison are from the southwest. These tend to drive detached masses of putrefying algae onto the shores and beaches of the lake especially around the northeast end of the mouth of the Yahara River at points beyond Starkweather Creek. Masses of decaying algae thus strengthened, if stirred with a stick look like human excrement and smell exactly like odors from a foul and neglected pig sty. [Quoted by Edmondson 1968.] This description can apply to conditions resulting from eutrophication with clean, pure phosphate in any lake.

The detestation of the word *pollution* showed up when the Soap and Detergent Association got permission to reprint a Cornell University Extension Service Bulletin, "Phosphates and detergents in water pollution." The *revised* version issued by the S & D Association held phosphate to be "a contributing factor to cultural eutrophication" rather than a pollutant as in the original. Other significant changes were made, including the introduction of the idea of carbon being involved in eutrophication (Rodgers 1973: 151). At least they were acknowledging that phosphate played some part in eutrophication, a rare admission by the S & D people. For more about the concept of pollution, see chapter 14.

### Lake Washington Again

Lake Washington seems to have been an embarrassment to the S & D people. It was fascinating to me to see how they dealt with it. Some ignored it, others minimized its relevance, one gave a factually incorrect account of it, and one invented his own data.

In addition to the published information, facts about Lake Washington were made available in the several congressional hearings cited in the References. The late Senator Warren G. Magnuson gave an effective narration of the development of the Lake Washington problem and the public action to alleviate it (U.S. Senate 1970). Others presented results of scientific studies. All of the key facts about Lake Washington were made clear in one or more of the statements. Nevertheless the S & D people went their own way.

The fact that Lake Washington had received effluent from secondary treatment plants was emphasized at the ASLO symposium attended by Paul F. Derr. In his FTC testimony, Derr showed that he realized that secondary treatment converts organic carbon to carbon dioxide, some of which is eliminated from the effluent:

> Secondary sewage treatment involves treating the overflowing water from the primary settling tank with large amounts of air (oxygen) to permit the natural aerobic bacteria to directly convert the carbon in the dissolved and suspended organic matter into carbon dioxide gas which again is expelled into the atmosphere.

However, earlier in his testimony, despite all the available information to the contrary, he stated:

> We are equally convinced that phosphates are not and never have been a cause of eutrophication. In the cases where scientists *thought* they had detected a relationship between increased phosphate concentration in a lake and increased algal growth such as in Lake Washington and in Lake Erie, it is now becoming clear that it was excessive discharges of carbon-containing organic wastes which caused both the increase in algal growth and simultaneously an increase in the amount of phosphate found in solution. Thus increased phosphate concentration is a result of organic pollution and eutrophication, not a cause!

These two statements are contradictory. In the first, he eliminates carbon by secondary treatment and in the second he puts it back in.

Another problem that had to be faced by the S & D people was that diversion of effluent was followed by a large change of phosphate and algae in Lake Washington but not a change of carbon dioxide. In the discussion of my paper at the ASLO symposium, Derr proposed that the reason Lake Washington had been rich in phosphate was that decomposing algae had liberated the phosphate. Dr. Joseph Shapiro, who is noted for his understanding and penetrating analysis of problems like this, said "To me it is like saying lung cancer causes cigarettes." When I asked Derr where the algae got the phosphate in the first place, his reply was "It was coming from the sewage introduced, obviously, and had no chance to be flushed out because algae have a great tendency to extract it from the water." (Edmondson 1974, discussion)

This kind of reasoning reminds me of the old story about a man who was accused of damaging a precious jar that he had borrowed. His lawyer opened the case in court by saying: "Your honor, we will offer three lines of defense. In the first place, we will prove that my client never borrowed the jar. In the second place, we will prove that it was returned in absolutely perfect condition. And in the third place, we will prove that it was already damaged when he was given it."

The ASLO symposium took place in February 1971. Unbelievably, Derr, testifying before the FTC the following June, repeated his explanation of Lake Washington, not mentioning cigarettes, but illustrating it with a graph in which he rearranged the data from one of my papers to show that algae caused phosphate (fig. 3.1). This time he did not explain to the commission where the algae got their phosphate. Apparently, Derr likes his explanation. I am told by Dr. Richard T. Barber of Duke University that Derr showed the graph as recently as April 1985, in connection with legislative hearings in North Carolina.

Derr was not the only member of the industry to misrepresent Lake Washington. In 1970, I published a preliminary account of the recovery of the lake in *Science*, a widely distributed journal that publishes small reports on topics of developing interest. I pointed out that the lake had received secondary ("two-stage") effluent and showed the results with a graph similar to fig. 1.5. Nevertheless, L. E. Kuentzel went out of his way to misrepresent the results by ignoring the information about the sewage treatment and guessing at what might have happened if it had been different. In a review (1971) he wrote:

# EDMONDSON'S LAKE WASHINGTON DATA

PHOSPHATE IS THE <u>CAUSE</u> – PER EDMONDSON, PHOSPHATE – P FOUND IN SOLUTION IN JAN.– APRIL DETERMINES THE ALGAE GROWTH IN JULY & AUG. OF <u>SAME</u> YEAR

PHOSPHATE IS AN <u>EFFECT</u> – ALGAE GROWTH IN JULY & AUG. DETERMINES THE AMOUNT OF PHOSPHATE – P RESOLUBILIZED FROM THE LAKE SEDIMENT AND FOUND IN SOLUTION IN JAN.– APRIL OF THE <u>FOLLOWING</u> YEAR

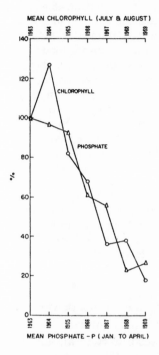

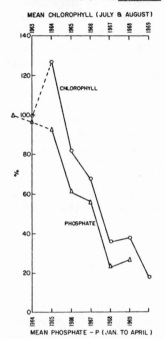

DATA FROM SCIENCE 169, p. 690 (1970)

*Fig. 3.1. A reinterpretation of data on Lake Washington made by Paul F. Derr, a member of the Soap and Detergent Industry, widely circulated by FMC Corporation, and shown as a slide in testimony before the Federal Trade Commission on 23 June 1971. Dr. Derr explained his graph as follows: "The attached two graphs show the data obtained and published by Professor Edmondson, University of Washington, after sewage was diverted from Lake Washington. The left hand plot is that presented by Prof. Edmondson to support his thesis that a decrease in phosphate input to Lake Washington caused the observed decrease in algae. The right hand plot is the same data plotted to show that the observed decrease in the mean phosphate for January–April is a result or effect of the decrease in the growth of algae the previous summer. This thesis further contends that the decrease in algae growth is directly attributable to diversion of sewage which contains all nutrients essential for algae growth. The excellent correlation readily seen in this graph supports the thesis that phosphate found in solution in a lake is a result or effect rather than a cause of eutrophication." The same data are shown in fig. 1.6.*

Finally, some comments need be made relative to a paper [foot-note to Edmondson 1970] describing recent studies on Lake Washington which have been used to support the contention that decreases in phosphate content of the lake's waters are responsible for its current improved condition. The decreases resulted after a sewage diversion from the lake which began in 1963. Studies of the lake's waters between 1963 and 1969 indicate that P has declined to about 30% of its 1963 value, that N declined very little and that the alkalinity and free $CO_2$ fluctuated somewhat but on an average changed very little. Meanwhile, the abundance of phytoplankton, as measured by chlorophyll, exhibited a steady decline. . . . The paper does not report any measurements on organic pollution or BOD. Before diversion of sewage, BOD in effluents to the lake *probably* were high [my emphasis]. After diversion, this source of BOD was eliminated. It would be expected that organic pollution in the lake would decrease steadily thereafter and decreases in algal growths would accompany this trend. It should be pointed out that even in 1969, at the end of the reported observations, the amount of phosphorus in Lake Washington still was greater than 10 ppb [footnote denotes equivalence to 0.010 ppm] and thus, as far as phosphorus is concerned, had the potential of supporting blooms as large as occurred in Lake Sebasticook.

Everybody familiar with *Science* knows that papers must be very concise and that there is no room for unnecessary information. The information that the sewage received secondary treatment renders Kuentzel's guesswork irrelevant. BOD data were presented in another paper. I have already dealt with the misuse of Sawyer's limit of 10 ppb.

It was interesting to see how some of the S & D people who bothered to acknowledge the existence of our Lake Washington study imagined what conditions might have been like, as Kuentzel did. Others actually made up data, as did W. J. Oswald in the 1970 House testimony.

In the case of Lake Washington based on Edmondson's data for chlorophyll, the natural concentrates [sic] of phosphate were probably [sic] on the order of 1–2 micrograms per liter, and addition of sewage phosphate probably [sic, again] brought this level up to 10 or 20 micrograms per liter. When the sewage was bypassed the natural concentrations were restored. Bypassing is, however, a luxury that cannot be widely applied because it is not unfair [another sic], if not illegal, to befoul one watershed to protect another.

Real data on phosphate in Lake Washington before eutrophication were published as early as 1939, and later values in a series of papers starting in 1956. The lake did not confirm Oswald's guesses about phosphate. As for the implication of the comment about befouling a watershed, in chapter 4 I will discuss the lack of significant effect of effluent diversion on Puget Sound.

In a review of the ASLO symposium, Legge dismissed my account of the Lake Washington experience, saying there were no new data in it. Actually, I reported some previously unpublished data on BOD measurements, highly relevant to the organic carbon idea, but not supportive of Legge's views. He rejected my interpretation of the behavior of Lake Washington because we had not consistently measured the concentration of organic carbon compounds in the lake. This is strange because we had abundant data on inorganic carbon, and the whole idea of the carbon thesis is that bacteria liberate inorganic carbon which is what the algae use. It was not necessary to measure organic carbon to get a satisfactory description of the condition and response of the lake. We knew that the secondary sewage effluent was not rich in organic material, as evidenced by low BOD values. In a complicated project with finite financing, one has to distribute the effort where it will do the most good, and routine measurements of organic carbon were not of top priority because they were not needed. Incidentally, Legge had slender evidence for his judgment. He had not attended the meeting nor seen copies of the papers that were later published. He had depended on "first hand reports of several individuals who attended."

In the same review Legge expressed admiration for a detailed study of the carbon cycle in a small lake in New Hampshire (Allen 1972). He neglected to mention that the lake had been fertilized with phosphate before the study began, and that its phosphorus concentration was higher than that of Lake Washington in 1958, the year of the Metro vote. That study was obviously not designed to determine the relative importance of carbon and phosphate. I cite this as an example of a way of causing a true statement to be misleading by omitting relevant information.

### Confusion Caused by the Detergent Debate

Here I will give some specific examples of the kind of confusion that arose during the debate. The S & D people seem to have had trouble in understanding the alga problem, and they were remarkably effective in spreading that misunderstanding by articulating their own confusion repeatedly and elaborately. Paul F. Derr in his submission to the Federal Trade Commission included a series of questions and answers. Question No. 7 is astonishing: "How did the scientific community reach this state of confusion concerning the possible causes of eutrophication?"

The community of scientists with experience in lakes was not in a state of confusion. It was the industrial scientists and engineers whose training and experience were inappropriate for the problem who were confused. Derr's answer:

> As noted earlier, this problem is by far the most complex scientific problem man will ever face. We have spent very little money to study the problem and therefore have a dearth of facts. Under these conditions theories can and do run rampant.
>
> We are greatly indebted to the scientists, primarily university professors and their students, who have worked in this area and provided us with the facts we do have. However, developing theories on the basis of only a few very limited observations must necessarily lead to many false starts, especially when the public is demanding explanations and actions.
>
> Years ago many researchers measured the amount of algae and only the amount [of] phosphorus present, because phosphate was the easiest chemical nutrient to measure. Since in some cases it appeared that phosphorus concentration (at some time of the year) appeared to correlate with the amount of algae, they reached the conclusion that there must be a relationship, i.e. high phosphate concentrations lead to high algal growth rates. For some unknown reason it never occurred to them to consider the corollary, i.e., that high algal growth leads to high phosphorus concentrations.

Actually, if an experienced scientist ever had such an idea, he would carefully consider it and then dismiss it for its absurdity.

Derr's introductory remarks had included the following statement:

> During these hearings you have heard statements from many scientific specialists who are recognized experts in a narrow field of science. When questioned in areas outside their field of expertise, some of these specialists properly declined to comment, but others gave you vague or even misleading information. FMC Corporation has had a unique *opportunity* as well as the varied capabilities required to study the many facets of this problem, and we believe we have developed a complete and coherent picture, part of which I shall attempt to convey to you in understandable layman's language.

Derr expressed this condescending approach further at a symposium held under the auspices of the American Association for the Advancement of Science and the American Institute of Chemists, as summarized by Krieger (1975).

> Derr cites seven reasons for the wide divergence in interpretation of data on eutrophication that, he says, has led to many cases of misuse of the data by scientists: withholding of data detrimental to a scientist's position; presenting only one interpretation for observed correlations; presenting correlations that appear to indict a single factor where many factors are involved; acknowledging only those differences in properties of different nutrients that support a particular theory; misapplying well-accepted theories or laws; designing experiments to prove a theory; and crediting success to removal of the theoretically assigned cause.

This is a perfect description of the behavior of the S & D people themselves. I wish that Derr had given some definite examples. Krieger continued: "A scientist should define the real problem and not substitute an apparently associated problem for it. All pertinent facts should be accepted and reported, especially those not appearing to support the theory. . . . And a scientist should be aware of his own vested interests as well as the vested interests of others." That is good advice for the S & D people.

The idea of the incomprehensible complexity of eutrophication came through in a statement by Jesse L. Steinfeld. He had been U.S. Surgeon General when NTA was banned. This experience evidently shook him, and he was strongly affected by the

S & D propaganda, writing: "*Eutrophication is an immensely complex process that cannot be linked to a single villain such as phosphorus.* It can be caused by other nutrients—manganese, iron, zinc, carbon, silica, molybdenum." (The emphasis is in the original.) As I have already pointed out, there is no evidence for this statement.

Perhaps the most shocking measure of the effectiveness of the S & D propaganda is that a scientist of the eminence and experience of Philip H. Abelson fell for it. In June 1987 he was awarded the National Medal of Science by President Ronald Reagan for his work in radiochemistry, physics, geophysics, biophysics and biochemistry. In 1970, as editor of the prestigious journal *Science*, he wrote an editorial entitled "Excessive emotion about detergents" in which he repeated several of the naive statements in the Legge and Dingledein articles, described by Abelson as "controversial but thought-provoking." He stated, "Massive algal blooms have occurred in lakes containing very little phosphate. The limiting nutrient is often carbon. Of considerable importance is a symbiotic relationship between blue-green algae and bacteria." I have already exposed the error of these statements. Abelson's reaction was remarkable in view of the fact that earlier in the same year, he had said in another editorial "To combat eutrophication, we must also reduce nitrate and especially phosphate." The later editorial brought him a number of protesting letters, three of which were published, including one, somewhat abbreviated editorially, by me.

The S & D people frequently tried to bolster their statements by referring to the eminence of their supporters. Again quoting Krieger's account of the AAAS symposium:

> In the area of phosphates, Derr explains that many scientists sincerely believe that phosphates are the cause of eutrophication, the excessive growths of algae and weeds that occur in some lakes. On the other hand, he says, other equally eminent scientists believe that eutrophication occurs only when all of the 15 to 20 nutrients essential for growth are present, phosphorus being simply an index of the total load of all nutrients to a lake.

Now in discussions like this, it does not matter how eminent somebody is. What matters is whether he is right. From the preceding discussion of the significance of phosphorus in the bottom sediments and other matters, it is clear that the possession of a Ph.D in physical chemistry may be poor preparation to understand what is basically a biological problem. An advanced degree does not guarantee good judgment. In the detergent debates, many eminent engineers and chemists exposed themselves as naive and ignorant of elementary biological principles, and not aware of the extent of their ignorance. Some of the testimony sounds as if they thought of algae as some kind of simple chemical reagent, not realizing that the cell is an active, energy-consuming structure that can make substances move and reactions take place in a way that does not happen in an inert nonliving system. There is no substitute for actual experience with lakes. I will return to this point in a discussion of the concept of experts in chapter 15.

### The Participation of Environmentalists

In the 1960s there developed a general public awareness of and unease about environmental deterioration. People who became especially interested and active were called environmentalists. Later, the use of the word shifted and it was applied to people who were especially active and annoying to the creators of the problems, sometimes qualified as "extreme," "rabid," or "hysterical." Much of the most contentious discussion centered on problems of the use of nuclear energy; however, almost all areas concerning the exploitation of environmental resources were involved, especially those that had to do with the control of pests by chemical means, spreading poison around the land and water. In terms of danger, eutrophication was not at the top of the list, but it was a legitimate concern.

The familiar technique of setting up a straw man was used frequently by stating falsely that the opponents of phosphorus detergents claimed that eutrophication was caused only by detergent phosphorus and that a ban of detergents would solve all eutrophication problems everywhere. These claims were then attributed to hysterical "environmentalists." For example, Legge, after taking credit for stimulating experimentation and field studies around the world with his 1970 polemic, wrote in 1971:

If the history of science teaches a lesson with respect to the algae/ nutrient debate, it is that some limnologists will likely go to their graves defending their phosphate-and-only phosphate positions. . . . It is no longer possible to accept the idea that the control of inputs of a single limiting nutrient can solve the continent-wide problems of accelerated eutrophication.

He does not tell us who held the "phosphate-and-only-phosphate" position. I have not seen such a statement by any responsible scientist. I wrote to several of the industry people involved in the Congressional and FTC hearings and asked for references. Several of them responded that they could not supply them because they had not seen any. The most relevant information that came back was a set of copies of newspaper articles with exaggerated headlines about death and destruction of lakes by eutrophication.

Without doubt, exaggerated statements were made about the dangers, with words like "ecological disaster," and 'killing lakes" being overworked. It embarrassed me to read about the "death" of Lake Erie. Who killed Lake Erie? is a non-question. Lake Erie had multiple problems, the worst of which was the addition of toxic materials from industry in limited areas. Because of the hydrological conditions, the water a few miles out from shore met U.S. Public Health Service drinking water qualifications. This point was frequently cited to counter claims that Lake Erie was "dead," assuming that the PHS standards were adequate. In any case, use of the word "dead" is inappropriate; death is not reversible, eutrophication is.

### Backwards Thinking

It looks to me as if the proponents of phosphorus detergents were working in reverse from the way science operates. Their publications were not scientific documents. The "scientific method" is not as cut-and-dried a pattern of thought as sometimes described in biology textbooks and publications on scientific philosophy, but in a normal scientific investigation there is usually a stepwise progression from formulating some definite questions or ideas (hypotheses), to gathering information in a systematic way that is relevant to the questions, to thinking about the information, and to coming to some conclusion. In an applied field the conclusion may then lead to some specific action.

The campaign against phosphorus was not like a scientific study. It is as if the people in the industry decided that it was important to retain phosphorus in detergents; that is an action. To justify the conclusion that would support the action, they had to round up reasons for it. Each reason could be an idea supported by a cluster of statements selectively culled from the scientific literature. For instance, the idea that phosphorus was less important than carbon was supported by a large series of statements, from which I have given a few examples ranging from the ridiculous (bottom sediments are an unlimited source of phosphorus) to the true but irrelevant (algae contain more carbon than phosphorus). Another idea was that to develop improved methods of treating sewage was a better way to go than to reduce the phosphate at the start. This may be true, but all of the supporting statements I have seen from the industry used faulty calculations of cost; no proper account was taken of the cost of disposal of sludge, among other things.

Because the campaign against phosphorus involved a great deal of misrepresentation of facts as well as a high degree of selection, we were presented not with a scientific evaluation of the problem, but with science fiction and intellectual pollution. An enormous amount of confusion was generated by throwing up irrelevances, like the chaff that confuses radar images.

### Detergent Bans

The industry won the battle about warning labels on boxes. The FTC dropped the proceedings when the manufacturers agreed to a uniform system of labelling the phosphorus content. However, they have not been able to prevent some legislative control of the contents of the boxes. At the time of writing, ten states and a number of municipalities and other communities have restricted the use of phosphorus in domestic laundry detergents. Phosphorus is still used in heavy-duty industrial and hospital detergents. The ban in Dade County, Florida was repealed on the basis that sewage treatment in that area was adequate to control eutrophication. The Wisconsin ban was passed in 1979, permitted to expire in 1982, apparently for lack of perceived effect, but was reinstated in 1984. The states with bans generally border on large lakes or have many small lakes. Canada was a pioneer in limiting phosphorus input into the Great Lakes.

The Chesapeake Bay is an interesting case. It receives fresh water from four major rivers near the north end and opens into the Atlantic Ocean at the south end. There is a gradient from fresh water at the north to full seawater at the south, with a corresponding limitation by phosphorus at the freshwater end, nitrogen at the ocean end. A very large sewage treatment plant with chemical precipitation has been built near the freshwater end. Nevertheless, Virginia, Maryland, and the District of Columbia have passed detergent bans, partly on the basis that restricting phosphate will reduce the amount of sludge produced by the plants, thereby reducing the cost of operation.

### Effectiveness of Detergent Bans

Much time, effort, and money have gone into the debates that led to banning detergents, and the bans have had pronounced economic and political effects. Have they had any environmental effects?

Already some excellent chances to answer that question properly have been wasted. Various studies have been made of lakes that have had the phosphorus input reduced by a detergent ban, but none that I have seen appears to have been well enough designed to answer the question definitively. In addition to published reports, through the courtesy of the Soap and Detergent Association I have seen several unpublished reports of studies sponsored by the association specifically to evaluate the effect of detergent bans in several states. While these reports seem to be competent studies in the field known as water quality, none fully meets necessary criteria for evaluating eutrophication, and all omit some essential data.

Any evaluation of the effect of phosphate reduction must be based on definite criteria that are relevant to the particular problem. It is not always made clear in reports whether the nuisance conditions were caused by phytoplankton, as is commonly the case, or by an abundance of rooted plants and massive littoral algae. It is not high phosphorus as such that bothers people. It is, most often, the planktonic species of blue-greens that make nuisances (not all do); thus the most relevant measurements to make would be of the abundance and composition of the phytoplankton with emphasis on the blue-greens. Because people object less to the simple cloudiness of a spring diatom bloom than to odorous, floating scums made by blue-greens during summer, it is important to follow seasonal changes. Transparency is desirable not only for esthetic reasons but is important to safety in swimming areas. None of the reports that I have seen on the effect of detergent bans gives relevant data on blue-greens. Few even mention specific kinds of algae, and some give no data on phytoplankton other than chlorophyll which is used as an index of total phytoplankton. This is surprising in view of the known sensitivity of the relative abundance of the blue-greens to changes in phosphorus supply, as in Lake Sammamish and Kootenay Lake. Some chemical data on nutrients and oxygen are of course essential, for one expects the phosphorus content of a lake to be related to the phosphorus input, but improvement of conditions as perceived by people may not be well measured by changes in phosphorus concentration.

The best evidence of the effect of a detergent ban would come from lakes known to have gone from a satisfactory condition to a production of algal nuisances, primarily under the influence of sewage effluent, with little change in any other circumstances that would affect the phytoplankton, as was the case with Lake Washington. The study should be made for a long enough time before the ban to establish the range of conditions and for long enough after the ban for the lake to come into equilibrium with the new level of nutrition. It would also be necessary to know of any changes in population, land use, or other conditions that might affect the production of phytoplankton.

However understandably, a serious lack in studies purporting to assess the results of detergent bans is in the duration of study, especially before the ban. In some this deficiency is partly compensated by studying lakes in pairs, one of which receives sewage effluent, the other not. Supposedly the ban would be followed by a change only in the lake receiving effluent. A change in both lakes would be interpreted as an effect of external influences, not of the ban. The problem is that some of the pairs used for comparison are of quite different depth, shape, and temperature, and therefore not comparable.

It is rare to find actual measurement even of loading, let alone the other minimal chemical data. In these studies, loading is usually estimated from the area of the watershed and the land use within it, using average values for the output of phosphorus from forested and cultivated land.

As it stands, it seems to me that there are cases in which a distinct change resulted from a ban, some in which the overloading of phosphate was so great that no improvement could have been expected, and many more in which no effect could have been detected by the techniques used. In such cases as the Great Lakes, where there have been changes in treatment facilities and land use as well as detergent bans, the results cannot technically answer the question about detergent bans; but we saw in Lake Washington that each reduction in phosphate resulted in a concomitant reduction in phytoplankton. In some cases a partial reduction because of a detergent ban in the phosphate coming into a lake might not visibly improve its condition, but would at least reduce the rate of deterioration, surely a valuable result. Such action could prevent serious problems during the time it took to develop adequate treatment facilities.

I see no reason for abandoning bans. However, proper studies should be organized where bans have been passed recently enough that results could be detected—and certainly in cases where bans are about to be imposed. There is a good opportunity here to improve our predictive capability, and it is unfortunate that better use has not been made of it.

## Suppose There Had Been a Rational Discussion of Phosphate Detergents?

Perhaps the outstanding feature of the campaign against control of detergents was that it was a response to a proposal not to ban them, but merely to put a warning label on the boxes and in advertisements. Evidently the industry felt seriously threatened by possible reactions to such a label. The proposal to label was a signal to call out the S & D big guns and to develop every possible argument against it, including the phony ones.

Some of the most amusing testimony before the FTC was aimed directly at the requirement to list ingredients on the box. This made some of the S & D people uneasy, and they had various objections to it. They made many references to "the housewife" and how it would do no good to list the ingredients because "she" could not understand them. "She" is unaccustomed to seeing negative statements in advertisements and would become confused by warnings. This cavalier evaluation of the female intellect is fully consistent with the general behavior of some of the S & D people toward scientific data and concepts. The women who testified made it crystal clear that they wanted genuine information about all their household materials, and felt that they were capable of understanding it. One of them quoted the kind of fake information about ingredients then available on boxes of detergent such as "advanced stain solvent formula," "micro enzyme action," "enriched borax," and "added cleaning muscle."

To be fair, we must recognize that there was something for the industry to be concerned about; actions by several states or smaller governmental units to limit the use of phosphorus had already succeeded. In fact, there did seem to be some defensible reasons to question the complete abandonment of phosphate in detergents at that time. It is interesting to speculate about what would have happened if the representatives of industry had concentrated on the real reasons and had not spent so much effort and credibility on their attack on the idea that phosphorus is a key element in forming algal nuisances.

Russell E. Train, then chairman of the Council on Environmental Quality, told the FTC very clearly:

The long-term solution to phosphates from municipal sewage must include both reduction or removal of phosphates in detergents and phosphate removal processes in municipal waste treatment plants. Action with respect to detergents alone, although essential, will not entirely solve the problem even if all phosphates were removed. Nor, from a cost-effectiveness standpoint, is it logical to achieve phosphate reductions solely through treatment plant removal processes.

The position of FMC Corporation was stated during the Senate hearings: "A partial solution is unacceptable. We must seek a total answer to the problem of eutrophication." It appeared that the only acceptable total solution was improved sewage treatment with no help from a reduction in the input of phosphate by control of detergents. A sure way to interfere with or halt action is to establish a worthy but impossible goal.

A few of the engineers and chemists who testified before the FTC on the S & D side acknowledged that phosphorus had a special importance and exhibited a reasonably good understanding of limnological concepts. Most of them supported the S & D position and expressed the judgment that to change detergents would not be worthwhile. This opinion of course involved combining science and economics and making a subjective or even intuitive evaluation against a scale of priorities; it was not a purely scientific decision. They rarely made clear how they had come to their conclusions, and inexperienced people could suppose that they were hearing a scientific statement. (See chapter 15 on experts.)

It seems to me that several points could have been argued better than they were if the S & D people had simply agreed that phosphorus had a special importance and that stopping its use would reduce the loading on all lakes that receive sewage. They could then have concentrated their argument on several clear points. The main one might have been to propose that while there could be some improvement, the overall improvement in lakes would not be of great enough benefit to the public to justify the disadvantages to the industry as measured by objective criteria. They could have discussed the basis for their judgment that so many lakes are overloaded with phosphorus that additional treatment would be necessary anyway, although it would be hard to do this convincingly while maintaining that phosphorus had nothing to do with the problem. Another point might have been that the known suitable substitutes for phosphate detergents caused deterioration of clothes and machinery.

They did state all these points, of course, but in a matrix of nonsense that clouded the real issues, as if they thought their position was not strong enough. In a rational discussion, there would be no room for the so-called "Lange-Kuentzel-Kerr" thesis, the mystical mutualism of bacteria and blue-greens, or for the actual misrepresentation of results of scientific work.

There might have been some problems about maintaining a rational discussion. One of them is the judgment that no suitable substitute existed, although hundreds of compounds had been screened. As far as I can tell, evaluation of the effectiveness of substitutes depended on work by chemists employed by or associated with the industries. However competent the chemists, there is a layer of administration between them and the public. An evaluation presumably involves more than objective data on chemical properties and whiteness of shirts. I suppose that a whole spectrum of facts would be used in judging the suitability of a substitute, including the availability and cost of raw ingredients, and profit margins. In other words, the financial interests of the company would have to be part of the information on which a judgment of suitability would be based. This brings up the ubiquitous problem of who pays for environmental protection.

Another problem concerns the substitute action that was proposed—to increase the treatment of sewage. As already pointed out, the more elaborate the treatment, the more sludge is produced, and disposal is costly, even when the sludge is used productively. Treatment does not really get rid of anything; you have the material either in the effluent, or in the air, or deposited in the sewage plant.

Both of these points, the substitute detergent and the choice of treatment, involve some subjectivity. In view of the serious mistakes and the falsification of the printed record of scientific work made by high officials of the industry, who now would trust their judgment when it comes to making the decisions required? If the discussion had been rational, perhaps there would have been no reason for distrust.

For my own part, I think that my strong reaction against the S & D position comes largely from my function in an educational institution. When an educator hears people expressing such fantastic errors of fact and judgment in his field, his natural impulse is to help out by exposing the errors and by presenting a better analysis. Some of the best explanations in the hearings were made by people with experience on university faculties and known for their ability to present information and ideas effectively, like Shapiro and Vallentyne.

In 1958 when Seattle Metro was voted, there was no treatment process commercially available that would have taken care of the phosphorus problem in Lake Washington. By 1971 when the detergent controversy was raging, improvements in treatment had been made, but had not reached the stage of development where they could have been routinely installed. It might have been predicted that adequate techniques would be developed eventually, but that would not have solved the immediate problems.

It could similarly have been predicted that real efforts to develop adequate non-phosphate detergents would be successful. The case made by the S & D people was that all known substitutes were unsatisfactory, and there seemed to be no forward-looking attitude that a solution would really be found in the future. The future has now arrived, and it appears that very effective substitutes may have been developed.

In other words, the proposition by Train that changes in both detergents and treatment would be necessary can be implemented. But nobody should think that these changes are without their own difficulty and cost, as will be shown further in chapter 4.

# Chapter 4

## Puget Sound

Puget Sound receives effluent from many different kinds of industries including pulp mills, oil refineries, and smelters, as well as sewage effluent from several sizable cities. For some decades increasing pollution in the sound has been of concern to members of the surrounding communities. While the problem of water pollution may be thought of as an entity, the difficulties besetting Puget Sound are in several ways fundamentally different from those that we encountered in Lake Washington. Attitudes toward public action have also changed during these years in ways that make the present problems harder to solve: the politics of confrontation have to some degree replaced the politics of consensus. I will return to this point later.

Before effluent could be diverted from Lake Washington it was necessary to evaluate the potential impact on Puget Sound. Some people misunderstood the situation and even referred to the diversion of effluent as "sweeping the problem under the rug," an evaluation based on misunderstanding of the character of Puget Sound and the nature of the effluent. Fortunately conditions are such that the Lake Washington algal problem was not simply transferred to the sound. For natural reasons, Puget Sound is very productive biologically. It is filled with upwelled water from the Pacific Ocean and, as is characteristic of such water, has high concentrations of nutrients, providing for a rich production of phytoplankton and seaweeds. Puget Sound is notable as a major source of seafood—fish, crustaceans, and molluscs. A popular song extolled the "Acres of Clams" of the Puget Sound country.

Natural concentrations of phosphate in the sound are higher than those in Lake Washington at its most eutrophic, while the concentration of nitrate is similar to that of the lake at that time. However, for physical reasons the production of phytoplankton in the main body of Puget Sound is not generally controlled by nutrients. Tides are of the normal Pacific type, with the greatest excursion between high and low occurring twice a month, at times of new and full moon (spring tides), and a smaller tidal change in between (neap tides). During summer, a weak stratification develops at the time of neap tides when the mixing action of the water is least. This limits mixing to the upper 50 feet (15 m) and the phytoplankton begins to increase. Typically, before there has been time for the algae to exhaust the nutrients in the upper water, the spring tides arrive, and the increased motion of water mixes the whole water mass of the sound from top to bottom. This in turn slows or even stops the growth of phytoplankton because the cells now spend so much time in the dim light of deep water (Winter et al. 1975).

Dense populations of phytoplankton can occur locally and temporarily, especially in bays and harbors of the sound where mixing is restricted, but these are not dominated by the blue-greens that were so prominent in the fresh water of Lake Washington. In any case, they cannot form floating scums in the open sound because of the vigorous motion of the wind and water. Occasionally decaying masses of seaweed create unpleasant smells, but their presence cannot be blamed on human activity.

The environmental problems of Puget Sound are thus very different from those of Lake Washington. Effluent and runoff containing a wide variety of toxic materials can damage the valuable biological productivity of the sound, while in Lake Washington toxic pollution was of minimal concern, and excessive production of undesirable organisms was what would make trouble. Perhaps the closest similarity between the two situations is that the troubles originate from activity in areas covered by different governmental agencies and coordinated efforts to alleviate them are difficult.

Industries produce effluents containing a variety of toxic materials such as metals like zinc, lead, and cadmium, as well as hundreds of organic compounds, some of which are manufactured precisely because of their toxicity, to be used as herbicides or pesticides. When released into a body of water, many of these substances can either kill organisms directly or can reduce some vital activity enough to prevent survival of a population. It is important to realize that toxic pollutants do not have to reach lethal concentrations in the water to do serious harm to a population of animals. Sublethal concentrations may injure them enough so that they are unable to fend off disease as they could normally. In some cases the immune system of the animals seems involved. During the summer of 1988 the harbor seals in the badly polluted North Sea (between the British Isles and Scandinavia) experienced massive mortality. Over half the population died on long stretches of coastline as the infection spread from Denmark to England in just a few weeks. While viruses were present, preliminary studies suggested that the basic trouble might have come from toxic substances in the fish that the seals were eating. Top predators like the seal are susceptible to this kind of effect because toxic material is concentrated at each step in the food chain; this process is known as food chain concentration or bioaccumulation. Moreover, several toxic materials in sublethal concentrations can be lethal when working together. One must know this when trying to identify the cause of a massive die-off. Each of several industries can claim to be blameless because its effluent is not creating a lethal concentration in the water. In all cases of single or multiple poisons, the concentration in the water after a die-off is irrelevant if the food chain is carrying the poison.

A poorly understood effect of pollution that is now receiving attention in Puget Sound is the induction of liver tumors and other defects in fish. There is a relation between the areas in which diseased animals are found and certain types of organic compounds and metals in the sediments (Malins et al. 1987). The exact cause of the tumors is being sought experimentally with promising results (Schiewe et al. 1989). The effect of the tumors on the fish is not well understood, but the afflicted fish are unsightly and people will not buy them. Crustaceans and molluscs also show damage. Thus enormous economic values are affected. Conversely, any measures to control the substances entering Puget Sound will be costly as well.

It is worth noting that human activity is not necessary to produce toxic concentrations of metals. There are places in the world where exposed ore deposits make standing water dangerous to drink. However, human activity has multiplied the number of elements that reach toxic concentrations and introduced them to places where they would not normally be; examples will be provided in chapters 14 and 16.

A different kind of chemical pollution results from the fact that some of the most toxic materials are organic molecules synthesized by artificial industrial processes, not by the normal enzymatic processes in organisms, and therefore are not easily decomposed ("biodegradable"). There are hundreds of such compounds such as PCBS, DDT, and dioxins. Some were intended to be toxic, but it has been difficult to confine them to the target organisms or locations. Some of the most toxic substances, such as dioxins, are produced as unintended by-products.

Pollution problems are produced in many places by efforts to control undesired organisms. "Fouling" is a term applied to the community of small marine invertebrates and algae that attaches to surfaces such as rocks, boats, and salmon pens. Since the speed and fuel consumption of ships are strongly affected by a load of barnacles on the hull, toxic antifouling paints have been developed to prevent the attachment and growth of fouling organisms. Naturally, some toxic material diffuses out from the paint into the water and can accumulate in lethal concentrations in confined waters where a large surface area of toxic paint is exposed. The effectiveness of antifouling paint was dramatically shown in the Bay of Arcachon, a center for French oyster culture. Spat production failed in five successive years (1977–81). Investigation showed that the problem originated in a nearby marina with restricted water circulation where boats had been painted with tributylin (TBT), described as the most toxic compound purposely introduced by man into natural waters. Fisherman have become ill after merely handling nets treated with TBT. The use of tributylin in Puget Sound has been somewhat restricted, but not completely banned.

Another kind of toxicity does not result from human activity, but can be increased by it. Some algae are naturally toxic, making poisonous substances that are contained within the cells or are secreted into the water. Toxic blooms are well known in eutrophic lakes, but also have been observed in marine waters polluted with sewage. In particular, toxic conditions seem to be increasing in frequency in the Baltic and North Seas. In 1988 there was a massive bloom off western Norway of an alga not observed there before (*Chrysochromulina*). It killed fish over a wide area including about $5 million dollars worth of salmon in pens. Blooms of certain other kinds of algae are known as red tides because of their characteristic color.

Another kind of toxic effect, widespread in marine waters, is indirect. Under some conditions dinoflagellates (algae) bloom and are eaten by shellfish. The toxin contained in the algal cells accumulates in the shellfish without harming them, but people can be made very sick or killed by eating the shellfish. This paralytic shellfish poisoning has been worldwide for a long time.

Obviously, the diversion of effluents from Lake Washington has not created any of these difficulties in Puget Sound. The effluent that had been entering Lake Washington was mostly of domestic origin and did not contain output from heavy industries of the kind that produce toxic effluent. For example, while the Boeing airplane company had a sewage treatment plant putting effluent into the Cedar River in 1958, its toxic wastes were not disposed of through the sewer at that time. Puget Sound does not have a eutrophication problem; indeed, we can regret that the phosphorus diverted from Lake Washington cannot be used productively by the Puget Sound community. The amount of nitrate diverted from the lake each year is approximately the amount contained in a cube one quarter of a mile on a side (a tenth of a cubic kilometer) of Puget Sound water. This is less than 0.07% of the volume of Puget Sound, not including the Hood Canal, and is a very small fraction of the annual input to the sound from other sources. Part of the nitrogen that had entered Lake Washington in effluent would eventually have reached the sound in any case. That the amount of nitrogen carried in the effluent has increased production in the sound appreciably seems unlikely.

Of course, any system can be overloaded. It is appropriate to ask if the total sewage input to the sound from all its cities has increased enough to cause a change in the character of the phytoplankton if not its abundance. The evidence I have seen does not show such a change. Red tides and paralytic shellfish poisoning are not new inventions.

Effluent was diverted from Lake Washington in two directions. The effluent from the southern part of the lake was first diverted in March 1963 to a new secondary treatment plant with an outfall to the Duwamish waterway, about six miles (10 kilometers) above its entry into Puget Sound. It was realized at the time that the capacity of the Duwamish was limited, and it would eventually be necessary to move the outfall to deep water in Puget Sound. The effluent from the northern part of the lake and adjacent regions was diverted to a new primary treatment plant at West Point with its outfall on the bottom in 280 feet (85 meters) of water, 1250 feet (380 meters) from shore. Operation of that plant started in 1966. In addition, 70 million gallons per day (265,000 m$^3$) of raw sewage that had been entering Puget Sound directly from Seattle was diverted to the West Point plant and given primary treatment, making an immediately obvious improvement along the waterfront. Finally, in 1987, the Duwamish effluent was diverted into a new outfall, the deepest and longest in the world. It consists of two pipes almost two miles (about 3 km) long, 64 inches (1.6 m) in diameter, and emptying at a depth of 600 feet (185 m) in Puget Sound.

The selection of West Point as the place to build the major new treatment plant has had some consequences that have now become important in dealing with the problems of Puget Sound. The main requirement was that the plant would be able to deliver its effluent to deep water, well away from shore at a place where currents would promote mixing and dilution. West Point fit the requirements and had an additional strong advantage. The entire land area, a high wooded bluff with extensive beach, was occupied by a military installation, Fort Lawton, built in 1898. The area was fenced and there were armed guards at the gate. It was not active militarily, and people were allowed to enter for picnics, hikes, and strolls along the impressive beach, but it was not a public park and there were no park facilities. Thus the area seemed an ideal, isolated place for the new sewage plant when Metro was formed in 1958, for no private or public property would be disturbed. City officials had previously tried to obtain the land for use as a park, but the federal government always refused, and there appeared to be no prospect of any change in the future. However, federal financial problems eventually developed and Fort Lawton was deactivated. Land was transferred to the city in 1974, and it opened as a park in 1975, eight years after the sewage plant was dedicated in 1967. There seems to be a prevalent local belief that Seattle made the horrible mistake of putting a sewage plant in a city park. The fact is that we put the park next to the sewage plant.

Secondary treatment was not needed at West Point according to the federal standards in force in 1958. Remember that the main purpose of secondary treatment is to decompose the organic material in the sewage so that the effluent will impose little demand for oxygen on the receiving water. Where the receiving water is large relative to the effluent and mixing and dispersal are adequate, lack of oxygen is not a problem. The central part of Puget Sound is such a place. The conditions around the West Point outfall were studied in detail by Metro by chemical sampling and underwater television, and it was found that plenty of oxygen remained and there was not a build-up of deposits around the outfall. This means that the sewage emerging from the West Point plant was being decomposed free of charge as part of normal recycling by the natural bacterial population of Puget Sound, along with wastes from the other local inhabitants, salmon, sea lions, sea urchins, and all the rest. By taking advantage of the local situation to use natural processes rather than using the energy-demanding machinery of secondary treatment, the handling of sewage at West Point seems very efficient. In fact, we might wonder whether the extra production of bacteria may have increased the food supply of beneficial microscopic invertebrates. In any case the present arrangement is an example of a way of handling environmental problems that can be described as co-operating with nature, not fighting nature. There are of course problems, disadvantages that accompany the advantages. Effluent is essentially fresh water and it tends to rise through the denser salt water. Sometimes at slack tide and with little wind, mixing and dispersal are reduced, and the effluent is visible. Some floating material makes its way to shore. Nevertheless, the arrangement seemed the best of several choices when the system was designed.

This relatively comfortable situation is going to change in a fundamental way. The Environmental Protection Agency has ordered that all sewage treatment plants in the country, including West Point, must be converted to secondary treatment. For some years Metro was able to get a waiver from this requirement, largely on the basis of the special features of West Point and Puget Sound described above, but this is no longer possible. The new requirement will impose a major financial cost of about 955 million dollars on the community. This might be acceptable if it could be shown that the results would be adequate, but the point is in question. I was bothered on principle by the blanket requirement for secondary treatment, on the basis that local conditions vary so much that treatment should be adjusted to meet them. I expressed this idea in a letter published in the *Seattle Times* on 26 January 1986: "Doctors do not prescribe the same medicine for all patients. They study the patients, diagnose the illness, and prescibe appropriate treatment. Aspirin might make a patient feel a little better, but it will not cure his cancer."

The motivation for the insistence on secondary treatment seems largely based on the fact that secondary treatment removes more than the oxygen-demanding organic matter, including some of the more prevalent toxic materials. For instance a typical finding is that primary treatment removes only 47% of the metals while secondary treatment removes 77%. While this may seem like an impressive improvement, it does not automatically follow that the remaining 23% will not cause serious damage. In any case, with increasing industrial development, the total amount could increase again to the original level or more. Nor will secondary treatment change the occasional tendency of the effluent to rise to the surface.

There is no question that secondary treatment will improve local conditions in Puget Sound somewhat, but is that good enough? Will that program drain away scarce funds from more effective plans? Would an alternative scheme produce the same or better results at less cost and disruption? For example, if the main goal is to remove metals, why not include a chemical precipitation stage in the new facilities? That of course would add some more cost. We can ask why the community should install facilities to remove materials that do not have to be in the sewage in the first place. Is it logical to permit dangerous materials to be put into the public sewer by private agencies and then take them out at great public expense? The alternative is to prevent the addition of potentially damaging wastes before the effluent goes into the sewer. An example is an experience with excess zinc, which was discovered in a sewer during routine monitoring by Metro in 1977. The sewers were then sampled upstream until the sources were identified, two newspaper printing plants. The papers had two options: changing the process that liberated the zinc or having the effluent treated to remove zinc. They elected to change the process.

Pretreatment has the advantages of providing more precise control of pollutants and of associating the costs of control specifically with the industry producing them, rather than spreading the cost to all users of a treatment plant. This of course may not be regarded as an advantage by an industry that produces large volumes of toxic effluent. There are other reasons for pretreatment; some materials interfere with the biological treatment process itself. Notably, dumping of substandard lots of antibiotics has been known to kill off the bacteria in a treatment plant, rendering it ineffective for several days until the microbial population could be reestablished.

Improvements have been made in the techniques of primary treatment since the West Point plant was built. If the present plant could have improved its operation and continued with the existing effective pretreatment policy, possibly the main goals of the requirement for secondary treatment could have been largely met at much less cost, freeing money to be used more efficiently against the other problems affecting the sound. The key factor in requiring the change at West Point is that Metro was unable to assure EPA that the effluent would meet certain of their requirements. The problem of defining effluent standards is a complicated one that has been studied repeatedly for many years, and the appropriateness of the requirement for Puget Sound conditions is not likely to be reviewed again. We can only hope that the cost of the change to secondary treatment will not interfere with the development of more effective programs of pretreatment.

The Puget Sound problems exemplify very well a common situation in which an industry can increase its profits significantly by cutting corners in a way that damages the environment. This accounts for the cases that have been seen of industries operating their drainage systems at night, putting highly toxic materials into the sound. It is not just a matter of offending the esthetic sensibilities of hard-core environmentalists; it is an activity that does powerful economic damage to another industry, the fisheries. To require the industries to take responsibility for their toxic wastes will increase their costs of doing business, but is it not time that they did this? For decades industries have been reducing their expenses by activities that were always damaging and at least are now being defined as illegal. The accumulated damage can be regarded as a debt that must be paid off. Preventing damage should be regarded as part of the cost of doing business. (See chapter 16 for more about this).

The production of abundant sludge is a universal feature of sewage treatment, and disposal can account for almost half the total cost of treatment. The conversion of the West Point plant to secondary treatment will approximately double the production of sludge. Fortunately, procedures have already been developed that will enable the increase to be handled, by treating the sludge as a recyclable resource rather than as an annoyance. For many years sludge has been used in various ways as a fertilizer or soil conditioner. The city of Milwaukee was a pioneer in this use with the well-known Milorganite. Because of the presence of toxic materials, however, the use of sludge has been limited mostly to non-agricultural areas. Locally, Metro and the University of Washington College of Forestry have collaborated in pioneering a coordinated system of equipment and procedures for using sludge to enhance the growth of trees in harvestable forests (Silvigrow). The effect on the rate of tree growth is spectacular, in some cases more than doubling the rate of increase in diameter.

Handling more than 90,000 tons of wet sludge in a year is not a casual operation. Moreover, there are some special difficulties with any method of above-ground land disposal of sludge. It requires special tank trucks, spraying equipment, and techniques of application. The rate of addition must be controlled so as not to overload the system and drain too much off into streams. If it is not handled correctly, streams and groundwater can become contaminated. The spraying process is unsightly and leaves the trees dripping with sludge. For various reasons the sprayed areas are posted with danger signs to keep people away, which in itself causes considerable concern. Recycling sludge is usually not profitable, but it has reduced the cost of managing sludge well below the amount required by a simple program of disposal, even if disposal sites were readily available.

While the effect on the trees seems clearly beneficial, one can ask if there might be unfavorable side effects on herbivores eating the leaves. This is suggested by the fact that, in an experimental situation, aphids feeding on collards fertilized with a sludge containing PCBs and cadmium showed reduced fecundity when compared with those feeding on plants fertilized with uncontaminated sludge (Culliney and Pimental 1986). The consequences of sludge fertilization could conceivably be either beneficial or detrimental, depending on the relative effects on pests and on useful insects. These effects illustrate the desirability of pretreatment to limit the introduction of trace metals into sewage and exemplify a side effect not foreseen in the initial planning; such effects have been called "unintended costs."

Disposal of sludge is a part of the sewage treatment process that is Metro's mandate. But there is not enough suitable forest in the area served by Metro to absorb the amount of sludge produced, so they have bought additional tracts of forest. As part of this activity, Metro took the initiative in forming a state-wide committee to work on the disposal of sludge as a regional problem. There are large rural communities outside the confines of Metro that are served by individual septic tanks which produce sludge and have to be pumped out from time to time. The Metro plant at Renton accepts such material from a region including parts of five adjacent counties, and treats it along with its own sludge.

The spraying activity has not brought favorable notice from everybody, and in fact has produced some difficult public relations problems for Metro. The sludge is welcomed for spraying in some places because it is used productively, but not in all. This problem was brought to focus in the spring of 1988 in a dispute about sludge-spraying on some of Metro's forest land. Citizens from Yelm, a small town nearby, raised strong objections. Dozens appeared in Seattle during a Metro Council meeting, shouting slogans and waving signs in a very confrontational manner. They wanted Metro to put "its" sludge in its own backyard. I saw this on a TV news program and was puzzled by the intensity and inappropriateness of the behavior, and the irrationality of some of the statements. While a community can have legitimate concerns about where and how sludge is sprayed, this type of meeting did not seem to be very productive of an exchange of views. The protestors seemed to want only to present their viewpoint and not to listen to alternatives. I wondered how many of the demonstrators stopped by the West Point Sewage Treatment Plant to ask to take home an amount of sludge equivalent to that which they produced during their stay in the Metro area. This question is relevant because the protestors live in an area served by septic tanks. Their sludge is disposed of locally on land, and used as fertilizer, a process that can contaminate ground water if not well controlled. Much later I learned some interesting things about the background of this particular protest which I will relate in chapter 15.

To return to the requirement for a change to secondary treatment for all effluent entering Puget Sound, this by itself will be inadequate to solve the sound's pollution problems. However, the most unfortunate effect of the change at West Point may be in the divisive effect it has had on the human community of the Metro area. This effect comes about from very different viewpoints about proper priorities for the use of land and waterfront and from different perceptions of governmental responsibility. For the West Point plant to carry out secondary treatment requires that it be enlarged considerably; an alternative plan is to dismantle it and build a replacement somewhere else. Each of these options has advantages and disadvantages, and each arouses, predictably, more heat than light in the present adversarial climate.

The advantages of retaining the plant at West Point are obvious: the site is optimal from the point of view of handling the discharge; enlargement of an existing facility would be considerable simpler and vastly less expensive than starting anew. However, this prospect is extremely offensive to a group of citizens who think that the sewage plant should not have been put on the waterfront in the first place, even under the conditions existing at the time. Siting such facilities on bodies of water has of course been practiced in many situations for the ease of discharging wastes. Cities were originally built on shores for that very reason. With increasing populations and decreasing recreational shorelines, this practice has come into serious question, and there have been many attempts to recover for better use areas that had been given over to industrial or similar functions in the days before land use planning became essential.

Relocating the Seattle sewage facility to an area less desirable for other uses may seem to be a good, adventurous idea. Some of the engineers I talked to in 1958 did not think that they were building the pyramids. They were used to the idea that buildings have a finite useful life, and when something becomes obsolete you replace it with something better. Cost alone should certainly not prevent the exchange of an undesirable condition for a long-term, even permanent benefit. There are, however, several difficulties about replacing the West Point plant with one somewhere else. Some of these are technical, some political, only some economic.

The number of possible sites is limited for such reasons as the availability of land and the configuration of the existing pipe system. All of the likely locations are farther south than West Point, and farther into the sound, so that mixing and dispersion of the effluent would be less. Any place south of West Point would be less satisfactory than West Point from that view, and any place north of West Point would present very complicated problems of design and operation. Most locations would require construction of a large tunnel through heavily developed areas of the city, a disruptive as well as expensive operation with which Seattle has been having some experience recently. The system would also include a continuing commitment to a large expenditure of energy for pumping.

From the community point of view, perhaps the biggest difficulty about abandoning the West Point is the cost. Even if a mutually satisfactory site could be found elsewhere, to dismantle the present plant, which is functioning well and could be converted to secondary treatment rather easily, would be massively expensive, as would be the construction of the substitute. The cost would show up in the monthly charges for household use. A representative estimate is that the monthly household cost would increase approximately $12 for moving the treatment plant, on top of $20 per month for adding secondary treatment. Former Mayor Royer of Seattle and a large portion of the city council were very supportive of the abandonment of West Point, while the suburbs have been almost universally against it. This is an important point because the shoreline Management Act of 1971 puts stringent control over land within 200 feet of the shoreline of Puget Sound, and the mayor and city council must agree to any change at West Point that would affect that area.

The decision about the proposal to abandon the West Point plant has to balance the advantages of having the beach at West Point unencumbered by a treatment plant against the disadvantages associated with building a new plant. Many people think it illogical to destroy an effective plant and build a new one simply to clear some of the beach at Discovery Park. The present plant does not prevent use of the beach; it occupies only a part of the area. Plans for expanding the plant include putting part of it underground to reduce its visibility. The degree of present use of the beach appears to be relatively small. The supporters of relocation of the sewage plant regard the park as a valuable regional resource, but Discovery Park seems not to be generally perceived as a regional facility, and some people in the suburbs have expressed themselves as unwilling to support a Seattle park of limited use by an increase in their sewer rates. Of course the degree of use is only one criterion of value. It is important to try to preserve natural areas with minimal disturbance. A beach of the quality of that of Discovery Park in an urban setting is a very unusual facility; it is not the only one available here, but Alki Point and Golden Gardens are heavily used.

Finally, even if the financial and other considerations were to be met, there is an additional problem about the possible relocation of the plant. The residents of other areas are just as intense in their opposition to such a facility as are those of the Discovery Park area. Each of the possible sites proposed has been declared absolutely unacceptable by large numbers of citizens who live in that neighborhood. Not in my back yard.

The divisiveness generated by the EPA requirement for secondary treatment has expressed itself vigorously at all levels. Within the Seattle community there is disagreement about the value of the beach at Discovery Park. Between Seattle and the suburbs there is disagreement about the value of the park itself. It seems to me that the community attitude now is different from that during the debates in 1958 about the formation of Metro. Disagreements are expressed in an ugly language not characteristic of the 1958 debates. Much of this centers on Metro as the cause of trouble. Actually, Metro itself has no choice but to provide secondary treatment, as a result of the action by EPA. There is no way to do that without changing the present plant somehow. In whatever way Metro responds to its legal responsibilities, a large segment of the population will be infuriated, and they will express the fury against Metro, not EPA.

Metro seems destined to be cast as either devil or angel. I once heard a television discussion between two high officials, one from Metro and one from EPA. Incredibly, they both agreed that "Metro is the biggest polluter of Puget Sound." Now in fact, Metro does not generate any pollution: we do. Its mission is to transport and treat wastes that are generated in households, commercial establishments, and industries. The statement quoted represents to me a gross distortion and misunderstanding of the Puget Sound pollution problem. With that idea being promulgated by officials, how can there be an effective general understanding of the problem and evaluation of possible solutions? This point is not trivial because much of the public discourse is based on anxiety and anger, with Metro as the object.

Professionally, however, Metro is held in high regard. Construction of the deep-water outfall to Puget Sound resulted in an Honor Award from the American Consulting Engineers Council in 1987. It was one of eighteen awards given nationally for outstanding engineering achievement, cost saving to clients, unique application of technology, and environmental and social concerns. The development and implementation of the Metro sludge program brought awards to Metro and to the manager of the program; in 1988 the program took first place in the National Beneficial Sludge Use Awards Program of the US Environmental Protection Agency. Metro's initiative in forming a state-wide committee to work on sludge disposal on a regional basis brought another award from EPA to the chair of that committee, who is also the director of the Metro sludge program.

Meanwhile, Metro continues to do its job. The EPA requirement for secondary treatment of sewage by Metro had not been fulfilled when this chapter was completed. The requirement itself and the possible ways of accommodating it had been discussed at open meetings. A variety of opinions were expressed with various degrees of emotion and dogmatism. The newspapers have printed many editorials and letters to the editor. Thus there was a public education campaign as there was in 1958, but with the greater diversity of problems, it seems less focussed. Hearings are being held on the requirements of land-use legislation and other regulations. The presence of a pair of bald eagles at West Point will complicate the process and construction since they are protected by law against disturbance.

I have emphasized the problem of sewage disposal at West Point, but this is not the only sewage plant discharging effluent into Puget Sound. All are affected by the EPA requirement to convert to secondary treatment. However well the conversion to secondary treatment is handled, the problem of toxic pollution will not be solved by that alone. Additional controls must be used not only because secondary treatment does not remove enough of the toxic materials, but because sewage treatment plants are not the only source of toxic effluent.

Sewage disposal is only one of many problems associated with the development of the Puget Sound region. Others will have to be faced. One that has been attracting notice and debate for several decades has to do with managing water transportation of oil to minimize the probability of serious damage. There have been already enough oil spill incidents in the sound or adjacent waters to demonstrate that a real difficulty exists. (See chapter 16.)

Recent developments of another kind suggest that Puget Sound is in for a major debate involving the conflict between preservation of environmental values and commercial interests. This development is the attempted creation of large salmon and seaweed farming industries in Puget Sound (Glude 1989).

Fish farming has been developed in many parts of the world so there is plently of experience to use as background for the proposed expansion in Puget Sound of farm production of Atlantic salmon (*Salmo salar*). The fish are raised in pens arranged in groups covering as much as two acres, and given large quantities of a variety of food materials which are often mixed with antibiotics to prevent diseases under the crowded conditions in the pens. Annual production of fish in a two-acre installation may be as much as 500,000 pounds (280,250 kilograms/hectare).

There are several negative effects on the biological community of Puget Sound and on human activities to consider. The potential damage to the sound comes from the fact that much of the food that is not used falls to the bottom under the cages along with a very voluminous production of feces. The material accumulates in a thick layer that extends far beyond the pens. It has a high oxygen demand and the area can then become unsuitable for the normal populations of fish and invertebrates for which the sound is valued. So this is another kind of sewage problem. The effect of the antibiotics is hard to assess, but the possibility exists that they could interfere with the normal microbial processes of the sound community and result in the flourishing of undesirable types of microorganisms. Attending to the pens and harvesting the fish generates considerable boat activity with attendant pollution.

Possibly the most serious potential effect of the salmon farms on the biology of Puget Sound would be a repetition of a very common kind of problem, the explosive success of a species when introduced into a new community. (See chapter 6.) The same phenomenon is exhibited by parasites when introduced to a host population that does not have immunity to them. Salmon, like all animals, are subject to infestation with a wide variety of animal and microbial parasites. One of these parasites, a small worm called *Gyrodactylus salaris*, has given severe trouble in Norway. The parasite damages the skin and gills of the fish, killing them. It appears to have been introduced into Norway in the early 1970s in a load of farmed salmon from Sweden. Inevitably it escaped, and infected the wild salmon in the Lakselva River where it caused a sharp decline in their numbers. Subsequently it spread to at least thirty other rivers, essentially eliminating the wild salmon from them. There is no reason to think that the same thing could not happen to Puget Sound salmon.

There are several other diseases capable of equal damage. The crowded conditions in fish farm pens facilitate the development and spread of infections, and inevitably fish will be accidentally lost from the pens. Thus it seems almost a sure bet that some kind of trouble for native fish stocks will be generated in Puget Sound from disease or parasites, if indeed it has not already been started by the existing farms in Puget Sound and the adjacent British Columbia Canadian waters.

Disease is not the only problem for penned salmon. Occasionally dense populations of algae that damage fish by toxicity or mechanical injury to the gills develop (Rensel et al. 1989). Free-swimming fish are less subject to damage and in any case may be able to avoid the densest parts of the bloom, while those in cages die. A bloom of diatoms caused the loss of several million dollars worth of salmon in September 1989 in part of Puget Sound. Another bloom did even more damage in 1990. Such experiences as well as the general cost of doing business and limited availability of suitable locations make the salmon farming business in Puget Sound very insecure economically (Crutchfield 1989).

A different kind of interference is with one of the properties for which Puget Sound is valued, its natural beauty. The salmon farm installations are very conspicuous and unsightly. Many private houses and resorts have been built for which the scenic beauty has a distinct economic value; property prices vary, as does the tourist industry, with the attractiveness of the view. Further, normal boat traffic and fishing operations would be disturbed by having large areas of fish pens.

The future of the salmon farming projects has been vigorously debated in the state legislature, with strong lobbying on both sides. The economic values of the farming projects are very persuasive to many people, including the governor of the state, who can document the values more precisely in terms of dollars and employment than can people primarily concerned with scenic and esthetic values, even those that have a strong touristic economic component. Actually, in view of the difficulties listed above, it seems unlikely that the salmon farms in Puget Sound will become more than a minor industry (Crutchfield 1989).

Nori, edible seaweed, is increasing in popularity in the Puget Sound region. While the techniques of growing it on rafts are not as disruptive and productive of wastes as the salmon farms, they have the same kind of impact on boat traffic and scenic values. Whether problems might develop from parasites, I do not know.

In response to the growing realization of the extent and complexity of the Puget Sound problems, in 1985 the Puget Sound Water Quality Authority was created by the state legislature. Its mandate was to make an extensive inventory of the problems of Puget Sound and to develop plans for control. This resulted in several large issue papers and a comprehensive Water Quality Management Plan. During the development of these studies, many public hearings were held. Because of the lack of essential information about some of the problems, in 1988 the authority proposed the creation of a non-profit Puget Sound Research Foundation.

The authority planned ambitiously and moved aggressively to develop real controls over the most serious kinds of pollution. Predictably this generated conflicts between the authority and the industries involved. Each year since 1987 the authority has had to scale back its plans because of insufficient financial support by the state legislature. In March 1990, the Water Quality Authority lost its authority when, again by act of the state legislature, it was transferred to the State Department of Ecology and its plans for cleanup were made advisory, not mandatory. Judging by news reports, this action was preceded by heavy lobbying in the legislature with important industrial interests overwhelming all others.

The unfolding story of the protection of Puget Sound provides rich material for a study of the interaction of industrial interests with serious environmentalism. It is especially interesting because some of the environmental interests have a strong economic component. The fishing and real-estate industries depend on maintaining certain environmental qualities in Puget Sound and the land around it. The fishing industry itself is divided between those dependent on maintaining natural populations and the fish-pen operators; they have very different requirements and their activities affect the sound differently. Real-estate values in such places as the San Juan Islands are based in part on isolation, or relatively low building density, but the developers, operating to maximize profits, destroy the qualities that brought people there in the first place.

In summary, then, the problems of Puget Sound are more complex and, particularly, the solutions are less straightforward than those for Lake Washington. But the real difficulties lie in the realm of public discourse. While politics may be the art of compromise, political compromise may not be the best road to the solution of technical problems. Nor is delay. As with many environmental problems, delay of positive action is a negative act. Any of several courses of action might be acceptable, but we need to determine and implement a rational long-term solution to the problems facing Puget Sound before it is too late.

# Chapter 5

# Mono Lake

For many years concern has been developing about the possible deterioration of Mono Lake in the Sierra Nevada of eastern California. Its case illustrates clearly the conflicts that arise when the solution of an environmental problem based largely on aesthetics and appreciation of a natural wonder has a large economic cost. The problem of Mono Lake does not have the immediate public obviousness that Lake Washington had, for the solution to prevent its deterioration would be costly to a distant large city without producing benefits visible to that city.

For climatic reasons Mono Lake is saline. The water supply comes from several streams, springs, rainfall, and melting snow. Mono Lake is in a delicate state of balance with its natural water input and evaporation. The lake has no outlet, and evaporation has concentrated the dissolved materials to about 2.5 times the salinity of sea water. A remarkable geological feature of great touristic interest is oddly shaped towers of tufa, a carbonate rock, that give the landscape a strange and powerful appeal. As the climate has varied, the water level has risen and fallen, but the lake has contained water for at least a half million years. In historical times the level has varied between 6428 feet (1960 meters) in 1918 and 6372 feet (1943 meters) above sea level in 1981. On the later date the maximum depth of the water was about 161 feet (49 meters). The salinity is high when the level is low and has varied between 51.3 and 99.4 grams/liter (approximately parts per thousand) in historical times; in contrast, sea water has about 35 grams/liter.

As is typical of alkaline saline lakes, Mono Lake is highly productive biologically and supports very dense populations of algae, and of invertebrates limited almost entirely to the brine shrimp (*Artemia*) and the brine fly (*Ephydra*). The brine shrimp filters phytoplankton for food. The larvae of the brine fly browse largely on algae attached to rocks and other hard substrates. There are no fish. The two invertebrates supply an important part of the diet of several species of birds. Mono Lake lies on one of the principal migration routes and during migration season hundreds of thousands of birds depend in whole or in part on *Artemia* and *Ephydra* for food. Gulls nest on islands in the lake, finding refuge there from predation by coyotes.

*Artemia* becomes so abundant that it is harvested with large dip nets, dried, and shipped to Jungle Laboratories, an aquarium supply company in Texas, for use as food for tropical fishes. This suggests that *Artemia* might constitute a definite and rather unusual economic value of the lake. I tried to find out the dollar value of the annual harvest of *Artemia*, but was told by a representative of the company that the information is not made public because it gives advantage to their competitors. Available information on the catch suggests that the annual production may be many tons (Chasan 1981). While this is probably a very small fraction of the *Artemia* production at this time, I wonder whether the people and the birds are in effective competition. There is evidence that predation by birds may be responsible for the decrease in abundance of *Artemia* during fall. This suggests that *Artemia* may be vulnerable to predation, including that by Jungle Labs.

Variation in water level and the coordinated variation in salinity have both direct and indirect effects on productivity. The consequences are most clearly shown by the abundance of *Artemia* and *Ephydra*, although that in turn is based on the high production of phytoplankton. In 1985 the level was at about 6380 feet (1946 meters) above sea level, and the populations were in good condition. The water level can drop to about 6360 feet (1940 meters) without much damage to *Artemia* and *Ephydra*. Decreases below that level would be accompanied by deterioration of both species for physiological reasons related to the increase in salinity, with consequent reduction in some of the bird spe-

cies such as the California gulls and the phaleropes. In addition
to the effects of changing food supply, birds that nest on islands
will suffer from a pronounced increase in predation by coyotes
on both adults and chicks as the water level drops and the islands become connected with the mainland. This happened to
Negut Island in 1978 when the level went down to 6375 feet (1944
meters). A fence was built across the peninsula in 1980 but gave
limited protection. Not only are there the biological consequences of decreasing water level, but some of the scenic value
could be destroyed by loss of tufa towers, either by submer-
gence at high level or by erosion at low level. If the level were to
rise too high, bird breeding areas would be submerged and conditions for production of *Artemia* and *Ephydra* would deteriorate. From this information and much more detail in the publications cited, we can see that the water supply to Mono Lake is
the major factor controlling the condition of the lake.

The environmental problem arises from the fact that the Department of Water and Power of the City of Los Angeles was
granted rights to divert water from streams feeding Mono Lake.
It has been doing so since 1941, and the lake has dropped by
about 40 feet (12 meters), with its area reduced by about 20 square
miles (52 square km). At present the area is about 70 square miles
(180 square km). This condition has generated much public concern among those who value Mono Lake for its unique scenic
qualities. Presumably private property values and the tourist industry would also be damaged if the lake loses its attraction.

If Los Angeles were to lose the use of Mono water, the city
would have several alternatives:

1. Buy more water from existing sources. Other sources are more
   expensive and the annual cost added might be about $50 per
   household. There might also be unfortunate environmental
   effects on the source of that water.
2. Develop new sources. Desalinization of sea water is expensive, but it is used on a large scale in Israel. At one time it was
   proposed to divert water from the Columbia River on the
   Washington-Oregon border to California. This would involve an enormous, expensive system of tunnels, pipes, and

pumps. The proposal was impracticable economically, politically, and environmentally. Congress refused even to appropriate money for a study.
3. Introduce a rationing or conservation program in Los Angeles. Such a proposal is sure to be strongly opposed by the inhabitants.
4. Control the increase in need for water by controlling the growth of Los Angeles. No more houses would be permitted to connect to the public water supply. Again, there would be strong public opposition.

All of these choices and others have a balance of advantage and disadvantage and involve very complicated financial and legal considerations. A fascinating thing about the Mono Lake situation, in contrast to most environmental problems, is the degree to which the pros and cons can be expressed quantitatively, although not necessarily in the same units. What would be the dollar value of the effects of a loss of *Artemia* production on the bird community? There are other kinds of values. Although Los Angeles technically has the legal right to buy water, what "right" do the people of Los Angeles have to destroy the values of Mono Lake to save themselves a mere fifty dollars per year on the household water bill? In 1941, when the rights were granted, nobody could have foreseen all the consequences. In 1989 the California Supreme Court ruled that "natural uses" of water can take precedence over the rights of diverters. This improves the likelihood of protecting Mono Lake if certain other problems can be solved.

Another remarkable feature of the Mono Lake situation is the detail and precision with which the consequences of a change in diversion of water can be predicted, at least in principle. By specifying a drop to a particular lake level, automatically one knows many of the resulting chemical and biological changes. The key problem is to translate different rates of diversion of water into a prediction of the lake level. Such information would be an essential tool in managing the system. It may not sound so difficult; the more water diverted, the lower the lake level and the higher the salinity. But when one comes to make a computation or a mathematical model of the system, it turns out to be extraordinarily complicated. For example, the rate of evaporation varies in a complex way with the salinity, area of water exposed, temperature, and wind. Nevertheless a satisfactory model has been made to calculate the effects of diversion. (Botkin et al. 1988).

A different kind of difficulty is the inability to forecast precipitation, temperature, and wind speed far in advance. In fact, the condition of the lake was changed in a fundamental way in 1982 and 1983 by unusually heavy snowfall coinciding with a temporary reduction in use of water by Los Angeles. The fresh water from the melting snow flowed out onto the lake and, because of limited mixing, formed a slightly less saline layer, about 33 feet (10 meters) thick floating on the denser water below; the lake became meromictic. Had such a condition persisted, the chemical and biological conditions would have been strongly affected because the freshwater would not mix through the entire volume of the lake and would have diluted the salinity of the upper layer strongly. In fact, because of reduced freshwater input and evaporation from the surface, the salinity of the upper layer increased and the lake mixed fully in 1988.

A similar change took place in the Dead Sea, a large, saline lake between Israel and Jordan. It had been meromictic since the first studies in the mid-nineteenth century. With increasing use of its inlet, the Jordan River, for irrigation, the input of freshwater decreased and the lake mixed fully in 1979.

The change in Mono Lake illustrates the point about its delicate balance. A great reduction in salinity could devastate the *Artemia* and *Ephydra* populations as much as an excess of salinity. A large rise in lake level could flood many of the best bird breeding areas. Any program of management must take account of both ends of the scale of elevation of lake level.

There is one fundamental contrast between the Mono Lake situation and most environmental problems of the Lake Washington type in which the people observe the deterioration close at hand and see the results of corrective action. Probably many people in Los Angeles do not know what Mono Lake is and would not care what happens to it if they did.

# Chapter 6

## Panama Canal

The Panama Canal presents an environmental problem rather different from those considered in earlier chapters, but similar in that it is based on the biological consequences of altering the chemical or physical environment. While some components of the system are highly predictable, as with Mono Lake, a major biological uncertainty complicates the solution of the Panama Canal problem, not to mention present political uncertainties.

The Panama Canal was built at one of the narrowest places in the Panamanian isthmus between the Atlantic and Pacific Oceans and at one of the lowest points. The system includes two long cuts with locks, each leading up to freshwater Gatun Lake about 85 feet (26 meters) above sea level. Gatun Lake fills an area that was a swamp before the canal was built. A high place became Barro Colorado Island, now operated as a nature reserve by The Smithsonian Tropical Research Institute. Gatun Lake receives water from many small streams and a large reservoir. The area has a typical tropical alternation of wet and dry seasons. In the rainy season the storage capacity of the system fills. During operation, the locks are filled by gravity with freshwater from Gatun Lake, so that the lake loses water with each lockage, is progressively depleted during the dry season, and its level drops. Toward the end of the dry season large ships loaded to capacity are not able to pass through this part of the canal.

With foreseen increases in world trade, the capacity of the canal will eventually become limited by its water supply. The basic question is how to increase the water supply. It turns out that there are more than a half dozen possible ways, each of which would increase the supply by a significant amount. Each has a cluster of advantages and disadvantages, economic, political, and environmental. Aside from the unpredictability of the weather, the costs and consequences of most of the methods are highly predictable, with one major exception. I will limit my discussion to that exception.

One of the proposals for increasing the water supply was to pump sea water up into Gatun Lake using large diesel-driven pumps. This idea was seriously entertained but became very unattractive during the oil crisis in 1973 because of the amount of fuel required. The environmental problem was that if the salinity of Gatun Lake increased enough, the lake would no longer serve as a freshwater barrier between the two oceans. It seemed more than likely that marine organisms brought in with the ships from one ocean would be able to survive and pass through to the other ocean. Specific consequences are unpredictable, but one can generalize from past experience with invasions of species into areas where they had not previously lived. There are many examples in which such invaders, apparently relieved of specialized predators, parasites, and competitors, went into a population explosion and created trouble by their impact on the invaded system. Well known examples include the rabbit in Australia and the Japanese beetle and starling in North America.

Many such invasions have been studied by ecologists because they offer excellent opportunities to get information about the way species interact (Mooney and Drake 1966). The Laurentian Great Lakes have provided good examples of major changes in community structure resulting from invasions of keystone predators. The opening of the Welland Canal permitted entry of the sea lamprey from the Atlantic Ocean with consequent near elimination of the lake trout. Currently we are seeing a less spectacular but no less significant new invasion by *Bythotrephes,* a planktonic crustacean that is common in Europe but had not been seen in North America before 1984. *Bythotrephes* has a body about the size of *Daphnia,* about a tenth of an inch (3 millimeters) long, but has in addition a tail spine several times as long. It is a keystone predator, and has eliminated *Daphnia* from parts of Lake Michigan, affecting the food base of several species of fish

(Lehman 1987). *Bythotrephes* itself is a nuisance to fishermen because its tail spine sticks to nets and lines, forming a "slimy" coating (John T. Lehman personal communication).

Remarkably, another European freshwater invader showed up in the Great Lakes at about the same time as *Bythotrephes*, an animal that may do even more damage. This is the zebra mussel (*Dreissena polymorpha*) which attaches to solid substrates. It becomes very abundant, clogging the intake pipes of city water supplies, reducing the flow, and fouling the water.

One could propose in general that if organisms were transferred through a salinified Panama Canal, there would be a good chance that some of the invaders from one ocean could make trouble in the other. One cannot be sure that any particular species would be a successful invader or would make trouble if it were. Ecologists are working to identify the characteristics of successful invaders to permit predictions. For Panama, there are some candidates. For example, there is a marine snake that lives among floating mats of seaweed off the Pacific Coast of Panama. It is extremely venomous, but in its native habitat it is not aggressive. If it formed a breeding population in the Atlantic, it would be a matter for concern in inhabited areas especially if, as is sometimes the case with invaders, it became aggressive. Stinging jellyfish may be more likely invaders. Different species in the two oceans are very bothersome on bathing beaches. A great increase in abundance of one of the species could be of considerable economic importance in resort areas.

A predatory starfish, *Acanthaster* (crown of thorns), has received considerable publicity for the damage it has done to coral reefs in the Pacific. Its activity is limited in part by a number of predatory invertebrates, associated with the coral, that harm *Acanthaster*. These protective invertebrates do not occur in the Atlantic, so it is likely that *Acanthaster* could cause severe trouble to Atlantic corals if it were transferred. Pathogenic microorganisms can eliminate their hosts from wide areas. In the 1930s eelgrass (*Zostera marina*) was essentially eliminated from the Atlantic by such an organism. It seems inevitable that considerable economic damage to valuable marine populations in one or both oceans would follow a major change in the ease of passage across the Isthmus of Panama. Likely candidates of economic value are crustaceans, molluscs, and sponges.

Because of the difficulties of greatly increasing the operation of the present canal, the possibility of a new canal at sea level without locks has been studied extensively. To minimize transfer of organisms, one of the plans called for a basin of very hot water to sterilize ships as they passed through, the heat being provided by a nuclear power plant! Despite a series of elaborate studies, there seems to be some doubt that a sea level canal will be built. Simpler alternatives are being considered that would have much less environmental impact with none of the dangers to marine populations. For transport of oil across the isthmus, additional pipelines can be built, and for other material, a conveyer belt parallel to the present canal and railroad has been proposed. There are several locations where such alternatives would be practicable, but at the moment there seem to be no specific plans to do more than restudy the problems. Since 1983 delegations from the United States, Panama, and Japan have been working to define the scope of yet another study to be made by an international consortium of engineering firms.

# Chapter 7

## Atmospheric Problems

Air, like water, is a fluid medium which can transport a variety of materials for great distances. There is little point in trying to decide which environmental problem is the single most dangerous or which is most urgently in need of solution, but some of the problems affecting the condition of the atmosphere could qualify as candidates for nomination. In this chapter I discuss four problems of pressing importance that have several features in common in addition to the fact that they modify the atmosphere. All have been gradually developing for several decades and are now receiving much public attention and scientific study. Only one has a simple, but probably unattainable, solution.

In order of decreasing scale of magnitude, the first is the continuing loss of ozone in the upper atmosphere, which is worldwide in extent and can make dangerous changes in conditions for life on earth. The second is the increase of carbon dioxide in the air which is also worldwide, but possibly of somewhat less danger, although it could make drastic changes in conditions for human life. The increase of the acid content of precipitation is more localized and possibly more controllable than the first two. These three problems are closely related because all depend on a substantial modification of the atmosphere by various effluvia of human activity. Some industrial processes contribute to more than one problem. It is only for convenience that I separate them. It may seem out of line to include as the fourth problem the health effects of tobacco smoking since the effect is directly on people, but the air is involved and the problem has close analogs in others I have discussed. One might suppose that this problem would be the easiest to control, but it is not under control now, although progress is being made.

Like the eutrophication of lakes, each of these problems involves a change in conditions during historical times in coordination with some human activity that can be shown with a high degree of probability to cause the change. However, unlike eutrophication, these changes are not easily subject to experimental verification. And even more than in the case of eutrophication, recognition of the changes and their interpretation has been confused by the fact that several conditions and processes have been changing at the same time. To sort out all the chains of cause and effect is difficult. Another point of confusion is that some of the effects are very hard to measure, and one can wonder whether an apparent change is merely the result of an improvement in techniques of detection and measurement. The problems involve a wide range of ecological phenomena. Each is based on the physiological reactions of individuals, but to make predictions requires an evaluation in terms of population and community processes. For example, carbon dioxide may increase the productivity of different species of plants by different amounts and change their competitive interactions and availability to consumers. With acid deposition, mortality rates are more prominent, and detection of early effects requires knowledge of population processes. While the tobacco problem is mostly a matter of individual human health, there are some interesting comparisons to make with the way corporations and individuals react to environmental problems.

## Atmospheric Ozone

As solar radiation penetrates through the atmosphere, its intensity is attenuated by absorption and scattering by gas molecules and by particles. Short wavelengths, especially ultraviolet (UV), are reduced more by these processes than are the longer wavelengths that include the visible and infrared parts of the spectrum. Radiation of certain wavelengths is strongly absorbed by particular molecules. Ozone is especially important for its absorption of ultraviolet radiation.

Most of the oxygen in the atmosphere is in the form of oxygen molecules ($O_2$), a combination of two atoms of the element. Another form, ozone, consists of three atoms of oxygen ($O_3$). It is unstable and easily enters into chemical reactions with many other substances. For this reason ozone has strongly damaging biological effects even in concentrations below 0.25 ppm (parts per million). Ozone is formed in the upper atmosphere (stratosphere) from oxygen molecules by the action of ultraviolet radiation. It has its maximum concentration at about 16 miles (20 kilometers) above sea level, and is barely detectable at sea level except under unusual meteorological conditions or near sources of its formation. Because of its instability, ozone is constantly breaking down, and its maintenance depends upon continuous production. The concentration maintained is a balance between the rates of formation and destruction, and a change of either rate will result in a change of concentration.

Once formed, ozone absorbs ultraviolet radiation very strongly, so much so that little of the short-wavelength ultraviolet radiation that enters the atmosphere reaches the earth at sea level. Strong ultraviolet radiation, such as that above the atmosphere, has a powerfully lethal effect on organisms. For instance, lamps that produce UV are used for sterilizing material by killing bacteria when the use of heat is inappropriate. The vicinity of UV lamps is one of the places where ozone has elevated concentrations at sea level. Ozone is also produced at sea level by photochemical reactions of oxygen with certain pollutants in air, such as some of the components of automobile exhaust. So, while ozone in the stratosphere helps protect against UV, at sea level it can be damaging.

It is obvious that the screen of ozone far above us is essential for the continuation of life as we know it. It is an astonishingly thin armor. If all the ozone were brought down to sea level and concentrated in a layer of pure ozone at atmospheric pressure, the layer would be about a fifth of an inch (5 millimeters) thick. This fact shows just how effectively the molecule absorbs UV radiation; it also suggests that the armor may be vulnerable. And it is vulnerable.

Ozone is not uniformly distributed around the world, and its concentration changes with time. There are increases and decreases in coordination with the changes in solar activity that are manifested in part by the sunspot cycle. There are also seasonal changes. The disappearance of the ozone over a large area of the Antarctic during austral spring each year since 1985 has received much attention in the public press because that is part of the evidence that suggests that ozone concentrations are tending to decrease. There has been uncertainty about the changes because of the difficulty of measuring ozone at enough places to get a secure global figure. Recently, through satellite technology, it has become possible to get data on a global scale. The total amount decreased by about 0.5% per year from 1979 through 1985. The localized Antarctic depletion has intensified, and the amount of ozone remaining reached a minimum in 1989.

Because of the seriousness of the potential consequences of a decrease in the amount of ozone, it is essential that we understand the reasons for changes in concentration. As mentioned above, ozone is part of a dynamic system, and the concentration maintained depends on the rates of formation and destruction. Since it is known that the radiation output of the sun varies over the years, there is a possibility that the formation of ozone has varied naturally and that a long-term but temporary decreasing trend could be natural, but such a trend would not continue indefinitely.

The increasing rate of destruction is another matter since it has more causes. Many materials produced on the ground mix slowly up through the atmosphere and reach the ozone layer where they react. Such materials are oxides of nitrogen, produced by natural biological activity in rich forest soils, and sulfur compounds from volcanos and from natural biological processes. But there is reason to think that human activity has been increasing the amounts of materials that react with ozone. Some of these are simply increases in natural processes, such as nitrogen oxide production in heavily fertilized agricultural land. The more important ones are generated or released by industrial and domestic activity. Automobile exhaust is a rich source of nitrogen oxides. High-flying airplanes inject much reactive material into the lower stratosphere; mostly these are supersonic military airplanes, but even passenger jets fly high enough that the cabin air sometimes contains annoying or even hazardous amounts of ozone. In the early 1970s there was worldwide interest in developing fleets of supersonic commercial aircraft; these would have injected potentially damaging amounts of exhaust into the stratosphere. The economic advantages of such airplanes was questionable, which may have been the dominating reason for abandoning the project at that time. As it is, only a few British-French Concordes have been flying, but interest in supersonic aircraft continues.

An even more serious threat to ozone is a class of synthetic organic compounds called chlorofluorocarbons (CFCs). They are widely used in a variety of products including refrigerants, components of plastic foam, and propellants in aerosol spray cans. They have been produced in rapidly increasing quantities since the 1930s. In 1974 it was recognized that CFCs were capable of reaching the stratosphere and reacting with ozone there. In fact, there is now good evidence, based on the byproducts of reaction, that this has happened.

It is important to try to predict the effect of changes in processes that affect the amount of ozone. It is difficult to do so because of the extraordinarily complex chemistry involved. Many different reactions are possible, but they compete for the same materials, and we do not always know which path of reaction will be followed. In addition there can be feedback effects when the accumulated product of a reaction changes the rate of that reaction. Another problem is that the future courses of some conditions, solar and atmospheric, cannot be controlled and are unpredictable. Nevertheless, one can try to calculate the effect of some specific, controllable change. For example, the production of CFCs is unlikely to increase indefinitely, and one can calculate the potential effect of adding various amounts up to a maximum rate, assuming nothing else changes. For each level of increase there would be a new, lesser amount of ozone in dynamic equilibrium between formation and destruction, and a new consequent intensity of UV at sea level.

The next step is to calculate the biological effects of the predicted intensity of ultraviolet radiation. UV covers a wide range of the spectrum of wavelengths shorter than those of visible light. Various wavelengths are absorbed by different kinds of molecules and therefore have different biological effects. Most effects are injurious to organisms, but to varying degrees. Different kinds of organisms have differing sensitivity and some can repair damage fast enough to stave off death. Again, we are dealing with a balance of opposed processes. Nevertheless, we know that increasing UV intensity would be generally damaging to the communities of the earth.

Many of the published predictions concern reductions of the amount of ozone of the order of 20% and the consequent increase in the incidence of various types of skin cancer. However, there is much more involved than the human physiological effects, for major parts of the food chain supporting the human population could be harmed. It is here that large areas of ecological knowledge can be relevant, because we would see the consequences of differential response of interacting species, predators, and competitors.

We can speculate on the conditions that would result from more drastic changes. The maximum damage would result if the full intensity of solar radiation blasted down onto the earth's surface. Most vegetation would be eliminated and the problem of human skin cancer would become moot for there would be no people. Fortunately, this is not achievable because there would be considerable attenuation of damaging wavelengths by oxygen ($O_2$). With the less severe depletion that is possible, humans might be able to adapt to a different life style that required full-time protection from sunlight, as by converting to a nocturnal existence, wearing protective clothing or improved sunscreen lotions, or staying in well-shaded places. This can hardly be considered a desirable condition.

The ozone situation is potentially so dangerous that even a suspicion of damage to the ozone layer must be taken seriously. The consequences of a mistake are just too great. Because of the danger, the United States government in 1978 passed regulations limiting the use and production of CFCs, especially in spray cans, and urged other nations to join the effort. A conference of twenty-four nations was held in 1987 under the auspices of the United Nations Environmental Program. It produced a treaty, ratified in August 1988, which will reduce the production of CFCs by 50% in the year 1999. Whether this response is adequate remains to be seen.

The initial reaction of the industry in 1974, when the potential effect of CFCs was announced, was the usual one of doubt, reference to natural variation in ozone, and emphasis on the economic loss caused by any control. As more and more evidence accumulated, it became obvious that the problem was real. In 1988 E. I. du Pont de Nemours & Company announced a 10-year plan to phase out the production of CFCs. So far, this is the most responsible and effective corporate action that has been taken.

### Atmospheric Carbon Dioxide

The temperature of the earth is determined by a balance between the incoming radiation from the sun, comprising a very wide range of wavelengths, and back-radiation into space, mostly in the infrared (heat) region of the spectrum. Several component gases of the atmosphere absorb infrared radiation strongly, the most important being carbon dioxide ($CO_2$). The concentration of carbon dioxide acts as a valve, controlling the flow of heat from the earth and at present maintaining temperatures high enough to support life.. Without carbon dioxide the mean temperature of the earth would be reduced by about 10° F (5.5° C), resulting in ice-age conditions. An increase in the amount of $CO_2$ would lead to an increase in temperature by reducing the loss of heat. This has been called the "greenhouse effect" because the glass used for greenhouses has a similar function in trapping heat.

In fact, the carbon dioxide content of the air has been rising since measurements with accurate methods were started, increasing from 315 ppm in 1958 to 340 ppm in 1981. Superimposed on the general upward drift are pronounced seasonal fluctuations related to the uptake of carbon dioxide by vegetation during the growing season and net release in the nongrowing season. While these annual changes show the importance of natural biological activity in controlling atmospheric chemistry on a global scale, it is not enough to account for all of the long-term increase. Large changes in land use can affect the cycling of carbon in different ways, depending on what is done, so that the consequences are complicated to calculate. The forests of the world contain more carbon than the atmosphere, so a relatively small change in carbon cycling could have a disproportionally large effect on the air. The amount of wood and other material containing recyclable carbon in the world is hard to estimate. But if an area of forest is cleared by burning, most of the contained carbon is released to the air. If the wood is converted to lumber instead, recycling is delayed. The balance of uptake and release will also be affected by the use of deforested land, whether it is reforested or converted to agriculture or urban use. The rate of deforestation in the tropics has increased dramatically in recent years: each year about 34,700 square miles (90,000 square kilometers) of forest is cleared. However, it appears that known changes in vegetation alone cannot account for the observed increase in atmospheric carbon dioxide.

The other obvious factor to consider is of course the burning of fossil fuels: coal, natural gas, and petroleum products. The amount of fossil fuel known to have been burned is more than enough to account for the increase in the air. In fact a considerable discrepancy exists; the increase in the air is only about half that known to have been released. Again, changes in the balance with vegetation seem to be insufficient to account for that difference. There has been considerable dispute about the identity of the "sink" for the missing carbon dioxide. The argument seems to have been settled in favor of the ocean rather than any terrestrial system.

The increasing amount of carbon dioxide will have some direct effects. Experiments show that plant growth will be increased, enhancing agricultural productivity. This is the one bright spot in the whole situation. The fact that much of the carbon dioxide has disappeared into the ocean leads to an examination of the carbon cycle there. In some places at least, the carbon dioxide that could be released is expected to react with calcium carbonate structures, causing them to dissolve. This means not only remnants of mollusc shells but coral reefs as well. If this effect takes place on a large scale, there will be repercussions in ocean productivity and fisheries.

The inevitable increase in temperature of the earth's atmosphere with an increase of $CO_2$, foreseen to be in the range 3°–8° F (1.5°–4.5° C), would have many consequences, some direct, some very indirect. There might even be temporary local decreases in temperature. The world's weather patterns would be drastically rearranged and the change in temperature would not be evenly distributed over the earth. In general we could expect new areas to be opened up to agriculture, subject to limitation by adequate soils and rainfall, while some presently cultivated areas would become unsuitable through lack of precipitation. There is considerable public concern that the prevalence of drought in the 1980s may herald the start of the greenhouse effect. There is also considerable disagreement among professionals.

A large-scale change that would cause major displacement of the human population is a rise in sea level that would accompany partial melting of glaciers. However, there is considerable uncertainty about the amount of rise. A possible rise by the year 2100 is about 12 feet (3.7 meters) (National Academy of Sciences 1983). While this may seem a small change, it would require the abandonment of many coastal habitations, including parts of some of the world's largest cities. The rise could be considerably higher.

Such vast rearrangements of the human population and its activities would not be fatal of course, but there would be enormous changes in world politics and economics. If the change is slow enough, but its course becomes clearly evident, presumably much of it could be accommodated by new construction on higher ground at the rate that would have been required by obsolescence of the old buildings anyway. A rapid change on the order of only several decades would be very much more disruptive economically. The rate of warming is not presently predictable within narrow limits. It almost certainly will be irregular, with the normal ups and downs being superimposed on the gradual increase.

It is also difficult to predict the degree of increase because of processes that compensate. Increased evaporation may increase cloudiness which shades the earth. Many industries produce smoke particles that scatter light and increase reflection of light.

That we can stop the warming soon enough to prevent a major change by controlling carbon dioxide production seems most unlikely, in view of the extent of disruption of present human activities required. To replace the energy provided by fossil fuels would demand such a large expansion of alternative sources that it seems impracticable in anything but a very long time. Already the use of atomic energy has presented major technical, political, and sociological problems. Sites for additional hydroelectric power are limited, and geothermal activity is too restricted to be a general solution. Solar and wind power have their own limitations.

It may be difficult to see a connection with the Lake Washington type of problem, where a clear solution was available for a well-understood and basically simple problem. Here, the problem involves a complex set of interactions responding to what seems like an inevitable change. As with Lake Washington, public understanding is essential, and that means that there must be an effort to present information effectively to the public, to think of all the consequences that may arise, and to plan how best to live with them. The National Academy of Sciences made a good start in 1983 with a technical presentation that contains this advice:

> There is a broad class of problems that have no 'solution' in the sense of an agreed course of action that would be expected to make the problem go away. These problems can also be so important that they should not be avoided or ignored until the fog lifts. We simply must learn to deal more effectively with their twists and turns as they unfold. We require sensible regular progress to anticipate what these developments might be with a balanced diversity of approaches. The payoff is that we will have had the chance to consider alternative courses of action with some degree of calm before we may be forced to choose among them in urgency or have them forced on us when other—perhaps better—options have been lost. Increasing atmospheric $CO_2$ and its climatic consequences constitute such a problem.

### Acid Deposition

Rain is not just water. Drops of condensing moisture tend to form around particles, and the water absorbs gases from the air. Various natural processes produce substances that cause the rainwater to be acid, including some also responsible for ozone depletion. Many human activities have added acid-forming materials to the atmosphere. Coal and oil contain compounds of sulfur and nitrogen, and automobile exhaust is especially rich in nitrogen oxides.

Atmospheric acids are carried down in rain and drain into lakes. This process has been called acid rain, but since acids are also carried by snow, fog, and dust particles, the more general term is acid deposition. While the emphasis of much research has been on the source and magnitude of industrially produced acid, many of the industrial sources also emit large amounts of toxic metals such as arsenic, zinc and lead.

Acids are substances that liberate hydrogen ions into solution. The degree of acidity is expressed as pH, which is related to the activity of the hydrogen ions in such a way that the smaller the number on the pH scale, the higher is the concentration of hydrogen ions. Solutions above pH 7 are alkaline, those below are acid. Because the scale is logarithmic, each pH unit is different from the next by a factor of 10, so that a pH of 5 is ten times as acid as a pH of 6. Rain in equilibrium with the carbon dioxide in an atmosphere uncontaminated by industrial activity would have a pH of about 5.6, but because of the content of other naturally produced acids it is actually close to pH 5.0. Rain downwind from heavily industrialized areas can have a pH below 4.0.

Freshwater lakes in soft-water areas tend to range from pH 7.0 to 7.5 in the winter when biological activity is low. Brown-water bog lakes contain organic acids which can bring the pH down below 4.5. Lakes in volcanic regions may have a pH as low as 3.0, the same as many vinegars. (Most lemon juice has a pH of about 2.2). Saline, alkaline lakes can have a pH of 10.0 or more.

There are strong correlations between the pH of lakes and the number of species of animals, plants and microorganisms present. While some species can tolerate or even require pH below 4.0, the numbers observed begin to drop off as one examines successively lakes of pH below neutrality. In general, conditions below 5.0 are unfavorable for most fish. Even if adult fish can survive at a low pH, the eggs may not develop. Some of the invertebrates that are eaten by fish are damaged by as mild an acid as pH 6.0, although some are specialized to acid water. Some groups of invertebrates are less resistant to acid than others; molluscs, with calcareous shells, are especially sensitive.

Chemical and biological changes in lakes subjected to acid precipitation became widely noticed in northern Europe, especially Scandinavia, during the 1950s. Much of the acid at first was attributed to airborne pollution from the industrial midland of England. It is now known that the process had been going on for many decades before; in fact, the term "acid rain" was coined in 1852. In North America the extent of acid precipitation became clear somewhat later than in Europe and was widely studied in the late 1960s, especially in eastern United States and Canada.

The processes leading to damage by acid are complex. For example, acid rain washing through the soil can dissolve aluminum from clay and carry it to a lake where it can be toxic under certain conditions. (But see the discussion of Green Lake in chapter 16.) In some regions the soils are capable of neutralizing considerable amounts of acid, and lakes in such regions show less effect than those in regions that do not have as much neutralizing capacity. Under some conditions the acidification is overcome by an increase of some chemical processes that liberate alkaline substances. The pH of lakes can also be affected by changes in land use around the lake. There can be more than one reason for fish disappearing from a lake, for example overfishing, and overuse of pesticides which can damage the fish directly or can eliminate insects that were an important part of their food. Thus some lakes have lost their fish populations before a great reduction of pH, and some have supported fish longer than expected at low pH.

The ecological basis of the acid deposition problem is clear, with two major components. One is the physiological effect of changed chemical conditions on longevity and reproductive success of individual animals and plants; these must be evaluated in terms of population birth and death rates. The second is the way the interaction between species is affected by changes in the chemical environment. If a sensitive keystone predatory species is eliminated, a more resistant prey species may increase.

Understanding and solving the acid deposition problem involves knowing the degree to which the acidity of precipitation and of lakes has changed and where. It was initially confused by the absence of definite records of the original conditions. In many regions where acid damage is suspected there is no historical record. Even when records exist, difficulties arise because methods used in the early 1940s for measuring pH were not as accurate as those used later and were subject to interference which could have biased the results. At most all one knows is that lakes that formerly supported good trout fishing no longer have fish and are too acid to support them now. Further, since effluent from tall smokestacks can travel very far before touching down, the source for a given area of damage may not be obvious. Nevertheless, it is possible to estimate the pH of lakes in the far past in areas that have had no direct effect of human habitation, eliminating the possibility of change due to agriculture, land clearing, and the like. For this one uses the paleolimnological record of diatoms mentioned in chapter 2. It is clear that changes in pH have occurred which cannot be explained by the various complicating factors mentioned. Since the Industrial Revolution there has been a genuine worldwide decrease in pH of lakes in regions that are sensitive to the effect.

As evidence accumulated, it became clear that damage was likely to get worse. It became important to identify the sources exactly to find out what means could be used to reduce the output of acid. The most obvious, but not the only, sources were the tall smokestacks of very large industries. Proposals to control that part of the problem resulted in considerable controversy. It is possible to reduce the amount of sulfur compounds going up the chimney, but the process requires expensive installations, maintenance and operation, and produces an intractable, useless sludge. Automobile exhaust was found to be a rich source of acid-producing materials. The reaction of some of the industries was again the common one: to deny that the problem exists, or if it does, something else is responsible, like natural changes; or that there is no cure, or if there is, that it is too expensive. There is a great similarity between the arguments about controlling sulfur emissions and those about detergents.

The controversy over the identity of the sources of acid rain and methods of control has led to confrontation between the governments of Canada and the United States. Much of the damage in Canada can be traced to sources in the U.S., and Canada wants the emissions reduced. The U.S. wants more study. Considerable attention has been given to this conflict in the newspapers.

Because of the magnitude of effort required to control industrial and automotive output of acid forming substances, efforts have been made to prevent damage at the site or to restore damaged soil or lakes. Acid can be neutralized by the addition of lime to soil or lakes. While this may reduce the acidity of the lake or soil, it can have side effects by binding essential elements. For example, excess liming of soil to counteract acid emission from a smelter causes a manganese deficiency in the herbage used by cattle and horses, resulting in characteristic deformity of newborn animals. This phenomenon is widespread enough to have been given a name, "smelter smoke syndrome."

A full evaluation of the acid deposition problem must be made as part of a study of the global sulfur and nitrogen cycles. While industries seem to like to blame natural variation for problems that they themselves have created or exacerbated, many pollution problems are, after all, exaggerations of natural processes, and we have to be sure in every case that we are making an adequate inventory of the naturally produced materials. (See chapter 16.) Some surprises have come to light recently. A very large amount of a volatile sulfur-containing material, dimethyl sulfide (DMS), is liberated by certain species of marine phytoplankton, and much gets into the atmosphere, joining all the other natural and industrial sources of acidifying materials. It is not known what fraction of the sulfur in acid precipitation originates from dimethyl sulfide on a worldwide basis, but locally it can be considerable at certain times. For example, the very productive waters around Scandinavia liberate 20–70% as much sulfur during summer as the industries. The Baltic and North Seas have been heavily eutrophied with sewage, so presumably the DMS output has not always been as great as it is now.

DMS may have a significant part in the control of the earth's temperature, working in opposition to the effect of carbon dioxide. That is, an increase of DMS leads to the formation of clouds by providing condensation nuclei. The clouds reflect light, reducing the delivery of radiation to the earth's surface.

The acid deposition problem illustrates nicely a point that comes up in connection with many problems; nothing is ever as simple as it seems at first, and interactions of two processes can produce effects different from the simple sum of both. One can reduce the effect of the other, as with DMS and carbon dioxide. One can amplify the effect of the other; for example, discrepancies in the timing of damage to forest vegetation led to the discovery that some acid deposition is so rich in nitrate that it serves as a fertilizer when absorbed through shrub leaves. Because leaf and bud growth was prolonged much later in the fall than is normal, the plants died by freezing when normally they would already have been dormant.

## Smoking Tobacco

Although the tobacco-smoking problem may seem to have only a small ecological component, it is relevant to the motif of this book for several reasons. A number of air pollution problems can involve a direct effect on human health as well as the modification of natural communities; smog and emissions from smelters are examples. There are places where a meteorological inversion traps air in a valley or other location with restricted air movement. If there are industries or heavy automobile traffic in the area, pollutants can accumulate instead of being dispersed by wind. The concentrations of sulfur and nitrogen oxides or other substances can be high enough to be injurious to people, initiating or worsening lung and heart disease. Vegetation in the area can be severely damaged by repeated episodes.

Because the tobacco smoke problem presents some aspects of air pollution and its control in a simplified, clear-cut way, an understanding of it may improve our understanding of air pollution in general. My main reason for including tobacco is that there are remarkable similarities in the nature of the arguments about tobacco and about other pollution problems. For instance, every component of the debate about detergents can be found here, but in magnified and exaggerated form, including misinterpretation of facts, omission of relevant information, and emphasis on irrelevant information. The conflict between economic and environmental (health) interests is especially strong. The tobacco case probably shows better than any other the extreme reaction by an industry to a threat to its economy. The tobacco industry spends billions of dollars each year on advertising alone and is a much more potent political force than the detergent industry, as evidenced by the fact that it is heavily subsidized by the U.S. Government with funds derived from taxes.

As I have not made as close a study of the literature on tobacco as of detergents, I will give only a general account. When I was a child, children were told that they should not smoke because it would stunt their growth. A little unbiased observation showed this to be false. Many smokers were big and husky, especially those in cigarette advertisements which made it clear that smoking was for classy people. Of course the adults had no way then of knowing the real danger of smoking. At that time a smoker could propose that if he wanted to expose himself to risk, that was his own business. During that era little attention was paid to the consequences of smoke on non-smokers, other than discomfort. Somehow smoking seemed such an important thing, and lighting up such an essential social custom, that many non-smokers felt intimidated, and only those who were especially sensitive to smoke would have nerve enough to complain.

It was not until about 1946 that an increasing incidence of lung and throat cancer began to draw attention. As more data accumulated and special studies were made, it began to seem more and more likely that the probability of developing cancer was related to the amount an individual smoked. Also, rates of heart disease and other ills were increasing. In 1964 the Surgeon General, Dr. Luther L. Terry at the time, issued the first report that reviewed evidence suggesting that the increase in disease was not a coincidence, but was causally connected with the use of tobacco. In 1972 federal regulations were established requiring warning labels to be put on cigarette packages and advertisements. Later local regulations were established in many states and municipalities limiting the places in which smoking was permitted. For example, no-smoking areas were designated in restaurants, waiting rooms, and airplanes.

The conflict between smokers and non-smokers was often presented by the tobacco industry simply as a difficult social interaction. If everybody would just be a good sport about it and behave courteously, smokers could smoke, exercising their Constitutional Right to Freedom of Choice, and non-smokers could non-smoke. When threatened with regulations limiting the public places where one could smoke, the industry reacted with ominous tales of the dangers of governmental interference with the rights to do what one wanted to do with one's own body. *Philip Morris Magazine,* distributed free by a cigarette company, is a good source of information of the character of tobacco company propaganda. Each issue contains newsy articles about sports, nature, and travel. The central section, "PM Notebook", is devoted to the industry's views on a variety of topics involving tobacco. Some present factual statements about recent court decisions, announcements of restrictive actions against smoking, or cute sayings of famous actors who need to smoke. Some are frankly fictional, designed to frighten people into worrying about the police state that anti-smokers are planning. For example, the Spring 1988 issue has a fantasy about the future in which the "Smoke Enforcement Agency" arrests and holds without bail people for the simple possession of a pack of cigarettes; the country is full of informers; a ten-year-old boy is given the Medal of Freedom for turning his mother in, a clear indication of the "smoke fascism that has overcome the land." "Paranoid" is a technical medical term and should not be used lightly, but this literature is of the character that is often popularly described by that word.

Smokers' viewpoints were expressed more soberly by fourteen authors in a symposium held in 1984, supported by several tobacco companies (Tollison 1986). Two major types of objection are elaborated in the book, scientific and social. Objections are raised against the scientific evidence of the unfortunate effects of tobacco on every possible ground. Cancer and heart disease have many causes; some people have a constitution that makes them subject to stress and disease whether they smoke or not. Social objections are based on ideas of human rights, civil liberties, the important social role of smoking and other such ideas. Since everybody is bothered by something done by or used by other people, we must exhibit tolerance and mutual respect for our differences; individual preferences must be accepted. As examples of objectionable products we are given alcohol, tea, salt, and red meat. Objectionable actions include open air burning of leaves and carrying guns. These things seem to be equated with tobacco and the effects of smoking, and are all implied to be equally acceptable.

The line of argument that pervades the book and the pro-smoking literature in general is that any governmental restriction on advertising tobacco or on the places where it may be smoked is an invasion of freedom by an evil, Big Brother government. Smoking is strictly a personal matter. It is important for smokers to oppose all controls on it because if the anti-smoking forces succeed, the way will be open for any number of additional repressions of liberty, and we will have a totally regulated society.

The situation had already changed before the symposium publication appeared. It was becoming clear, to a high degree of probability, that environmental tobacco smoke was damaging to non-smokers ("passive smoking"). On that basis, smoking still is a matter of individual choice, but where the smoking is done is not. The findings about "passive smoking" changed the character of the conflict between smokers and non-smokers in a basic way. No longer could a smoker tell another person that his smoking was strictly a personal matter. The non-smoker could object to being forced to inhale smoke for stronger reasons than his mere personal discomfort. This idea had already brought vigorous denials at the symposium. One author admitted that environmental tobacco smoke may be annoying to some non-smokers, but he denied that scientific evidence supports the view that it is a significant health hazard to nonsmokers. Reported adverse reactions to environmental tobacco smoke were thought to be possibly "psychosocial in origin." This idea has interesting implications. Are psychological problems unreal?

The tobacco industry has directed much effort to attacking the validity of studies of the medical effects of environmental tobacco smoke. They reacted strongly to a report by the National Academy of Sciences on environmental tobacco smoke, as shown in another symposium edited by R. D. Tollison (1988). As with the first symposium, this one deals with a wide range of social and political as well as the scientific issues. One of the more remarkable propositions is that limitations on smoking in the work place are more properly dealt with in collective bargaining with labor unions than by governmental legislative action. Just think that one through!

The book emphasizes the complexity of the air pollution

problem, citing the multiple sources and kinds of irritating particles in the air, the inadequacy of ventilation systems in large buildings, and the difficulty of getting accurate data on anything. We are told that cleaner indoor environments require better ventilation systems, not smoking bans. This reminds me of the position of the detergent people that better sewage treatment was the answer to the phosphate problem when they were advised against putting detergents into the sewer system.

An appendix reviews a selection of studies of environmental smoke. While I am not familiar with this literature, I was struck by an uncanny resemblance of the style of the appendix to that of the criticisms by the soap and detergent people of the scientific literature on phosphorus and eutrophication, quoted extensively in chapter 3. As during the detergent controversy, many true statements are cited in such a way as to appear to contradict the conclusion that tobacco smoke is damaging. The tobacco people emphasize the complexities of air pollution and medical research. They point out that much of the evidence against tobacco is indirect, correlational, or circumstantial, and therefore there is "no scientific proof" that smoke is damaging. Actually, the kind of experimentation with people that would lead to so-called scientific proof is illegal.

The difficulty here is one that is common in epidemiology and environmental sciences. The effect of a change in some condition is expressed by a change in the characteristics of a group or population. For example, since a person dies only once, the concept of death rate can be applied only to groups, not individuals. Thus the tobacco industry can claim that there is no proof that a particular cancer was caused by tobacco smoking; cancers are caused by a variety of agents, and individuals vary in their susceptibility to them. Some heavy smokers never contract cancer, and some non-smokers do. Because most scientists are careful to indicate the areas of uncertainty in their results, especially in preliminary progress reports, the tobacco people can pick out sentences that mention uncertainty and quote them as if they applied to the whole body of research results.

In 1986 Surgeon General C. Everett Koop issued a report on the environmental smoke issues, commenting:

Critics often express that more research is required, that certain studies are flawed, or that we should delay action until more conclusive proof is produced. As both a physician and a public health official, it is my judgment that the time for delay is past; measures to protect the public health are required now. The scientific case against involuntary smoking as a health risk is more than sufficient to justify appropriate remedial action, and the goal of any remedial action must be to protect the nonsmoker from environmental tobacco smoke. (U.S. Department of Health and Human Services 1986).

In fact, the evidence was studied in great detail by a committee of the National Academy of Sciences and found to be anything but insubstantial. Each chapter ends with a summary and a listing of "What is known" and "What scientific information is missing" with recommendations for specific research to be done.

It is worthwhile calling attention to the character of the academy reports, many of which are cited in this book. The National Academy of Sciences is a private organization created by an act of Congress in 1863, during the administration of Abraham Lincoln. Its function is to further science and technology and to advise the federal government upon request. It does this largely by making studies of particular scientific problems which can then be used by the government as bases for action, such as legislation. The National Research Council is the operating agency of the academy. A report may not make recommendations for specific actions other than any needed to define additional research, since the findings must be combined with other considerations in the legislative process. I was struck by a point made by a representative of the tobacco industry during a television debate about the environmental smoke report. He emphasized that "Even the National Academy of Sciences did not recommend banning smoking," somehow making it seem that the academy supported the industry's position, which it did not, since that kind of evaluation was not the function of that report.

In this connection, another NRC report has special significance. It was a detailed examination of the condition of the air of commercial airliners, undertaken because there had been much complaint about the air quality, especially about tobacco smoke.

On the basis of its finding, the committee did in this case suggest a series of specific actions including: "The Committee recommends a ban on smoking on all domestic commercial flights, for four major reasons: to lessen irritation and discomfort to passengers and crew, to reduce potential health hazards to cabin crew associated with ETS (Environmental Tobacco Smoke), to eliminate the possibility of fires caused by cigarettes, and to bring the cabin air quality into line with established standards for other closed environments." There was solid basis for this action. The airline cabin is a special kind of environment; it has limited air circulation and filtering capacity. Despite separation of the smoking and non-smoking sections, smoke is re-distributed to all parts of the airplane. It is the work place of the cabin attendants, and tobacco smoke topped the list of their complaints in a survey about their working conditions. Mr. Tollison's second symposium contains a comment agreeing that exposure to ETS could be viewed as a problem by some crew members and passengers, but holds that more study is needed before a definite response can be made to the recommendation to ban smoking in airplanes. This is a common delaying tactic. Subsequent federal legislation nevertheless banned smoking on all flights within the United States.

Objective evidence of an actual transfer of smoke material to non-smokers has been found in the form of cotinine in the blood, saliva, and urine of non-smokers who have been in a smoky environment. Cotinine is uniquely derived from nicotine. This fact by itself of course does not prove that the non-smokers had an enhanced risk of cancer, but the observation shows that a mechanism exists by which carcinogens can be transferred from smokers to non-smokers.

Superficially it would seem that the solution to smoking would be simply to stop, and many people have. Unfortunately, some significant fraction of the population is addicted and physiologically unable to stop, and such people are very uncomfortable if they cannot smoke even for short periods. The Surgeon General's 1986 Report states:

> Changes in smoking policies regarding the work place and other
> environments necessitated by the data presented in this Report

should not be designed to punish the smoker. Successful implementation of protection for the nonsmoker requires the support and cooperation of smokers, nonsmokers, management, and employees and should be developed through a cooperative effort of all groups affected. In addition, changes are often more effective when support and assistance is provided for the smoker who wants to quit.

Cigarette smoking is an addictive behavior, and the individual smoker must decide whether or not to continue that behavior, however, it is evident from the data presented in this volume that the choice to smoke cannot interfere with the nonsmokers' right to breathe air free of tobacco smoke. The right of smokers to smoke ends where their behavior affects the health and well-being of others; furthermore, it is the smokers' responsibility to ensure that they do not expose nonsmokers to the potential harmful effects of tobacco smoke.

The character of advertisements of cigarettes and statements issued by the tobacco industry has shifted over the years in coordination with the developing knowledge of the effect of tobacco smoking. At the time of World War I, when cigarettes became very popular, there was little or no awareness of a real health problem, and advertising was designed to attract people to smoking largely by emphasizing the social advantages. Later, there were simple denials that tobacco had anything to do with cancer or any other disease. More recently the advertisements ignore the dangers, except for an obligatory warning about one of the dangerous features of tobacco smoke. The industry asserts that there is no attempt in advertising to attract people to smoking, but merely to help smokers decide which brand to choose.

The shocking behavior of the tobacco industry in response to limitations on the places where people may smoke gives a fascinating insight into the way that an industry faced with a threat to its economic well-being can illustrate that it is a jungle out there. When Northwest Airlines decided independently to ban smoking on all its domestic flights, it hired an advertising company to make a television commercial to announce the fact. The same company had been making commercials for some food industries that were part of a large conglomerate which included several tobacco companies. When the vice-chairman of the conglomerate saw the commercial, he became furious and cancelled all the food contracts held by the advertising firm. The value of the contracts was 84 million dollars, and 120 workers were to be laid off. The tobacco industry itself retaliated directly against the airline by publishing criticisms of its service and encouraging smokers to use other airlines.

There are several legal, social, and medical problems that are not strictly relevant to this chapter, although they are important and are being widely debated. One has to do with Medicare costs for hospital treatment of smokers with lung cancer. I doubt that anyone would seriously propose that medical care be withheld from smokers, for smoking is not the only cause of cancer. Nevertheless, the cost of private health insurance is increased by inclusion of coverage of health problems related to smoking. These considerations center on who pays the bills. Because taxes and insurance premiums are increased to pay some of those bills, public pressure to reduce smoking may result. One of the most unsettling aspects of the tobacco situation is that tobacco growers are heavily subsidized with tax money by the federal government. The senators and congressmen from the tobacco-growing states have been very successful in perpetuating this dubious practice.

The Office of the U.S. Trade Representative is aggressively encouraging the sales of U.S. cigarettes abroad, and the packages do not carry the warning label required here. The Reagan Administration threatened sanctions against Asian markets that have resisted importing American cigarettes. With friends like that, who needs enemies? The president of Philip Morris defended the governmental policy simply on the basis that it is a matter of free trade and the right to sell American products in foreign markets. This situation is similar to others in which we sell abroad products that are not permitted in American markets, like nutritionally inadequate baby food.

## Summary

Finally, because air and water are both effective transporters of material, the atmospheric and detergent problems are comparable. In each case the effects are felt at a distance from the source, there are strong economic motives for not controlling the problem, and this has provided motivation for the kinds of obfuscation we saw in the detergent debates. In all these cases, material produced for the benefit of, or used by one element (person, industry, or country) causes damage to another without a compensating benefit. This generates dissent or even conflict and is as true for water as it is for air. The Great Lakes were a center of contention between the United States and Canada because Canada was faster about introducing water pollution control, especially of phosphorus. Relations between the two countries became strained during the Reagan administration because the efforts by the United States to control acid-forming emissions were thought inadequate by the Government of Canada. The conflict was largely resolved by the International Joint Commission.

A conflict may develop between the two countries in the other direction. Most Canadian cities on marine coasts have little treatment of sewage; it is mostly discharged raw. Vancouver, B.C. is the only West Coast Canadian city to use even primary treatment. Since water tends to move along the coast in many places, the sewage can move over a considerable length of coastline. Such contamination may force the closure of clam and oyster beds, among other things, as has occurred along the East Coast of North America. Puget Sound (U.S.) and the Straits of Georgia (Canada) are capable of affecting each other by the same kind of transport of various pollutants.

# Part 3

## Long-Term Environmental Research

In the first chapter of this book I gave an account of the Lake Washington study, one that exemplifies a particular way of working that has become known as long-term research. The phrase means more than simply that the project takes a long time to complete. The essential feature of long-term research is that its rate of progress is determined by the rate at which the system being studied operates, not by the diligence of the scientists. One cannot complete the project in half the time by working twice as hard any more than nine women can produce a baby in one month. The time scale is not necessarily set by the life span of organisms; it may depend on long-term variation in the physical environment.

In the case of Lake Washington, the buildup of enrichment continued for eight years after *Oscillatoria rubescens* gave its signal of impending trouble. The diversion program took five years, and we then intended to continue the study for as long as needed for the lake to complete its adjustment to the new nutrient conditions, perhaps five or ten years. Once it seemed to reach a balance with its new conditions, the study would have to be continued only long enough to get a good sample of the normal year-to-year variation so that we could accurately describe its "equilibrium" condition. Because weather tends to show short-term fluctuations, so will some aspects of lakes. This feature of the control of lakes makes it essential that studies to evaluate the effect of a restorative action be continued long enough to detect genuine trends. As one of my graduate students, D. A. Culver, explained to me: "There is no such thing as a representative year; what we have is a series of abnormal years."

An experimental whole-lake study is not necessarily a long-term project. Some processes are fast enough that results are obtained promptly. In the following group of chapters I have selected examples of truly long-term projects to illustrate the concept further and to show some of the difficulties inherent in such work. All of the examples have several things in common. Each is concerned wth a definite environmental problem of practical importance. Each concerns the response of a natural system to disturbance. Each has an ecological component that can appeal to a scientist for its own basic interest and would be worth investigating even if there were no immediate practical benefit. Each has its own time scale for completion; some entail much less time than others, and some may have no definite completion. They all demand a continuous, sustained effort for however long it takes. Because of the different periods needed and the necessity for continuity, it has been proposed to abandon the phrase "long-term research" and refer to this kind of project as *sustained environmental research*. (See Strayer et al. in the references for chapter 13).

In chapter 13 I will try to generalize from the examples to identify more explicitly the character of sustained environmental research and its special needs that are different from those of other kinds of research. I will also discuss current developments in the financial support of long-term or sustained research.

# Chapter 8

## Hubbard Brook

The Hubbard Brook Ecosystem Study has become to many ecologists the prime example of what is meant by long-term research. It was started in 1963 by F. H. Bormann and G. E. Likens, both then at Dartmouth. They realized at the beginning that a strong commitment to continuity over a long period of time must be made and that this required a study area that could be maintained without disturbance. The Hubbard Brook Experimental Forest in New Hampshire, established by the USDA Forest Service in 1955, was such a place, and the success of the project has depended on cooperation between the agency and the scientists.

The project started on a small scale with modest, but specific, objectives. Funding was provided by the National Science Foundation in grants varying from one to three years in duration. The plan was modified as the project continued and the initial findings led to new ideas. The number of scientists and helpers varied appropriately as needed. The primary goal was to make an experimental study of the biogeochemical cycling processes in a forested terrestrial ecosystem. The basic procedure was to measure the input of material carried by precipitation and the output in the streams draining the area; thus a budget could be calculated for each chemical element measured. The effect of the project on the thinking of scientists has been out of proportion to its magnitude. For example, after some unexpected results about the pH of rain led to an extension of the chemical analyses, the project produced the first and longest continous record of the development of acid precipitation in North America and was influential in the design of other studies of acid deposition.

The watershed consists of several subwatersheds, each drained by a small stream leading to the main stream, Hubbard Brook. The experimental aspect consisted of subjecting subwatersheds to different treatments and comparing the subsequent output with what it had been before modification and with that of an unmodified reference watershed. For instance, when the forest was clear-cut, nutrient loss was increased due to changes in chemical cycling and increased erosion and therefore removal of material from the soil to the stream. If vegetation was prevented from regrowing by application of herbicide, the maximum output was seen. When vegetation was permitted to become re-established, erosion was reduced and the chemical output reduced.

The study included Mirror Lake, a small lake with its outlet leading to Hubbard Brook downstream from the main experimental watersheds. The detail and intensity of the chemical and biological work on the lake progressively increased and included a paleolimnological study that extended the time scale to 14,000 years.

For purposes of illustrating the problems of carrying out long-term research, I will mention two of the events as recounted to me by Dr. Likens. There had been considerable interest among environmentally concerned people about the toxic effects of airborne lead liberated by burning leaded gasoline in motor vehicles. So lead was obviously an appropriate substance to measure in the precipitation. The published graphical record of the concentration of lead in the precipitation falling on the Hubbard Brook valley shows a decreasing trend from 1975 through 1982, consistent with a reduction in the use of lead in gasoline. There is a gap of one and a half years in the graph, explained by the authors briefly: "The break in the data occurred because of an interruption of funding for the study."

The second event was a decision by one of the program officers at NSF to stop funding the Hubbard Brook project. Perhaps this derived from the fact that granting agencies are accustomed to projects that produce definitive results and are finished in a few years. A long-term project may seem to be repeating the same thing without producing anything new. In any case, a special committee was appointed to visit the project and consult about the best way to terminate it with minimal damage. As a result of interviews with members of the project and an examination of the record of accomplishment, the visiting committee recommended that the project be continued with enhanced funding.

These kinds of events are familiar to people who try to do long-term research projects. A recurrent theme in discussion among investigators is the difficulty of maintaining a continuous flow of funds and of staving off termination at each time of renewal. This point will be illustrated in each of the next five chapters and elaborated in chapter 13.

# Chapter 9

## Lake Tahoe

Although Lake Tahoe is very different from Lake Washington limnologically, there is some similarity in the relation between the scientific studies and the approach to the environmental problems. Lake Tahoe, on the border between California and Nevada, lies at an altitude of 6225 feet (1899 meters) in strikingly beautiful mountainous country. It is large, 192 square miles in area (499 km$^2$), and the third deepest lake in North America, tenth in the world, 1645 feet (505 m). For many years it has been attracting increasing numbers of tourists and full-time residents. Because of its size, great clarity, low productivity, and unusual chemical characteristics, it is also an attractive object for limnologists, and for that reason has been studied intensively by Dr. Charles Goldman and associates at the University of California, Davis.

Goldman's initial study in 1958–59 provided valuable baseline information about the general characteristics of the lake. He did not follow it up with a regular program of full sampling until 1967 because initially he was not able to get enough financial support for such a study. Because of its size and exposure to strong wind, Lake Tahoe has special requirements for field equipment and other facilities, and therefore, special requirements for funding. In the interval, Goldman made occasional trips to the lake from Davis, about 100 miles (160 km) away, sampling from a small aluminum boat. During one of the trips he encountered a group of sanitary engineers who were doing a study of problems of sewage disposal from communities around the lake. Naturally they were interested in what he was doing, and the meeting led to a useful association and development of a new sewage disposal plan for the basin.

By the time Goldman started his concentrated study in 1967, the lake had changed distinctly. The rate of primary production by phytoplankton was about double that in 1959, and the transparency was less. The sewage problem was effectively solved by building an elaborate chemical precipitation treatment plant and exporting its effluent along with other sewage from the Tahoe drainage basin. But another serious pollution problem was developing, one that was much harder to control. Because of the increasing resident population and numbers of visitors there was a large increase in development of land for houses, condominiums, casinos, roads, parking lots, and other urban facilities. The work of clearing the land with bulldozers was apparently done with little or no attention to its effect on the lake. Erosion increased and many tons of topsoil were washed into the lake through the inlet streams, some of which became rivers of mud during spring runoff or thunderstorms.

Lake Tahoe is different chemically from Lake Washington and most other lakes in the northern U.S. and southern Canada in that the chief limiting nutrient during most of the last 30 years has been nitrogen, rather than phosphorus. Thus, Lake Tahoe was particularly susceptible to pollution with nitrate from topsoil, and from accelerated runoff from numerous roads, parking lots, and roofs. The effect on the lake has been profound. The rate of primary production by phytoplankton tripled between 1958 and 1984, and the phytoplankton abundance has increased with a consequent decrease in transparency. However, the most evident change has been inshore where everybody can see it. In the earlier years the rocks along the shore remained seemingly bare all year long. Now, in areas that receive drainage from developed land, they become covered with a thick layer of attached algae, largely diatoms, that form mats of slimy material. The mats break away from the rocks in late spring and are concentrated in a decaying scum along the shore by the wind. The algae attach to boats as well as rocks and are a nuisance there, reducing speed and increasing fuel consumption.

The major difficulty about protecting Lake Tahoe against continued deterioration is that the land developers have been very resistant to any control of their activities that would have a financial impact. The real estate industry is particularly concerned, and together with the developers has organized a group called the "Tahoe Preservation Council." The gambling industry is also deeply involved, since a continuous flow of large numbers of people is essential to keeping the casinos operating at high profit margins. The economic interest is enormous, involving many millions of dollars each year. Some of the activities of the land developers have been similar to those of the soap and detergent industry described in chapter 3, by first denying that there was a problem and then saying that if there was, nothing could be done about it or if it could, it would be too costly. The proposals for control have varied from requiring land-clearing operations to be done in such a way as to minimize erosion to moratoria on all further land development.

A major conservation force in the Tahoe basin, the League to Save Lake Tahoe (LTSLT) has made extensive use of Goldman's limnological data and has been fairly successful in the battle for public opinion. Together with the California attorney general's office, they have successfully forced the Tahoe Regional Planning Agency to adopt stricter building regulations in the basin. Unfortunately, the courtroom continues to be the main arena for settling these disputes.

Goldman's activities with reference to Lake Tahoe have been similar to mine with Lake Washington in that he has taken advantage of the external changes being imposed on the lake to make a scientific study that will improve our understanding of the way lakes work. He has been assiduous in educating the concerned public through documentary films and public lectures about what has happened to the lake and what its future would be under different treatments. His manner of working is different from mine in that he has been very aggressive in making specific recommendations about the control of land development. These activities have made him unpopular with the developers and some of the dependent industries. The developers are well financed, have been vigorous in their opposition to proposals for change, and continue to have considerable influence on governmental agencies.

The antagonism toward Goldman's efforts to protect Lake

Tahoe has been expressed in unpleasant and harmful ways. The University of California was given 10 acres of waterfront land as a site on which to build a laboratory to replace the converted fish hatchery where Goldman had been working. Goldman got $100,000 from the National Science Foundation to build it. The limnological study would do no more damage to the lake than any other operation with a small boat, and the laboratory would not produce harmful effluent. Nevertheless, the California-Tahoe Regional Planning Agency refused to issue a building permit on the excuse that the University of California is a commercial enterprise [sic] and the land was zoned for non-commercial use! So the Tahoe Research Group continues to work under crowded conditions in the old hatchery. As far as I know, there was no trace of this kind of vindictive activity in the Lake Washington experience. Fortunately the NSF permitted Goldman to use the building grant to buy a new research vessel, which did considerably improve his ability to do field work.

The study of Lake Tahoe has been prolonged, detailed, and complicated, requiring work by a large number of people. It started before federal agencies had much experience with long-term research problems and it has been more expensive and more prolonged than studies they have normally supported. Goldman has managed to keep the work going, mostly with help from the National Science Foundation, supplemented in recent years with additional funds from state and other agencies. The level of support has fluctuated. The work of finding the money with which to operate has been a major effort in itself.

The lack of public response to predictions about trouble may be influenced by the fact that even now Lake Tahoe is one of the clearest lakes in North America, with a Secchi disc reading averaging about 75 feet (24 m) during 1984; but that is 23 feet (7 m) less than it was in 1968. By contrast the average transparency of Lake Washington was 9 feet (2.7 m) in 1963 and 21 feet (6.4 m) in 1987, its clearest year. The transparency of Tahoe is decreasing at about 1.5 feet or 0.5 meters per year. Whether it maintains that rate of decrease until it becomes objectionably cloudy will depend on decisions and actions being taken now and in the immediate future.

# Chapter 10

## Long Lake

A remarkable episode in Long Lake near Spokane, Washington deserves detailed exposition. Long Lake got into the news in September 1976 when four important dogs died after drinking from the lake. Somebody once asked me why I described the dogs as "important." My reply was that by definition a dog is important if its death leads to a multimillion dollar lawsuit. Indeed, the dogs were pedigreed, and the owners sued the city of Spokane and the state Department of Ecology for $5,200,000, attributing the deaths directly to actions by the city and indirectly by the state.

What had happened was the result of a fairly frequent, well-known but poorly understood phenomenon, the development of a dense bloom of toxic blue-greens. Under some conditions, certain species develop a toxic material, contained within the cells or liberated into the water, that is fatal to warm-blooded vertebrate animals if ingested in large enough quantities. This has been an economic problem in the Midwest of the United States and Canada where productive ponds and lakes are used by cattle for drinking water. Long Lake is not the only example in Washington; Moses Lake had such a bloom in October 1982, killing two dogs. American Lake near Tacoma had a persistent toxic bloom in December 1989, the first such bloom reported west of the Cascades. Equally surprising were the deaths of two cats as well as some dogs.

Many kinds of algae can produce toxic compounds although the best known ones in lakes are blue-greens. In Long Lake it was *Anabaena flos-aquae*, responsible for a large proportion of toxic blooms in North America. As reported by Soltero and Nichols (1981), dogs were not the only victims of the bloom: "The deaths of four dogs were attributed to drinking reservoir water containing *Anabaena*. In addition seven dogs, one horse and one cow were suspiciously sick after drinking reservoir water. The reported deaths of two ducks and a beaver were not verified."

The lawsuit was based on the premise that the bloom was caused by an action of the city of Spokane that allowed raw sewage to enter the lake for three and a half days while the sewerage system was being connected to a new treatment plant. The state Department of Ecology was blamed for permitting Spokane to do this without having issued an environmental impact statement as required by law.

A description of the site of Long Lake and a review of the history of sewage disposal by Spokane are essential background for understanding the Long Lake problem. Long Lake is called a lake by courtesy only (fig. 10.1). It is a dammed stretch of the Spokane River, about 22 miles long (35 km), averaging less than half a mile wide (572 m), and with a maximum depth of 180 feet

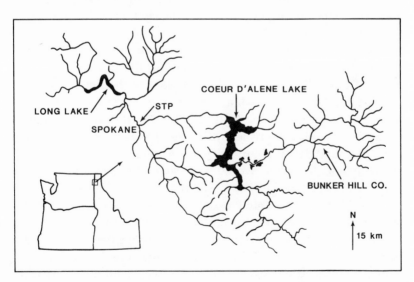

*Fig. 10.1. Long Lake, Spokane, and vicinity. The direction arrow gives scale. Location of the Spokane sewage treatment plant (STP) is shown.*

(55 m). The dam was built in 1915 to form a reservoir for hydro-electric power. The Spokane River originates as the outlet of Lake Coeur d'Alene in Idaho, whose principal source of water is the Coeur d'Alene River which runs through country with many metal mines. The water of the Spokane River flows in an orderly manner through the narrow Long Lake and out the downstream end. The volume of water entering the lake during a year averages about thirty-three times the volume of the lake; that is, the water is replaced by inflow about thirty-three times during a year. This is a retention time of less than twelve days. (See chapter 2.)

The outfall of the sewage treatment plant in Spokane empties into the Spokane River. The city is about 15 miles (24 km) upstream from Long Lake. Spokane developed a sewer system carrying raw sewage to the river in 1889. In the 1920s visible evidence of the sewage became obvious, but only in 1957 was the situation improved somewhat by installing primary treatment. This was regarded as inadequate, and the state Department of Ecology required expansion to secondary treatment. In response, Spokane went further by building an advanced wastewater treatment plant with chemical precipitation. The new plant was connected in October 1975, and started its advanced treatment in December 1977.

There were practical problems associated with the changeover. The sewage continued to come, but the flow of raw sewage had to be diverted from the old plant to the new. The idea was explored of using holding tanks to prevent raw sewage from entering the river, but the volume to be stored during three and a half days was the equivalent of a tank 50 feet deep and the area of five football fields, about 100 million gallons (or 382 thousand cubic meters). Since this would have been highly impractical and very expensive, the decision was made simply to let the raw sewage flow. Presumably it was felt that this would cause minimal damage since raw sewage is little different from primary effluent in its chemical effect. Also, in October people had little personal contact with the lake. Since inflow is highest in the winter, the slug of raw sewage would be washed through the lake soon and be replaced by normal river water.

Eleven months later, in September 1976, the *Anabaena* bloom occurred. The basis for the resulting lawsuit was that the bloom was supposed to have been caused by the brief flow of raw sewage much earlier. I was called to testify as one of the expert witnesses for the defense. My view was that there is no known set of limnological processes that could have connected the bloom with the previous flow of raw sewage. During the interval of eleven months the water of the lake was replaced about twenty-five times, giving a retention time of about thirteen days. There was simply no way for the lake to have retained the material so as to produce a bloom. Further, the water flowing into the lake since the episode was of higher quality than earlier because of the new treatment plant.

The expert witness on the other side had a different idea. He said there were two spectacular events in the lake that year, the sewage bypass and the death of the dogs. The bypass came first so it must have been the cause. This is a perfect example of a post hoc propter hoc argument. To connect the bloom to the sewage bypass it would have been necessary to show that the raw sewage added something to the lake that could account for the added growth of algae and that there was some chemical or physical process that would permit that material to delay showing its effect for eleven months.

In the end the owners of the dogs lost the part of the suit about the cause of the bloom, but there was a financial settlement because the state Department of Ecology had not obtained the required Environmental Impact Statement.

The question remains, what did cause the bloom to happen when it did? After all the lake had been enriched for decades; why did it wait until 1976 to bloom?

The fact was that the phytoplankton crop in Long Lake was much smaller during the years before the bloom than would have been expected on the basis of the nutrient input. This suggests that some inhibitory condition must have existed. This question can be examined in definite ways. It was known that the mining upstream in Idaho involved production of wastes rich in zinc. Zinc in small concentrations can reduce the ability of algae to grow, and at higher concentrations can be fatal to them. Chemical and bioassay studies before the 1976 bloom showed that the Spokane River carried concentrations of zinc high enough to inhibit some algae.

The next question then must be, what happened to the zinc? There had been no consistent program of measuring zinc in the water or of continuing the bioassay study, but there is relevant information. The Bunker Hill Corporation had mines along the Coeur d'Alene River and operated a very large smelter. The Environmental Protection Agency had pressed for a cleanup of the operation to reduce toxic pollution. During 1971–73 improvements were made in the handling of effluents and emissions. Although there were no consistent measurements of zinc or bioassay tests in the river or lake during 1973–76, there is paleolimnological evidence that the concentration of zinc decreased. Long Lake lays down sediments in clear-cut, visible annual layers. Analyses of metals in the mud showed a graded increase in the zinc concentration of the mud from 1957 to about 1970, and then a decrease to 1974, the time the core was taken.

Additional evidence of changes is provided by a study of the zinc content of the wood growing near the Spokane River, dated by tree rings, and in cores of sediment from Lake Coeur d'Alene itself. The changes in concentration are in reasonable agreement with known changes in mining activity along the Coeur d'Alene River. This information shows the value of the paleolimnological data discussed in chapter 2 and of tree-ring analysis for evaluating the development of environmental problems when adequate historical data do not exist.

It appears probable then that the year 1976 was a sort of crossing point for two kinds of chemical influence on Long Lake. A potential for algal blooms had developed much earlier because of sewage, but it could not be expressed because of inhibition by zinc. When the concentration of zinc was reduced, inhibition was lessened, permitting the lake to bloom in 1976 and the following two years. By 1979, two years after the new Spokane treatment plant started chemical precipitation, phosphorus had decreased enough to reduce the production of algae once more.

The blooms of 1977 and 1978 were not dominated by *Anabaena* and there was no evidence of toxicity. It is not yet known what environmental conditions are required to develop a toxic bloom.

*Anabaena* blooms are not always toxic. Another blue-green, *Microcystis aeruginosa,* has genetically different strains that differ in their ability to produce toxin; some can and some cannot. Potentially toxic strains produce more or less toxin, depending on environmental conditions. We are not now able to predict a toxic bloom before it happens on the basis of the environmental conditions in the lake; we need to learn more about the conditions that precede toxic blooms. This means, among other things, making systematic measurements of conditions thought to affect toxicity in lakes known to produce toxic blooms, and doing it often enough to give a reasonable chance of encountering one. Nor is environmental analysis enough by itself; there must be appropriate physiological studies of algae organized with reference to the environmental studies. Conventional studies of nutrient physiology will not necessarily answer ecological questions.

Long Lake had been studied for several years before 1976 by Soltero and his associates, but nothing is known of its condition between the spring of 1976 and the end of summer when the bloom occurred. That is because Soltero's research grant had expired and the funding agency thought that they knew enough about the lake already (personal communication, R. A. Soltero). Here again is an example of termination because of an interruption of funding of what, in retrospect, should have been a sustained study. In this case, the goal of the funding agency had been to provide a description of the lake before the new advanced treatment plant went into operation, and that was done. The agency apparently felt that treatment was sure to improve the quality of Long Lake and therefore further study was not needed. Even in the face of limited funds, such a decision seems mysterious. It would seem prudent to have had the objective evidence of the effect of such an expensive installation that could have been provided by the relatively inexpensive completed limnological investigation. We cannot assert that the problem of predicting toxic blooms would have been solved if the study at Long Lake had continued through the summer of 1976, but such a study would have provided information of a kind that is very rare. At the same time, the results would have permitted more exact evaluation of the effect of the reduction in zinc.

Since the mining operations appear to have had an impact as far downstream as Long Lake, one can wonder how Lake Coeur d'Alene responded to the changes. While something is known about conditions in 1971–72, unfortunately there appears to be no long-term record of limnological conditions in Coeur d'Alene.

The experience with Long Lake is typical of many cases of environmental deterioration. A condition develops that was not expected, and it becomes necessary to explain it in retrospect by using whatever evidence happens to be available. This kind of experience has led to proposals to establish monitoring programs in major bodies of water, where problems might be expected because of planned or possible developments in the drainage area. For example, in the Great Lakes the smaller downstream lakes are responding to protective actions, while Lake Superior is beginning to show signs of deterioration. Monitoring will be discussed in chapter 16.

# Chapter 11

## Saline Lakes in the Lower Grand Coulee

When, in 1948, after the retirement of Professor Trevor Kincaid, I was invited to join the faculty of the University of Washington Department of Zoology to teach limnology, my wife and I looked at a map of the state to see what was there. We noticed, right in the middle, something called Soap Lake. That sounded interesting and was one of the factors that led us to decide to come, a most fortunate decision. As soon as possible after arriving in the spring of 1949, we drove over to have a look. We found one of the most haunting landscapes in the world, and two of the most interesting lakes I have ever worked with.

The Grand Coulee was formed by complicated, cataclysmic geological events and had achieved its present form by the end of the Ice Age about 12,000 years ago. When we got to it, the southern half was occupied by six major lakes (fig. 11.1). Because of the aridity of the area, the Coulee lies in a region of internal drainage, in which surface streams dry up before they reach the ocean or a major river. The southernmost lake, Soap Lake, has no surface inlet, receiving only groundwater and surface runoff. It has no outlet. Because of evaporation Soap Lake had accumulated about 37.1 grams/liter (approximately parts per thousand) of total dissolved solids (TDS) in the surface water by the late 1940s, about 20% more than seawater. The next lake to the north, Lake Lenore, has intermittent surface inflow but no surface outlet. It had 12.9 g/l of TDS. Chemically, the dissolved material is quite different from sea salt, having much more sulfate, carbonate and bicarbonate in addition to sodium and chloride. Both lakes were alkaline, with pHs at or close to 10.0. The other lakes, Blue, Park, Dry Falls, and Deep were fresh, with a range of 0.200–0.390 g/l TDS.

Alkaline, saline lakes are of intense interest to aquatic ecologists because relatively few species of specialized animals can survive and breed in them. Fish are absent. That means that the community structure is very simple. Also, such lakes are highly eutrophic because nutrients are concentrated, and they support very high rates of production. In the 1950s little was known of the ecology of salt-lake communities, so we had a good opportunity to get novel information. Two of my graduate students, George C. Anderson and the late Gabriel W. Comita, were just starting their Ph.D. research, a comparative study of different kinds of lakes with emphasis on the seasonal changes of abundance of the plankton. They included Soap and Lenore in their series, and found some highly interesting things worth studying in detail. For instance, Soap Lake had only three species of planktonic invertebrate animals, two rotifers and one cladoceran crustacean. Lake Lenore had the same three species, plus two copepod crustaceans (fig. 11.2). This is a strong contrast with freshwater lakes; Lake Washington has nine species of crustaceans and nineteen species of rotifers that become relatively abundant at some time of year. The spring phytoplankton bloom of Lake Lenore was dominated by the diatom *Chaetoceros elmorei*, which was absent from Soap Lake. The genus *Chaetoceros* is common in the ocean, but only a few species are found in lakes, all saline and alkaline.

When Comita and Anderson had finished their exploratory study, it was clear that we should continue to examine some of the questions about community structure and seasonal population dynamics. Nothing about this problem required a very long

*Fig. 11.1. The south end of the Lower Grand Coulee showing Soap Lake, in foreground, and Lake Lenore, 13 May 1953. The surface of Soap Lake at that time was 1078.5 feet above sea level, and water had been invading basements of houses near the lake. U.S. Bureau of Reclamation.*

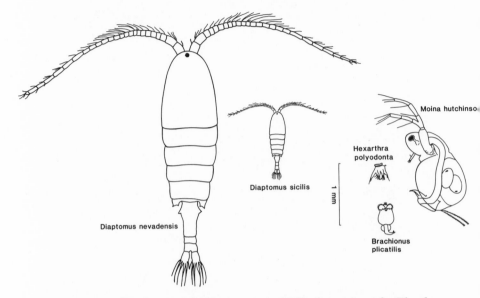

*Fig. 11.2. Planktonic animals present in 1950, drawn to scale. The three species at the right lived in both Lake Lenore and Soap Lake. The two species of copepods at the left lived in Lake Lenore, not in Soap Lake.*

investigation. Probably two or three years of field work plus two or three more for some follow-up experiments in the laboratory would have been enough to answer the questions that we could have thought of then. (Of course those answers probably would have generated more questions.) I expected to make such a study, waiting for an interested graduate student to appear. It did not seem urgent to start immediately.

That relaxed attitude ended abruptly on 26 June 1954. My wife and I had attended a meeting across the state in Pullman and decided to drive through the Grand Coulee on the way home just to see the lakes again. Soap Lake was a very conspicuous green so I took a sample home and found a dense bloom of *Chaetoceros*. This surprising biological difference from the condition just four years earlier meant that something affecting the lake must have changed. An analysis showed that the TDS in Soap Lake had decreased from 37.1 grams/liter (parts per thousand or ppt) in

1950 to 27.1 in 1954, and Lenore had decreased from 12.9 to 10.8. These large differences implied that some major change had taken place in the water supply. As I later found out, there had been a general increase in moisture at somewhat different times in various parts of the arid Northwest, and the levels of a number of saline lakes rose. For instance, Great Salt Lake in Utah rose four feet between 1946 and 1954, then dropped. Locally, rain and snow had been unusually high in the Coulee area during 1948 and 1951. The levels of Soap Lake and Lake Lenore started to rise in 1949, but then they continued to rise, more than could be accounted for on the basis of precipitation.

Geologists and hydrologists in the Bureau of Reclamation found that the source of the excess water in the Coulee lakes was the irrigation project based on Grand Coulee Dam. The bureau was responsible for building the dam and operating the project. Water applied to the fields soaked down and flowed in aquifers to the lakes. We could look through the clear water of Soap Lake and see little trickles of fresh water rising from the bottom. In 1952 the level of Soap Lake rose to 1076 ft (328 m) above sea level. This generated considerable anxiety for the people of the town of Soap Lake, which is at the south end of the lake, and only slightly higher in elevation. Corrosive lake water was getting into the basements of houses near the shore, and a continued rise threatened to submerge the town.

To keep the town from drowning, the bureau in 1953 installed large pumps to remove water from both lakes. The level of Soap Lake was stabilized, but the new situation was nearly as worrisome to the people of the town as the rise in lake level. Salt water was being pumped out, fresh water was moving in, and the salinity of the lake was consequently decreasing (fig. 11.3).

The trouble with that is that the town of Soap Lake is a health resort. The waters of the lake have a reputation for health-giving properties, and many people came to bathe in the water and plaster themselves with malodorous mud. Most of them stayed in hotels, ate in restaurants, and bought souvenirs. Four companies had produced salt by evaporating surface lake water for use by people at home. The price of a pound of Thorson's Soap Lake Salts in 1954 was $3.00. (Now it is $5.50.) There was an ad-

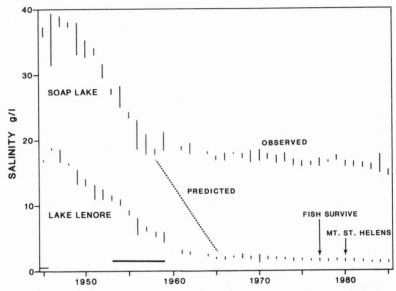

*Fig. 11.3. Dilution of Coulee lakes. Salinity is expressed as total dissolved solids (TDS). The vertical bars show the range of values for each year. (Data before 1955, from the Bureau of Reclamation, were taken twice each year. Subsequent data from our study were taken more frequently.) The bar above the baseline shows the period of pumping directly from the lakes. The tick at the extreme left shows the salinity of ground water taken from wells near Soap Lake.*

ditional use of the water. Soap Lake is meromictic. (It never mixes completely.) The deep monimolimnion had about five times the salinity of the surface water. The dense, dark-colored sulfurous water was sold in bottles to be taken internally in teaspoon-sized doses. It was collected by Mr. Thorson by cleverly using a principle of physics, not scientific equipment. He simply lowered a heavy bucket into the monimolimnion and waited a few minutes. During that time the relatively light surface water floated out of the bucket and was replaced by the dense water around it. It could then be hauled up slowly with essentially no mixing.

Thus, the salinity of Soap Lake was a real economic resource essential to the survival of the town, and fresh water entering the lake could be considered a very damaging form of pollution. At first sight, the situation might have seemed hopeless. There was no way the Columbia Basin Project could stop its multimillion dollar irrigation operation to preserve the salinity of a salt lake. So, the mayor of Soap Lake, M. R. Newell, in May 1956 went to Washington, D.C., where he discussed the problem with a number of legislators. He took with him a detailed statement of the history, character, and use of Soap Lake and the potential economic impact of dilution. Bills were introduced into the Senate by Senators Warren G. Magnuson and Henry M. Jackson and into the House by Representative Roy Holmes. The result was that Mr. Newell was able to go home assured of a special appropriation of $233,000 to solve the Soap Lake problem.

The solution was simple. Instead of pumping from the lake, the bureau pumped from wells located to intercept the ground water before it reached the lake. Pumping directly from Soap Lake ended in March 1959, the salinity has been fairly stable since then, and the lake is still an attraction for visitors.

Lake Lenore did not have the economic value of Soap Lake and there has been no attempt to preserve its salinity, which therefore has decreased much more than that of Soap Lake. In fact, in 1946 the War Assets Administration office in Seattle asked the Washington State Department of Game to select the "most useless" lake in the state, and Lake Lenore was nominated for the honor. For reasons that I cannot imagine, at the end of World War II the WAA found itself with six large metal barrels containing a total of 21,000 pounds (9,545 kilograms) of sodium metal submerged in oil. The barrels were corroding, creating a dangerous situation because pure sodium is extremely reactive chemically. The WAA arranged to sell the sodium to a California firm, but the Interstate Commerce Commission refused permission to ship it because of the danger. Sodium combines with water, releasing hydrogen gas which is immediately ignited by atmospheric oxygen. I remember a demonstration of this in a high school chemistry class. A tiny bit of the metal was dropped into a sink half full of water. The reaction of the sodium with the water produced a burst of flame and left the sink with a solution of sodium hydroxide.

The army recreated this experiment on a somewhat larger scale since the amount of sodium was enough to produce 162,000 cubic feet of hydrogen and to add another 4% to the sodium already dissolved in the lake. The barrels were rolled off a cliff onto the frozen surface of the lake where they were machine-gunned to expose the sodium. The resulting column of flame and steam was reported to have been spectacular, and several dozen passing motorists stopped their cars to watch as a gentle mist of corrosive sodium hydroxide came down over a wide area. The army paid for repainting the cars.

It is noteworthy that long before the passage of federal legislation requiring environmental impact statements, the Washington Department of Game and the War Assets Administration made a thoughtful evaluation of the effects of the disposal of sodium into Lake Lenore on the environment, wildlife, and people. They calculated the volume of hydrogen that would be generated and realized that the operation would have to be done carefully to avoid injury to the workers. They knew that the sodium added was a small fraction of what was already in the lake and that the increase in pH would not be a problem. They had no information about the effect on the ducks, but knew that ducks made use of Soap Lake, which had even more sodium and a higher pH. There were no fish in Lake Lenore and no trees around it. They correctly decided that the operation would not cause environmental problems. Apparently the only thing they missed was the effect of sodium hydroxide on postwar automobile paint.

Today Soap Lake has a salinity of about 15 g/l, similar to that of Lake Lenore in 1950, and Lake Lenore is nearly fresh, about 1.3 g/l, close to that of the ground water pumped from the wells which varies between 0.35 and 1.0 g/l. I am glad that Soap Lake was kept as saline as it is, for it is still ecologically interesting. The people of the town of Soap Lake appear to be happy too, for different reasons.

A monument was erected on the public town beach to commemorate the work of Mayor Newell, and dedicated with an appropriate ceremony on August 22, 1970. I was invited to attend but unfortunately was unable to do so. The monument, a handsome polished granite slab 44 inches long and 20 inches high, stands on a stone foundation five feet high. On one side is inscribed:

M. R. NEWELL
MAYOR OF SOAP LAKE IN MAY 1956
PRESENTED THE SOAP LAKE PROBLEM TO THE U.S. CONGRESS
WHO APPROPRIATED FUNDS AND DIRECTED THE BUREAU OF
RECLAMATION TO INSTALL INTERCEPTION WELLS AROUND THE
LAKE TO PREVENT FRESH WATER FROM ENTERING THE LAKE FROM
UNDERGROUND SOURCES. IT HAS BEEN SUCCESSFUL IN
PRESERVING THE SALINITY OF SOAP LAKE WATER AND ITS
CURATIVE QUALITIES FOR FUTURE GENERATIONS.

The other side reads:

MINERAL CONTENT OF LAKE

| | | |
|---|---|---|
| SODIUM | MAGNESIUM | ALUMINUM |
| CARBONATE | POTASSIUM | LITHIUM |
| SULFATE | ORGANIC NITROGEN | FLUORIDE |
| BICARBONATE | OIL (ICTHYOL) | COPPER |
| CHLORINE | CALCIUM | IRON |
| SILICA | PHOSPHORUS | RUBIDIUM |

Most knowledgeable people, if asked to name a lake in the state of Washington that had been saved from deterioration by public action, would say "Lake Washington." But the action to save Soap Lake took place two years before the vote that formed the Seattle Metro.

As soon as I realized that the change in Soap Lake was not temporary, I could expect further changes in the biota. In effect, an unusual experiment was being done for us, the kind that later became known as whole-lake experiments. (This is further discussed in chapter 12). This fact changed the time scale of our study. No longer could the problem be settled by an intensive study for a couple of years; it needed to run as long as the condition of the lake was changing and then some. The maintenance of salt lakes requires a delicate balance between a supply of precipitation large enough to keep them provided with water and one small enough to prevent them from being flushed out. That is why salt lakes are limited to semi-arid regions. They tend to fluctuate in level and salinity with changes in climate, as does, for example, Mono Lake, discussed in chapter 5. The condition of the Coulee lakes would let us study in some detail the consequences of what amounted to an episode of moist climate.

To get funds from a granting agency would take nearly a year, but that was too much delay to face in view of the rapid changes in the lakes. So I made a visit to the Dean of the Graduate School, Harold W. Stoke. In just a short conversation he grasped the significance and urgency of the Coulee project and provided enough money from a local fund to hire an associate until I could get a grant from the National Science Foundation. That fund was the State of Washington Fund for Research in Biology and Medicine. It was also known in the university as the "liquor money" because the money was provided by the license fees paid by restaurants and bars for serving individual alcoholic drinks, the result of a public vote in 1948 on Initiative 171. Some people assumed that the fund was for research on alcoholism, but much of it was used for the basic biological sciences. (This fund had already been important at the beginning of my lake work because it financed the new equipment that I would need. Among the items that I ordered were a panel truck, a small boat, and an outboard motor. When the order arrived in the purchasing department, the comptroller of the university made a personal visit to my office to inquire about my interest in fishing. After I assured him that fishing bored me, he approved the order.)

Fortunately, George Anderson had just finished his Ph.D. work, which included a study of the phytoplankton of Soap and Lenore Lakes, and was looking for a position. He agreed to extend his work on the Coulee lakes. I applied to the National Science Foundation for support of a project called "Arid Land Limnology." I took the same line that I used later for work on Lake Washington; we had been given a biological signal of an important change in a lake community, and it was in the interest of basic science to exploit the situation as a large-scale, whole-lake experiment. The foundation supported the study for five years through the spring of 1959.

During the dilution of the lakes, large changes took place in the populations. The two species of copepods that had been limited to Lake Lenore appeared in Soap Lake and thrived. The cladoceran that had been in both lakes, *Moina hutchinsoni,* needs a high salinity. It disappeared from Lake Lenore and was replaced by *Daphnia,* first *Daphnia ambigua* and then *Daphnia pulex. Moina* is still present in Soap Lake but in smaller numbers than before the dilution. Not all the changes in the zooplankton can be attributed simply to tolerance to salinity. Between 1969 and 1977, three species of zooplankton successively appeared and disappeared in Lake Lenore although the salinity did not change appreciably in that period. Probably some biological interactions took place between the species that we could not anticipate and were not prepared to recognize and study as they happened. However, we now know what species were involved, what to look for in other lakes and what experiments to do in the laboratory. The benthic insect larvae also changed greatly in Lake Lenore, but did not change much in Soap Lake. Apparently the dilution of Soap Lake was not great enough to affect many of these species.

The phytoplankton of Lake Lenore changed much more than that of Soap Lake. During the dilution period the chemical conditions in Lenore changed enough to permit growth of the blue-greens that make algal nuisances in normal freshwater eutrophic lakes; they had been scarce or absent in 1950. Lake Lenore is surrounded by sagebrush desert and receives no waste nor enriched drainage. It is eutrophic for natural reasons and now maintains dense populations of blue-greens all summer. In this case, pollution with freshwater changed conditions to favor blue-greens.

In 1959 I received a Senior Postdoctoral Fellowship from the National Science Foundation and was away from June 1959 to September 1960 doing research at several institutes in Europe. It was a better time for me to be away from Seattle than any other. We had been able to study the Coulee lakes through most of their dilution. The Seattle Metro had been voted, but diversion of sewage from Lake Washington would not begin for several years.

When we returned, I started the detailed study of Lake Washington. This took so much attention and funding that we made only occasional trips to the Coulee lakes, each time taking samples but not doing any serious work. Many of the trips were made to show the area to various visiting European limnologists who were always impressed by the beauty of the region and the scientific interest of the lakes. One visitor, Vittorio Tonolli from Italy, said, "There can't be lakes in a place like this." On another occasion, because of pressure of time, we had to choose between going to see Grand Coulee Dam or spending more time with the lakes. Clifford Mortimer from England said, "Now the dam is merely a marvel of modern engineering, isn't it, but the lakes are unique." More recently, after we took G. E. Hutchinson of Yale University on a trip there, I heard him comment that the Grand Coulee is "the most magnificent piece of geomorphology that I have ever seen." Since I knew that he had done limnological work in the Himalayas on several lakes higher than the top of Mt. Rainier, I asked him about them. The reply was, "Oh, they're just mountains."

Our neglect of the Coulee lakes continued for eight years, and we stayed busy with the recovery of Lake Washington. I had become aware from our occasional visits that changes were still going on in the Coulee lakes and was uneasy about missing something. Just at that time the Atomic Energy Commission was starting a program to support basic research in environmental sciences, and one of their staff people suggested that I apply. I defined the goal broadly enough to think of the grant as supporting our non-Lake Washington limnology, but the emphasis was on the saline Grand Coulee lakes.

With support from AEC we resumed a regular sampling program in the Coulee and continued it as the agency metamorphosed into the Energy Research and Development Administration (ERDA) and then the Department of Energy (DOE), its present form. Our emphasis was no longer on the response to changes in salinity, but on special features of the communities. While we were not able to study the functioning of a simple three-species community, graduate students and other associates found plenty of interesting things to work on.

There was a difference in color of the species of large copepod in the two lakes: in Soap Lake it was a conspicuous deep red but in Lenore was quite pale. The small species was red in both lakes. The simple question, why?, was the subject of an entire Ph.D.

research project by Nelson Hairston, Jr. that involved a detailed characterization of the behavior of the populations in the lakes through two years, as well as coordinated laboratory experiments with the animals. The red coloring is a carotenoid called astaxanthin, an organic material that occurs in many organisms and is known to protect them against damage from solar radiation. Thus the red copepods could cruise around in the clear water of Soap Lake in summer at all depths without damage. Laboratory experiments confirmed that red animals exposed to light survived much longer than pale animals. So why were the big copepods not red in Lake Lenore?

There was a good reason for the big red animals not to survive in Lake Lenore. A behavioral difference between the large copepods in the two lakes provided a clue: in Lake Lenore they stayed out of shallow water, swimming near the bottom. It turned out that the chemical protection of the red animals against light damage also made them very visible to sighted predators. In Lake Lenore both salamanders and damsel fly larvae on the bottom are able to see and catch large red copepods much more easily than pale ones, as demonstrated by experiments under controlled conditions. Such predators are not a problem in Soap Lake; there are no salamanders, and damsel fly larvae are scarce. However, the small copepods can be red in both lakes because they are too small to trigger the feeding reaction of the predators. The copepods in these lakes present an excellent example of how biological adaptations work. An adaptation that is very effective in one environment may assure death in a different environment.

By 1977 it appeared that we had exploited the situation about as much as could be justified, and we could stop the intensive sampling; but an event then took place that renewed our interest. The Washington Department of Game had already been interested in Lake Lenore because they had a program of planting rainbow trout (*Salmo gairdneri*) in lakes throughout the state. Lake Lenore would be an excellent candidate for the program because of its high productivity. Unfortunately there was a technical problem; the fish always died. Several trials were made in the 1970s with fish in cages in the lake where they could be observed. The fish survived for a few days at the most, although they survived well in water diluted to two thirds. However, it was known that a subspecies of cutthroat trout, the Lahontan trout *Salmo clarki henshawi*, thrives in Pyramid Lake, Nevada, which is similar to Lake Lenore in its chemistry. In July 1977, 30 adult fish from Pyramid Lake were placed in a cage in Lake Lenore. They survived for two weeks, so the Department of Game liberated them and developed plans for repeated planting of hatchery-reared fry and fingerlings. In the fall of 1979, 37,000 small fish were planted, and more have been planted every year since. They do not reproduce in the lake, but grow and survive very well. Some of the original 30 were sighted as much as three years after they were introduced.

The introduction of a voracious, sighted, cruising predator, very different from the existing sluggish benthic salamanders and the insect larvae, could be expected to have a major effect on the structure of the community. Because of the known feeding habits of the trout we could make some specific predictions of those effects. To check the predictions required a census of the benthos and plankton several times a year. Accordingly, on April 8, 1980, we made a very complete sampling of Lake Lenore, occupying the full time of four technicians for two days. This was to serve as the major baseline against which to compare future conditions.

We had not planned to sample Soap Lake very often, but our plans were drastically changed on May 18, 1980 when Mt. St. Helens exploded and dropped volcanic ash into both lakes. This was a matter of great anxiety to us because we were worried that the ash would affect the community of Lake Lenore so much as to spoil the predation experiment. Normally experiments are supposed to vary only one condition at a time. Here we had two changes that might affect the lake strongly.

Ten days later, as soon as it was safe to enter the area, we repeated the sampling of Lake Lenore and also sampled Soap Lake extensively. The samples were supplemented with first-hand observations by a scuba diver who took core samples to define the thickness of the layer of ash. Fortunately, it turned out that the ash had a minimal effect on the lakes, especially Lenore, which received less ash than Soap. The thickness of the layer of freshly deposited ash was about a quarter of an inch (6 mm) in Soap Lake and the southern part of Lenore; the north end received even less. The ash had the consistency of toothpaste, and the small benthic invertebrates were able to burrow up through it. Salamanders were still active, as evidenced by their tracks on the bottom. The ash had settled to the bottom promptly, and the zooplankton showed no signs of damage.

It seemed evident that further work would characterize the effect of trout predation clearly, without confusion by effects of volcanic ash. So, we proceeded, and were able to study the bottom fauna and plankton during the first eight years of influence by trout. As usual we backed up the field program with appropriate experiments in the laboratory or in the lake itself to increase the interpretability of the field data. Part of the work formed the basis of a Ph.D. dissertation by Chris Luecke. He determined the degree to which trout of different size selected food items of different kinds, mostly aquatic insect larvae, and the rate at which they fed. The field data showed that some of the invertebrates became less abundant in the lake in a way that was consistent with the laboratory findings. The biggest changes took place in the deeper water, where the food animals lived on or in the mud and were not protected by vegetation.

While there have been some early changes, one of the more interesting predictions will evidently require more time to evaluate. The trout is able to eat salamanders and damsel fly larvae, but the fish are too big when planted to prey heavily on copepods. Therefore, a likely consequence of the addition of the trout to the community of Lake Lenore will be an eventual replacement of the pale copepods by the red form, once it is relieved of visual predation. To keep track of the color of the copepod population does not require such intensive sampling as was needed for the initial study of the effect of the trout, and the completion of Luecke's Ph.D. dissertation marked a time when we could greatly reduce the program in the Coulee.

As it happened, DOE had decided to eliminate many of its environmental programs including ours, and support ended in January 1986. This was no surprise. The work had been supported by annual grants since 1968, and for about half that time the program officer had been telling me at each renewal time that continued support was in question. Nevertheless, the money kept coming in until the program finally was terminated a few months before my retirement. This timing was fortunate, for termination a year earlier would have interfered with the completion of an essential part of the work. On the other hand, after that I would have found it difficult to justify a continuation of the full-scale sampling program we had needed earlier. I do not suggest that there are no more interesting things to be done in the Coulee with intensive work right now; on the contrary; but my part of it can be reduced. I have no bad feelings about my eighteen-year relation with AEC-ERDA-DOE, which ended on a very pleasant note.

To take notice of my retirement, some of my former graduate students arranged a symposium in June of 1986 at the annual meeting of the American Society of Limnology and Oceanography. The DOE participated in a most unusual way. At the end of the program, Dr. D. Heyward Hamilton, the person at DOE who was in charge of my grant, appeared and presented a Certificate of Appreciation:

> For two decades of outstanding contributions to the Department's Basic Ecology Program. Through more than 30 years of research and teaching on the lakes of the Pacific Northwest, you have had a strong influence on the development of limnology, while educating the public, this, and other agencies of government in the wise use and stewardship of the nation's freshwater resources.

I have written many thank-you notes (known as "Final Reports") to granting agencies. This is the first and only note I have had from a granting agency thanking me for spending their money.

However, retirement does not mean inactivity, and with support from the Andrew W. Mellon Foundation we are able to sample the Coulee lakes occasionally to check the color of the copepods and to sample bottom fauna. If the large red copepods do appear in Lake Lenore, it will be important to make a detailed census of their predators to ascertain whether the predators have indeed been reduced enough to account for the change.

As a limnologist I have mixed feelings about the events in the Coulee. Soap Lake in its original state was a more interesting object for research than it is now, but the opportunity to study the effects of dilution as an experiment was most rewarding. Likewise, I would have preferred to see Lake Lenore maintained at its original salinity, but again the opportunity to study the effects of dilution and especially the effects of the introduced trout on community structure has been very productive.

It is interesting to speculate about what might have been done if the dilution of Soap Lake had been anticipated before irrigation began. It would have been possible to avoid dilution by either of two methods. One would have been to start pumping from wells earlier, before fresh water reached the lakes. The other would have been to avoid irrigation within the drainage area of the lakes. The first might have been difficult to do because of a lack of the hydrological information, which was obtained only by studies made after the level of Soap Lake increased. The second would have been easy to do. There is still plenty of unirrigated land in the area, and the loss of a relatively small area near Soap Lake would not represent an important loss of agricultural production. The results of a cost-benefit analysis would be most informative. It would compare the estimated costs of the two protective programs with the actual cost to the Bureau of Reclamation of the program that was carried out. It is worth emphasizing that the pumping program was paid for by the responsible federal agency, the Bureau of Reclamation, not by the town of Soap Lake.

Can we say that the dilution of the Coulee lakes was pollution with fresh water? Even though Soap Lake still attracts tourists, in its diluted condition it is not as attractive as it was. To prepare salt for sale requires evaporation of about twice as much water as before. If Soap Lake had been permitted to become freshened enough to enable nuisance blue-greens to survive as they do in Lake Lenore, the lake would have become unattractive to swimmers, and the economy of the town seriously damaged. On the other hand, fishermen certainly would regard Lake Lenore as vastly improved. I discuss the concept of pollution further in chapter 14.

Our studies of Lake Washington and of the Coulee Lakes have much in common. In each case a descriptive study established the condition of a lake. In each the condition was subsequently changed in a distinct way by human activity, presenting an excellent opportunity for basic limnological research. And in each there was a succession of unplanned or unexpected changes that maintained interest in the lakes for a longer term than could have been foreseen at the beginning.

# Chapter 12

## Experiments with Whole Lakes

M any of the external conditions that affect lakes vary during the year in a coordinated way. It is difficult or impossible to know by simple observation what is causing a particular change. Something must be done to separate the interacting processes. While bioassay, bag, and enclosure experiments come increasingly close to sorting out what is going on, experiments with whole lakes are desirable where they can be made. Inadvertent changes imposed on lakes by human activity can be considered as such, but the investigator has no influence over them.

Experiments in laboratory studies always involve a control; experimental vessels are manipulated in a very specific way while others, the controls, are left without manipulation. This is essentially impossible to do in experiments with whole lakes because even very similar neighboring lakes are not identical in all important regards. Nevertheless one can find substitutes, at least partial ones, for controls and replication. After making some kind of manipulation of the lake that affects only one or a few processes, the response of the lake is determined by measuring properties that are expected to be affected. A study of the data will show coordination among some of the properties. Special experiments are then done to find which changes can be causally connected. (See Hairston 1989 for a review of ecological field experiments, strictly defined.)

Only isolated parts of the lake system can be handled this way; there is still need to correlate conditions in the lakes with the results of the experiments, since the goal is to understand the operation of the whole system. That is how we treated the experience with Lake Washington. While we had no control over the kind or quantity of enrichment of the lake, we could proceed as if we had arranged to have it fertilized. When *Daphnia* appeared unexpectedly, we were able to develop a highly probable explanation based on information largely derived by doing laboratory experiments with *Daphnia* and *Neomysis* collected from the lake, combined with data from local agencies.

Experimental studies of lakes have been made by deliberately adding measured quantities of something that changes the rate of a process in a relatively simple way. For example, the addition of lime to a brown-water bog lake bleaches the organic stain that colors the water and increases the penetration of light, permitting increased photosynthesis by phytoplankton. The addition of alum reduces the release of phosphate from sediments and can help control algal nuisances by reducing recycling of phosphorus. The introduction of planktivorous fish increases predation pressure on the zooplankton. However, most whole-lake experiments have been done by fertilizing lakes with inorganic nutrients. Some of these were designed to elucidate the function of various nutrients in the control of productivity. Others were done for the practical purpose of increasing the production of fish.

This chapter presents three research projects directed at applied, practical problems that produced advances in basic limnological knowledge, just the reverse of the sequence of most examples given so far. The first is a study of the process of eutrophication with emphasis on the relative effect of different elements. The other two are projects to increase the production of salmon by fertilizing the lakes in which the young fish spend the first part of their lives.

## Experimental Lakes Area

One of the most unusual developments in long-term limnological research was the establishment by the Canadian government of the Freshwater Institute at Winnipeg, Manitoba in 1966. In response to growing awareness of the deterioration of the

Great Lakes, a Eutrophication Section was included to increase basic knowledge of the process. In a wide search, the scientific staff was recruited from Canada, the United States, Poland, Norway, Italy, Switzerland, and Japan, with emphasis on the scientists' originality, creativity, and willingness to apply themselves to the central problem. The program was developed with considerable freedom of imagination but clearly focussed on eutrophication. The financial commitment was very strong, enough so that long-term experiments could be completed as planned (Johnson and Vallentyne 1971).

The most unusual feature, perhaps unique among limnological research institutes, was the way that the research material, a group of lakes, was selected. A large region was studied on maps and a promising area containing more than 1000 varied lakes selected for examination; 463 of them were surveyed and sampled by helicopter. This became known as the Experimental Lakes Area (ELA). A well-equipped field laboratory was built. Forty-six lakes were chosen for eutrophication experiments. In 1968 agreements were reached between the Government and logging companies to stop activity in the drainage areas of the experimental lakes for 20 years, with an option to renew. This option has been exercised, extending control to the year 2005 with first option to renew again.

The first whole-lake enrichment experiment was done in June 1969. By 1971 it was possible to devote an entire issue of the *Journal of The Fisheries Research Board of Canada* to the preliminary results of many of the projects on different aspects of the lakes. All of the experiments have been directed at specific questions and carried out to give effective answers. Some of D. W. Schindler's results were described in chapters 2 and 3 in connection with the relative importance of phosphorus, nitrogen, and carbon in the control of productivity.

The conditions of limited public access and, with one exception, the lack of unplanned disturbance permitted an unusual degree of control over the experiments, with consequent security of results. The unplanned disturbance was a forest fire that affected several lakes. As a result, the ELA area was enlarged to include more lakes. Evidently much of the work on the principles of eutrophication has been carried about as far as is useful in the ELA, but other major problems remain—acid deposition, for instance.

## Bare Lake, Alaska

In 1950, Phillip Nelson of the U.S. Fish and Wildlife Service approached me for advice about how to conduct a lake fertilization project on a small lake on Kodiak Island. The motivation was that the catch of sockeye or red salmon (*Onchorhynchus nerka*) from the large lakes in southeast Alaska had been decreasing. The service wanted to discover the reason and, if possible, correct the problem.

The background was that the salmon-producing lakes in Alaska are oligotrophic and therefore relatively unproductive in a limnological sense. Although the number of salmon taken by the fishery was impressive, it was made possible by the size of the system, not the intensity of production. The young fish spend from one to four years in the lakes before migrating to the ocean, where they spend several more years growing to adult size before migrating back to the lakes to spawn. Thus, most of the total mass of the fish caught by the fishery is produced in the ocean and does not depend on the productivity of the lakes.

The percentage of fish returning depends in part on conditions in the streams and lakes that affect success of spawning and survival of the young fish in freshwater. The idea arose that the bodies of the salmon returning from the ocean to the lakes were an important source of phosphorus, and therefore part of the chemical support system of the food chain leading to the next generation of salmon. When the spawned fish die and decompose, nutrients are released to the water. Some of the corpses are eaten by scavengers, but many of those are insects and crustaceans of kinds eaten in turn by young salmon. The hypothesis was that so many adult salmon trying to return to the lakes were being caught by the fishing industry that a large part of the phosphorus supply was being intercepted, with a consequent decrease in the later production of fish. The reduced food supply would result in slower growth and higher mortality of the young salmon while they were growing in the lake. It was assumed that there had been no major change in predation, disease, or physical conditions during the period of decreasing salmon. This phosphorus limitation hypothesis was based on a very good foundation of ecological information and concepts of productivity and community structure. It could be tested easily by fertilizing a lake so as to increase its productivity, enhancing the standard of living of the young salmon.

We established a fertilization program for Bare Lake on Kodiak Island, but it was not easy to carry out. This small lake was selected to minimize the amount of fertilizer needed, but even so, each year it took a total of 9000 pounds of phosphate and nitrate fertilizer. The lake was isolated and everything had to be transported by float airplane. At frequent intervals during the summer, samples were taken for chemical analysis, plankton and benthos counting, and measurement of primary production. Fish coming to and going from the lake were counted, and appropriate measurements made.

The design of the experiment was determined by the life history of the salmon in Bare Lake. After hatching from the egg, most fish live in the lake for two or three years before migrating to sea, where they live for another two or three years before returning to their home lake to spawn and die. Some fish take longer, in some cases totalling seven years. Thus there would be a minimum period of six years before we could expect to see a large number of returned fish that had spent their entire freshwater life in the fertilized lake; earlier returners would have spent their first year or more in the lake before it was fertilized. Beyond that, several more years of fertilization and sampling would be required to determine the amount of year-to-year variation. Finally, fertilization should be discontinued and the lake studied for long enough to see the consequences of decreased productivity on the fish. Clearly, this would be a genuine long-term study. Anything shorter would be incomplete, although work would not have to go on indefinitely.

The first fertilization was in 1950 and the initial results were very promising. Primary production increased as did the abundance of small algae of the kind used by many kinds of zooplankton and benthic insect larvae. The survival of the fish in the lake increased nearly fourfold during 1951–53 over that in 1950.

The growth rate of the fish increased each year, so that the fish that migrated each year were larger than those the year before. There was an unexpectedly close correlation between the size of the fish at migration and the mean rate of primary production (photosynthesis) in the lake during the time those fish were in the lake.

Data were obtained on only a few returning fish that had lived in Bare Lake after it was fertilized, just enough to suggest that survival at sea had been increased significantly. But sampling stopped too soon to give data on fish produced during the entire time of fertilization and there was no follow-up study in a period without fertilization. Unfortunately, the experiment had been terminated prematurely.

The primary reason for the failure to complete the Bare Lake experiment was that a change of administration in the Fish and Wildlife Service led to a change of priorities and to reassignment of the people who had the greatest interest in the experiment. There had been some skepticism within the service about its usefulness because the growth of fish is affected by more factors than just the productivity of the system they are living in. Some people felt that the results from the small lake could not be extrapolated to large lakes. Some supposed that in any case fertilizing large lakes was entirely impracticable even if the Bare Lake experiment showed that it would increase salmon production in a small lake.

From this experience it seems clear that when a promising long-term project is started, some administrative device should be used to insure continuity through changes in administration and key personnel. This may be hard to do because newly appointed administrators generally are expected to do something new. Unless there is an increase in funding, something new probably requires that something else be canceled. Organizations that do long-term research should have some procedure that requires a special review and justification before an established project is canceled; otherwise much time and money may be wasted in getting a project started and not accomplishing the goals. At least the Bare Lake study confirmed the central importance of phosphorus and the responsiveness of the salmon population to an increase in lake productivity. Much later, studies showed that returning salmon can indeed contribute a large amount of phosphorus, depending on the size of the run which can vary by a factor of 24 over a four-year cycle. In 1965, a peak year for Lake Iliamna, a major salmon-producing lake in Alaska, the fish contributed 1.48 times as much phosphorus as came in through the inlets. In the previous year, a very small return of salmon contributed only 4% as much as the streams (Donaldson 1967).

## Vancouver Island

The final example carries on from Bare Lake and is more of a success story. We used to think that the only practicable way to fertilize a large lake was to let sewage effluent do it; but usually that is overdone, making nuisance conditions. Besides, for scientific purposes, the limnologist needs to be able to control the amount and kind of fertilizer. However, when you use some imagination, do a little arithmetic and calculate the amount of phosphorus actually needed to make a significant increase in production, it turns out to be practicable to fertilize lakes that are large enough to support a commercial production of sockeye salmon. All it takes is the will and the money to do it. Scientists in the Canadian Fisheries and Marine Services did some pilot experiments in 1970-73 on Great Central Lake on Vancouver Island, B.C. Although the lake has a smaller area than Lake Washington, it is much deeper and has nearly four times the volume, 2.6 cubic miles (10.8 km$^3$). They found it possible to shovel enough fertilizer from barges to increase the productivity of the phytoplankton to a satisfactory level, but that was a cumbersome operation. On the basis of the early success, they were able to plan a more ambitious program starting in 1977. A group of thirteen lakes was selected, varying from 0.7 to 5.0 mi$^2$ (1.8 to 64 km$^2$) in area and 82 ft to 696 ft (25 to 212 m) in mean depth. To make effective delivery of many tons of agricultural fertilizer they use a converted four-engine passenger airliner that swoops down over the lake, leaving a trail of fertilizer behind. The salmon production has been greatly enhanced. The total cost of the program has been about $2,000,000 (Canadian) per year, while the commercial value of the fishery has been about

$6,500,000. Included in the program cost is $700,000 for research and assessment.

This program illustrates very well the points I want to make about the interaction between scientific research and applied work. The fertilization is done strictly for the practical purpose of increasing the commercial catch of salmon. But to find out whether it is effective, the work must be accompanied by a monitoring program to see what, if anything, happened, and to permit improvements. In this case, monitoring is required by law, and must continue for two years after fertilization stops. As it happens, the director of the study, Dr. John Stockner, is a limnologist who has organized the project as a limnological experiment. Thus the study provides not only an essential evaluation of the practical value of the program, but also a major advance in understanding the role of nutrient supply to lakes.

# Chapter 13

## Special Requirements of Long-Term Research

As shown in the preceding chapters, many basic ecological problems require study of a changing system over a relatively long time. Furthermore, the successful solution of many environmental problems depends on having a record of the prior conditions and a record of the response of the system to efforts to alleviate it: that means long-term research. There has been much interest recently among ecologists in long-term research, and much activity in trying to find ways to foster it. While the intense discussion of this topic among scientists may be of little interest to people not engaged in it, anyone seriously interested in environmental problems needs to have some understanding of what ecologists are up against in trying to do their work. In this chapter I give some of the background needed by anyone who wants to understand the present state of long-term ecological research in the United States. Inevitably I will make some reference to my own experience in getting support for projects on Lake Washington and the Coulee lakes.

There is more similarity than difference between long-term research and ordinary research. Both use the same kind of thinking. Both depend on having clear-cut questions or hypotheses. Both require effective design of programs of observation or experiments. The main difference is that with a prolonged study of a natural system, the scientist is not in charge of the schedule. He must continue to work until the system has completed the change that is being studied. Not all lake experiments are long term. In some cases the events of a single summer provide the answer. A more practical difference is external to the science, having more to do with the mechanism of evaluation and support than with the scientific procedures. In this country recent efforts to develop long-term research have led mainly to developing complex new administrative procedures to force groups of scientists to work together in a specific field, as I explain below.

I have wondered whether personal characteristics of scientists may determine the kinds of problem they take up. (There is good reason to think so [Roe 1953].) An individual who starts a long-term project can expect it to occupy a major part of his scientific career before he sees the full results; this requires patience. He can maintain interest by working on a variety of problems, or by finding within the long-term project small subprojects that can be completed along the way. Some of us have been led inadvertently into long-term projects and have found it rewarding.

When we look at examples of long-term projects that are generally regarded as successful, two generalizations emerge that show the similarity between long-term and other kinds of research. With few exceptions each project was conceived and organized by one person; in a few cases, two or three individuals became voluntarily associated because of mutual interest in the problem (Strayer et al. 1986). And most work was funded in the same way as short-term projects, with a long series of short-term grants; a recurrent difficulty in the research projects discussed in chapters 8 through 12 has been lack of money.

To understand the conditions under which projects are financed, it is necessary to know something about the sources. Some money is available from university funds, various governmental agencies such as the Environmental Protection Agency and the Department of Energy, and from some private agencies. But the main support of ecological research in the United States since World War II has been the National Science Foundation (NSF), founded in 1950 with the primary purpose of supporting basic scientific research (Matzuzan 1988). Support is provided in response to applications that specify the problem, the reason for studying it, the way it will be studied, the cost of equipment, supplies, salaries for helpers, and anything else needed. Many university faculty are on nine-month appointments and some get summer salary from research grants. Most applications come from individual scientists, although some come from two or more cooperating scientists, as with the Hubbard Brook study discussed in chapter 8. Any application will be reviewed by a panel of scientists in that general field and also mailed out to several specialists in the particular area of the proposed work. Whether the proposal is funded depends not only on its worth but also on the amount of money available to the panel for distribution. There is intense competition and only a small fraction of even very good applications can be supported. Foundation policy limits grants to five years, but most are given for three.

It is important to realize that this system gives full initiative to individual scientists or to groups who have voluntarily associated themselves. The panel and *ad hoc* reviewers may have suggestions to the applicant, but once the grant is given, the foundation has no part in directing the work; that is the responsibility of the scientist. If he encounters an unanticipated interesting diversion, he is free to follow it as long as he stays within the general bounds of the proposal. If he wants to deviate he is expected to inform the foundation, in which case he is likely to get a letter (I have several) saying:

> The Foundation believes that the principal investigator, operating within the established policies of the grantee institution, is best qualified to determine the manner in which grant funds may be used most effectively to accomplish the proposed research. In accord with this stated policy, the Foundation interposes no objections.

The system of evaluation known as peer review is widely used by granting agencies. There is much debate about it, but most scientists agree that no better system has been invented (National Science Foundation 1988). Errors can be made in the reviewing process because of a workload too large to handle, or a lack of attention, competence, or thought on the part of individual reviewers or panel members, but those are not failings of the system itself.

Nothing I say in the following section is to be taken as criticism of the general operation of NSF. The National Science Foundation was founded on excellent principles and in general it has functioned excellently. The panels and the reviewers have worked exceedingly hard to make it function. The staff has a very heavy workload and is often met with hostility for decisions not fully within its control. I offer here criticisms of some of the policies and operations, but I offer them in a spirit of helpfulness, not of carping. I have served on the Ecology Panel and have an admiration, even affection, for the NSF. I should say that, within the limits in which the foundation can operate, I have been treated very well, so my comments are not the expression of a disgruntled rejectee. Without NSF our knowledge of what happened to Lake Washington would be pretty trivial.

It is easy to see why many long-term projects were funded in the same way as short-term ones. There was already an effective mechanism in place for evaluation. Nothing would prevent a scientist from applying repeatedly for grants to continue a project, as I did with Lake Washington. In some cases, one could not know at the beginning how much time would be required. For instance, when *Oscillatoria* appeared in Lake Washington our goal was to follow the lake's response to increasing enrichment. At some unpredictable time, enough information would have accumulated that continuation would not be interesting. I had no idea then that the pollution would be corrected so soon. When Metro was voted it was easy enough to predict approximately how long it would take for the lake to recover: the year 1975 or a little later might then have been predicted to be an adequate stopping place for the sampling program. The question became moot in 1976 with the *Daphnia* population explosion. That started a whole new problem with its own time scale. The new problem was appealing to the NSF panel and it too was funded.

There is an inherent difficulty with this way of handling long-term studies. Panels must have criteria by which to judge applications. Such terms as "fresh new hypotheses" or "cutting edge of science" are used. When the panel receives the third application to continue a particular long-term study, set up six years earlier with clear hypotheses to be tested by prolonged observation, they may get the impression that it is simply to continue "monitoring" without much purpose; whereas in fact the proposed program would provide essential information. Without it, the work of the preceding six years could be wasted. Nevertheless such an application may take a low priority relative to one that seems to have a new idea. The membership of the panel will have changed since the original application and the new members will not be aware of the considerations that led to funding the original proposal. Apparently when a genuine long-term continuation application comes in a package with new short-term applications, it is hard for the panels to think of it in a different way. Actually, there are few really new ideas, and ecologists have become adept at inventing catchy new names for old ideas. Somebody who reinvents the wheel would not say so; he would call it an RTD (rotational transportation device).

The difficulty of handling long-term projects is compounded by a shortage of funds available to the foundation. In recent years the Ecology Panel of NSF has been able to fund only about 15% of the applications and few of those get the full amount requested. This intense competition puts heavy pressure on the panels and means that decisions to fund projects are not based on excellence of science alone; that criterion selects a group that will be further screened according to other criteria, such as novelty, multidisciplinary nature, or involvement of a group of investigators. Also, the foundation has long been under pressure to distribute its funds "fairly," that is, widely among the states and universities, so that excellence may well not be the determining factor in choosing one particular project over another.

After the problem of funding, the problem of personnel probably gives investigators the most trouble. Most ecological studies involve so much work of different kinds that no one person can do it all, and require assistants at different levels of professional status. This is closely tied to the funding problem, because salaries are geared to the level of qualification. Rather than try to generalize from the experience that long-term researchers have had with personnel, I will illustrate from my own experience that produced the results described in chapters 1 and 11. I present this simply as an example. I would be interested in knowing how this problem has been handled in other long-term projects.

The 1949–50 study of Lake Washington was made by two graduate students as part of their Ph.D. dissertation research, financed by local university funds. In 1955 when the nature of the developing problem became evident, I did what was becoming common procedure at the time: I applied to a federal granting agency for support for the salary of a postdoctoral research associate who could provide the full-time attention and continuity needed. It turns out that most postdoctoral associates are looking for full-time faculty positions, and are no more permanent than graduate students. After the third post-doctoral associate left for a permanent position I decided that the project needed more continuity than that. In 1960 I found a technician experienced in water chemistry. He was agreeable to staying with the project and was in charge of the chemical work until 1982.

The biological work required a different kind of specialization and experience. I found technicians who were interested in and able to develop expertise in the plankton work. So the group of technicians increased, and since 1965 three or four have been working with me on various lake research projects, helped by part-time undergraduate and graduate students. All have benefitted educationally by the experience as well as financially. The technicians on the lake projects have really worked as scientists, thinking about what they are doing and why. To avoid monotony, none does just one thing all the time. Each has a specialty, but all know some of the chemical and field procedures so work is never held up when somebody is absent. All share in the field work, which is generally regarded as a fringe benefit of the job. And the continuity of experience provides an additional long-term advantage.

While there are tremendous advantages to having such a group of technicians for long-term projects, problems arise because of salaries. State employees receive regular raises and promotions commensurate with their experience and length of service. A reviewer of one of my Lake Washington applications complained that the technicians were being paid as much as associate professors. He chided me for not being "sufficiently strict in exercising budgetary control over his salaried personnel." Now possibly a skilled technician who has been working for fifteen years may make more than a newly appointed associate professor in a small institution, but the implications of that comment worried me. Is a technician's salary to be frozen at a starting level for life? When a technician starts to make a decent salary, must I fire him and start over with a beginner, losing those years of experience so valuable to the continuity of the work? The NSF would never tell an investigator that he had to do that. But usually an applicant does not get as much money as he needs. He is given the responsibility of deciding how much he must reduce his plans, and that may require dismissal of an expensive helper. In fact the amount of financing available from NSF for Lake Washington was not enough to support my assistants, so they divided their time between Lake Washington and other projects funded by other agencies.

Graduate students can have a very important function in long-term research, but they cannot be used effectively as substitutes for full-time technicians in doing the routine work because they have obligations to class work and to their own degree research. The Ph.D. research project is supposed to be an independent study in which the student learns to function as a creative scientist. The data he would get doing the routine work on a larger project could not properly be used as the sole basis of a dissertation. However, most long-term studies can include special problems that are ideal as material for Ph.D. dissertations or M.S. theses, for they can be worked on quite independently as units, but still be proper parts of the whole. Collecting samples or measurements for the special sub-project automatically produces material for the main investigation. For example, when it became obvious that *Neomysis* had a special significance in the changes in Lake Washington, we needed to get information about its selective feeding and distribution in the lake. This could have become part of the work of the technicians, but at the time Paul Murtaugh, one of the graduate students, was looking for a good Ph.D. project, and the ecology of *Neomysis* was an ideal subject. His work in turn provided an essential element in the analysis of the population explosion of *Daphnia*. The color of copepods in the Coulee lakes was no part of my thinking when Nelson Hairston, Jr. was looking for a thesis topic. (See chapter 11.) I had suggested considering something about zooplankton population dynamics, but when he went to look, he was taken by the question, why was there a difference in color of the big copepods in Soap Lake and Lake Lenore? I think the resultant dissertation was much more interesting than anything that could have been done on the original problem. Every trip he made to the Coulee also produced samples for the main project that were not used in his dissertation, and we now have the material needed for the analysis of zooplankton population dynamics.

I have given my own opinion of the proper nature of long-term research, its values, and the problems that can interfere with progress. Attempts are being made by agencies to promote long-term research, but some of these attempts are based on concepts very different from mine. I will conclude by explaining this difference and proposing changes that would improve the support of genuine long-term research.

In 1979 NSF announced two new programs in long-term research. In view of the foundation's strong record of effective support of ecological research, one might have expected this action to have alleviated the kind of problems I have identified above. Actually, it does little. Before explaining that, I will trace how the programs were created. They were developed during three conferences of eminent ecologists and administrators held in 1977–79, and the evolution of thinking is recorded in three reports. The first report (1977) starts promisingly with a four-page summary of the general state of long-term research at the time and of the needs for improvement. Here is a selection:

> Ecology requires long-term studies. They are indispensable and must be initiated. All ecosystems are in a process of long-term change. Some changes may be long-term cycles, others unidirectional. Some may be due to natural climatic, geological and biological events and processes, some to subtle long-term anthropogenic influences. At present, few research strategies allow us to separate long-term cyclic from unidirectional changes; or anthropogenically induced changes from natural ones. This and other central ecological issues make clear the need for long-term quantitative data sets, which have irreplaceable theoretical and applied utility. . . .
>
> There are two basic approaches to long-term studies, one through individuals and one through institutions. A scientist who has done good work and wants to do it for a long time seems a safe bet to maintain accuracy and precision in his measurements and to be motivated to seek insights from his observations. Our society's methods for funding research have tended to obstruct, rather than promote, the continued, long-term studies of good scientists and good projects. . . .

We recommend that mechanisms be developed that make possible and promote longer studies by competent scientists. . . .

*Long-term measurement programs should not compete for funds with proposals for short-term research projects. Such long-term programs should not be interpreted as mechanisms for new sets of huge, encompassing analyses of whole ecosystems.* [The emphasis is added because that is not what happened (Callahan 1984).] The purposes of the programs suggested here are quite different: to select crucial factors which are essential to major ecological issues. While the time scale is large, and while in the long run such programs should exist in many locations, there is a need to determine the minimal level of monitoring necessary. . . .

In these excerpts we can clearly see the birth of two NSF programs, *Long Term Environmental Research* (LTER) and *Long Term Research in Environmental Biology* (LTREB). However, most attention was given to LTER, and LTREB has not been well known. After the introduction, the report makes a curious reversal of normal scientific practice. Usually when one starts an investigation he has some observation to explain, a question to answer or an idea to test. He selects those properties of the system to measure which he thinks are relevant to the problem. However, this report dives right in with long lists of "parameters" to be measured in each type of habitat. There was little mention of the kinds of questions the "monitoring" would illuminate. There were even recommendations about such details as how many times a year a lake should be sampled and at how many depths. The goal was to set up a system of routine measurements for a descriptive, comparative study of ecosystems. The programs as described would have been inappropriate for such studies as the eutrophication of Lake Washington or the dilution of the Coulee lakes, where dynamic seasonal changes have to be defined on a much finer time scale within the long-term duration.

The domination by ecosystem concepts became clear in the title of the second report (1978), *A Pilot Program of Long-Term Study and Observation of Ecosystems in the United States.* Again, there is a strong emphasis on what to measure, how to store the numbers, and how the administration should be organized. In this report there was much emphasis on data. But facts are meaningless by themselves. They take on meaning only in a context of investigation in which they were collected with respect to some question. All the "parameters" listed are meaningful to some problems and irrelevant to others. Some meaningful ones were not included in the list.

The third report (1979) begins to pay attention to scientific problems and concepts, and at last assures us that "The proposed program would have to answer significant ecological research questions if it were to be considered for support by the National Science Foundation."

It seems pretty clear that early in the development of the LTER program, ecosystem ecologists saw a great opportunity for support and grabbed it. The outcome was a program very different from that prescribed by the first report in the final paragraph quoted above. Now there is nothing wrong with a group seeking support for their field of research, but in this case they misappropriated the concept of long-term research to a different purpose that does not easily accommodate some important types of long-term research, as I will show below.

## LTER Program

Of the two programs, the major one is identified as Long-Term Ecological Research (LTER). It reverses the usual procedure, taking initiative away from individual investigators by establishing goals that are to be met by investigators who organize as competing groups and write proposals showing how they will meet the research goals and criteria established by NSF. There have been three such "competitions" in which applications meeting various very restrictive requirements were invited.

The announcement of the first competition in 1980 included in part the following specifications:

> The Division of Environmental Biology will make available support for pilot studies in Long-Term Ecological research (LTER). The goals of LTER are to (1) initiate the collection of comparative data at a network of sites representing major biotic regions of North America and (2) evaluate the scientific, technical and managerial problems associated with such long-term comparative research. Initially, the Foundation expects to fund three to five projects at funding levels not to exceed $300,000 per year.

LTER will involve groups of investigators working at representative sites located over the continent or within geographic regions. Investigators must focus on a series of core research topics, coordinate their studies across sites, utilize documented and comparable methods, and be committed to continuation of work for the required time.

The core research areas are (1) pattern and control of primary production, (2) dynamics of populations of organisms selected to represent trophic structure, 3) pattern and control of organic matter accumulation in surface layers and sediments, (4) patterns of inorganic inputs and movements of nutrients through soils, groundwater, and surface waters, and (5) patterns and frequency of disturbances.

The principal investigator must be prepared to make long-term time commitments and should consider (1) continuity of leadership, (2) institutional cost sharing, (3) physical facilities, (4) site integrity, (5) conflict in use of a site, and (6) long-term agreements with site owners. Attention must be given to the following items: (1) baseline information, (2) bibliographies and libraries, (3) reference collections, (4) data storage and retrieval, (5) information synthesis and publication, (6) site promotion and (7) external review of project operation.

During the early phases of a project, attention must be given to the tasks of assuring information comparability and inter-project coordination. These tasks will be facilitated through workshops and meetings between LTER investigators. Adequate provision for these meetings should be made. Baseline studies of macroclimate, geology, soils and sediments, flora and fauna, and past disturbances may be initiated as they relate to the five core areas. Researchers should coordinate their studies with those working at other reserves and nature areas, such as Biosphere Reserves.

The first paragraph states two goals, one of which is to get descriptive, comparative data at sites in different biotic regions; nothing specific is said about long-term needs. The other stated goal in effect is to conduct an experiment in the administration of complex scientific projects. It seems not well designed as an experiment and is an expensive one. The character of the statement is rather aggressive, with its strict directions about things that "must" be done. What the plan does is to establish a limited number of research centers around the country with instructions to make certain kinds of measurements so that the operation of different types of ecosystems can be compared.

There is nothing in the formal description that calls for the passage of time. The justification seems to be that ecosystems are always changing.

My initial reaction to the announcement was pretty negative. One could spend his entire professional career doing such descriptive, comparative studies of a large number of lakes. It would take a long time, but it would not be long-term research in the sense in which I have been using the phrase. As far as I can see, the main justification for calling LTER a program in long-term ecological research was that it would take a long time to develop the administrative organization of the centers and a long time to do the complex work.

Now in practice, administration of programs is often much more flexible than the formal descriptions. Very recently, more than ten years after the LTER program was announced, several progress reports have been published (Magnuson 1990; Swanson and Sparks 1990; Franklin, Bledsoe and Callahan 1990). As could have been expected, not all projects at LTER sites are as narrowly bound to comparative descriptions of ecosystems as would be suggested by the initial NSF announcements. It is important to realize that some of the institutions selected for the LTER program were at sites where substantial long-term research had already been done, so LTER inherited bodies of first-class research. For instance, the Hubbard Brook Project (chapter 8) started in 1963 and had achieved worldwide recognition long before it associated itself with LTER in 1987. Some new genuine long-term projects have been started that involve more than comparative ecosystem studies. But it is hard to tell how many of these could have been done more easily by self-organized groups with more conventional support, possibly at more suitable sites than those in LTER locations. Undoubtedly some very good unitary studies will come out of the program, almost as byproducts of the main goal, that could have been done as part of a normal research program. Some of them will in fact be real long-term experimental studies in which the response rate sets the time scale, but LTER is a cumbersome mechanism for that. This type of experiment has been done before, without such strict administrative control, as the International Biological Program, and as a program of biome studies supported by NSF. Initial opinions of their value were mixed, and the results received mixed reviews. Some day the value of the LTER program will have to be reviewed by an independent group. Could the same support have been more efficiently used for a less complex, less limited effort? How do the results compare with the potential results of top-rated projects that were not funded? Will new insights have been generated that could not have been gained by conventional cooperative work, or at least with less cumbersome arrangements? Will they have been worth the effort? How much of the accomplishment really pertained to the announced goals of LTER? Does the accumulated information on the mandated properties to be measured provide an adequate explanation for the changes observed over long periods? How has the comparison of data among ecosystems been used? What really new concepts have arisen? As far as I can tell from published reports, the really new thing to appear is the development of a network of communication for sharing data among the LTER groups. This will certainly facilitate synthesis, a valuable function. The current LTER effort is receiving considerable scrutiny and criticism. Possibly positive responses to those criticisms can avert some of the problems.

## LTREB Program

The other new NSF program announced in the same flyer as LTER was "Long-Term Research in Environmental Biology" (LTREB), described simply in a brief sentence: "Individuals or groups may submit proposals that identify questions requiring acquisitions of data over long periods of time." The acronym was not used in the 1979 announcement, evidently through inadvertence, but appeared in a later bulletin. This sounds more like the kind of program that I would regard as appropriate for long-term research as I see it, but there were some limitations:

> Such support will not normally be for an investigator's major line of research but ancillary to it. Major studies of a long-term nature will be considered as part of the regular proposal review mechanisms not through the LTREB route. It is expected that LTREB awards will not exceed $25,000 per year.

So, this at first seems to be no real solution to the long-term research problem. For one thing, it covered only small projects. An intensive study of a long-term problem requiring full-time work would continue to be subject to the traditional process. However, while little use has been made of LTREB by NSF, its scope has not been as limited as suggested by the description and some genuine long-term projects have been supported. In fact, the LTREB program has been important in helping maintain the continuity of my Lake Washington project which had been supported by NSF since 1959 by a long series of ordinary three-year grants. At first the foundation funded my applications fully, but in the late 1960s support to universities from the foundation was reduced, the requests to the foundation increased, and grant applications were only partially funded. In 1980 I applied for another grant, for five years this time, at the same level that was provided during eutrophication. What I received instead was a terminal three-year grant at a greatly reduced level. Apparently it was thought that we knew enough about Lake Washington. I was told that if something exciting seemed to be happening I could apply for a new grant to study it. I was not sure how I could be expected to know if anything was happening in the lake if I was not sampling it. In any case, continuity of the record would be lost, very risky in view of the speed with which changes can take place. For example, just suppose I had stopped working on the lake in 1973. The sudden increase in transparency in 1976 was publicly noticed and I would have started to get telephone inquiries. How could I have explained it?

The inconspicuous announcement of LTREB had attracted little notice even within the foundation. The program director in charge of my terminal grant did not tell me about it, and his successor had to do some telephoning to find out what it was when I learned about it and called to find out how to apply. Eventually I secured an LTREB grant to support continued sampling of Lake Washington to 1989. This is fortunate, for otherwise we would have missed the increase of alkalinity in 1988. Because of that change, NSF granted a three-year renewal through 1992. Fortunately, the Andrew W. Mellon Foundation has a program in conservation, and they have generously provided grants to maintain my group of helpers so that we can complete the analysis of our long run of data and prepare definitive publications, work not covered by the LTREB grant.

## Conclusions

Plainly, LTER as described would have been no use to me in 1954 and 1955 at the start of the Coulee Lake and Lake Washington long-term projects; nor, unfortunately, would it be of use were I starting today. LTER calls for the creation of an enormous administrative effort aimed at closely specified areas of research, in a controllable site, with insufficient funding and with much of the direction coming from administrators remote from the site and outside the group doing the work. There is no room in it for an individual investigator with a good twenty-year idea, modifying the goals as new discoveries are made. LTREB holds the greatest promise for support of real long-term research. As described, it is too restricted in scope and magnitude of financing. With some modification it could serve to support some long-term investigations very efficiently.

Certainly nobody could expect to be given a full grant at one time to cover a twenty-year study, but changes could be made to improve the effectiveness of the present process. For example, with a commitment to a longer funding period, a principal investigator could attract research associates who otherwise would not make themselves available. Additional specific recommendations that could be made for improvement may not interest those not doing the work, but such improvements would in the long run affect the cost to the public and the availability of ecological data for solving environmental problems. NSF intends to maintain the LTREB program and actively encourage long-term projects, within its financial constraints.

The LTER program seems to be part of a fairly recent tendency on the part of granting agencies to establish very large projects and especially research centers with rather strictly defined aims. This would disturb few scientists if there were an unlimited amount of research money available; in fact it never has been unlimited, and is now decreasing in terms of buying power. Further, there is considerable worry that the large new projects in many scientific disciplines will drain away money that otherwise would be available for application by independent individual investigators in the traditional way. The worry is not simply that the immediate supply of NSF money is commandeered. Universities that obtain funding for a center are expected to commit some amount of matching money from their own funds. Automatically, acceptance of funds for a Center limits options for future developments.

The system of unsolicited application and peer review has been well tested by many years of experience, while more grandiose systems have failed or proven to be inefficient. There is growing fear among scientists that the progress of science will be damaged by the new kind of development. For an example of the reaction of two experienced aquatic ecologists to the recently announced policy of NSF, see reviews by Paine (1989) and Lehman (1989).

This problem was discussed at length by both biological and physical scientists at a meeting of the National Academy of Sciences in April 1988. A widespread feeling was expressed in a statement offered to the council of the academy:

> The membership . . . reaffirms its commitment to the preservation of the role of the independent investigator, which is so central to the health of many areas of American science. Accordingly, we continue to express our concern over the increasing emphasis by the National Science Foundation on channeling its support of basic academic science through mechanisms other than the traditional grants to individual investigators. Such mechanisms include the designation of so-called "priority areas" of basic research and the proposed establishment on a large scale of science and technology research centers and of programs for the selective support of group research. If implemented, these changes could affect adversely the patterns of scientific research and education in our universities, for example, by suppressing or distorting the original contributions of emerging investigators. . . .

Concerns that Big Science will limit the support of creative, independent, individual scientists are widespread. Currently a vigorous debate is proceeding among physicists about construction of the superconducting supercollider (SSC), an instrument that, with an estimated cost of four billion dollars, is described as the most expensive single research project in history. The argument seems not to be so much about the value of the information that it would produce as about the damage it would do to other areas of physical research by draining away support. All these arguments should not be taken to mean that the only support for science should be through the individual investigator system. There are good reasons for having government laboratories with teams of investigators focusing on definite problems in limited areas, but they cannot be expected to do the same kind of work as is accomplished by the projects originated by individual creative scientists.

# Part 4

## Retrospect and Prospect

The purpose of this section is to discuss features that are common to more than one environmental problem and to give thought to what future prospects may be. On the basis of what we now know, we ought to be able to do better with our problems than we have been doing.

Not all environmental problems are due to pollution, but many are, and we need to take a broad view of what pollution is, as I will discuss in chapter 14. The testimony of experts has a major influence on the success or failure of environmental protection, so it is important to be able to recognize one. Chapter 15 gives some guidelines. In chapter 16, I comment on a variety of topics that are common to much of the preceding work. In chapter 17, I recognize, but do not solve, the major problem facing us.

# Chapter 14

## What is Pollution?

M ost of the problems of environmental deterioration discussed in this book are clearly the results of pollution. But
the detergent people objected to describing phosphate as a pollutant, evidently on the basis that it was not inherently objectionable of itself. Raw sewage would certainly be called a pollutant with no quibbles because it is objectionable as a component
of water to drink or to swim in, but how about well-treated secondary effluent? I have been told that after the development of
effective secondary treatment techniques, some sewage plant
operators would drink the effluent from their plants to show
visitors how well the purification process had worked. Secondary effluent is not offensive by this standard, but it is capable of
generating odorous blooms such as that described so vividly for
Lake Monona. Further, most inorganic compounds of phosphorus are not foul smelling, but they too are capable of generating
nuisance blooms, as in Little Otter Lake. Freshwater damaged the
value of Soap Lake, but I find that few people would describe that
as a case of pollution as I did. That word has been preempted to
mean something inherently objectionable.

So what, really, is pollution? Obviously pollution is what we
define it to be, but definitions should make sense. We may need
to choose among several possibilities, each one suitable for a
particular purpose. The definition of a technical term to be used
in drawing up legislation might be more elaborate and specific
than one that would be appropriate for normal conversation about
environmental problems. For example, the Clean Water Act as
amended in 1987 presents nineteen definitions of terms in Section 502. Of these, two are related to this discussion:

(6) The term pollutant means dredged spoil, solid waste, inciner-
ator residue, sewage, garbage, sewage sludge, munitions, chemical wastes, biological materials, radioactive materials, heat, wrecked
or discarded equipment, rock, sand, cellar dirt, and industrial,
municipal and agricultural waste discharged into water. . . .
(19) The term 'pollution' means the man-made or man induced al-
teration of the physical, biological, and radiological integrity of
water. [Integrity is not defined.]

For less formal uses, pollution is usually defined in terms of
what it does, rather than what it is. "Water pollution, as generally defined, is the addition of something to water which changes
its natural qualities" (See Francko and Wetzel [1983] in chapter
2 references.) The same authors define pollutant as "any substance which becomes dissolved in water and impairs its usefulness." The first definition implies an undisturbed natural state
which is changed by human activity. The second introduces the
idea of usefulness, presumably to people. I prefer a slight modification: "Pollution of a lake is the addition of anything to the
lake that interferes with its best use." The word *best* requires
thought. This definition is centered on human use of natural resources. It does not automatically exclude our doing things that
change lakes, only those that interfere with our proper use of the
lake. It recognizes that the human species is a natural part of the
community, having evolved right along with the rest of the living world, and that we have a right to function in the community in accordance with our needs. All animal species use their
natural resources and affect their environment. Each species has
its particular requirements. However, this definition cannot serve
as an excuse for needless, wasteful treatment of the world as a
dump. It assumes that we will employ our brains, and that our
treatment of natural resources will be responsible, based on a
decent sense of ethics and a set of social values and priorities.
Because these are very subjective matters, the definition is open
to misuse. This is not a trivial point. *Homo sapiens* is the only
species capable of having discussions like this and making decisions that can cause enormous irreversible damage to its own
support system.

Disagreements arise because of differences in priorities among
people. The best use of a particular lake may be to leave it alone

in an undisturbed watershed. Conversion of a beautiful, clear mountain lake into a eutrophic producer of the conditions described for Lake Monona may strike some people as an environmental disaster, while others will think of the lake as merely messy, and not care much about it. An ancient forest with trees centuries old strikes awe in many people. Some loggers are bothered by the sight of "over-ripe" trees going to waste. Often the priorities are based on economic factors. Even if everybody agrees to spend money to achieve a highly desirable goal, there may be arguments about how to do it, and the cheapest way is usually the one that wins, even if it is not the best as judged by a wider set of criteria.

There is a story appropriate to this emphasis on economic priorities. It is almost certainly apocryphal and has not been funny since 28 January 1986, but it is worth knowing, anyway. Just at the start of one of the Apollo trips to the moon, one of the astronauts, strapped in his seat in the capsule, looked around and realized that everything around him had been built by the lowest bidder.

One sometimes sees the term "natural pollution." The term refers to the fact that there are many places in the world where there are ugly or even dangerous conditions for natural reasons with no human assistance. It usually occurs in statements by representatives of industry or by politicians in defense of sloppy practices with waste disposal or manufacturing processes. Take some examples comparing natural conditions with those created by man:

We are unfortunately aware of the damage done by oil spills at sea. Often they are the result of incompetent operation of ships, but there have been many episodes when oil has gushed uncontrollably from holes made by offshore drilling rigs. However, there are also places where oil deposits are a short distance below the bottom of the sea, permitting oil to escape naturally and float up into the water.

Many lakes are eutrophic and produce dense populations of blue-greens without sewage or other sources of human enrichment. Birds or wallowing mammals may contribute fecal enrichment to lakes, but some lakes are eutrophic for geological and climatic reasons. Examples are Soap Lake and Lake Lenore. (See chapter 12.) In some regions with mineral deposits, the surface water may contain lethal concentrations of arsenic or other toxic elements.

There has been concern about the effect of heated water from nuclear and fossil-fuel power plants on fish (thermal pollution). A similar effect is seen in geothermal regions where hot springs flow into lakes or streams. In some places, such as Yellowstone Park, some of the springs are so hot that a person who falls in has no chance of emerging alive.

A number of natural processes mimic air pollution; I have already discussed natural sources of acid precipitation in chapter 13. Conifer trees liberate aromatic organic compounds, some of which make pine forests smell so nice and piney. On a warm day with no wind, enough of these compounds can accumulate to exceed the legal limits permitted by the Clean Air Act. Abandoned coal mines are not natural objects, but can be dangerous places because natural processes produce methane which accumulates beyond lethal limits. A local example is Cougar Mountain, a former coal mining area near Lake Washington. Several people have died during explorations of the old mine shafts. The area is now posted with signs reading:

DANGER

POSSIBILITY OF DEADLY GAS

POSSIBILITY OF ODORLESS, COLORLESS
DEADLY GAS COMING FROM ANY MINE
RELATED OPENINGS IN THIS AREA
IT IS NOT KNOWN WHICH OPENINGS
MAY BE RELEASING GAS
BECAUSE YOU CANNOT KNOW WHEN
YOU ARE BREATHING THE GAS
STAY AWAY FROM
ALL MINE OPENINGS

Probably the most dramatic example of a natural event producing lethal air conditions was caused by the West African Lake Nyos, otherwise known as the Killer Lake. For reasons that are not fully understood, this meromictic lake accumulated a vast amount of carbon dioxide dissolved in the monimolimnion. The gas was suddenly released during the night of 21 August 1986, as from a shaken bottle of soda water, and spread close to the ground for distances up to 10 miles (16 kilometers) from the lake. About 1700 people and 3000 cattle died of suffocation. Two years earlier nearby Lake Monoun had done the same thing on a smaller scale, killing 37 people. (See Stager 1987 for a general account; Kling et al. 1987 for technical details; and Kerr 1989 for recent developments.) The Nyos episode was a weird echo of an infamous industrial accident in Bhopal, India on 3 December 1984. An error in the operation of a chemical factory released a large amount of a toxic gas, methyl isocyanate, that spread in a way similar to the carbon dioxide from Lake Nyos, killing about 2,000 people and injuring 50,000 more.

It seems illogical to describe the natural conditions listed above as "natural pollution." They are simply natural conditions that people find unpleasant or dangerous. I think that "pollution" should be limited to effects of human activity. Sometimes attempts are made to ameliorate natural conditions in order to improve them for human use. Such efforts cannot appropriately be called restoration.

# Chapter 15

## Experts

Even the experts disagree—what's a poor citizen to do? This
sentiment has been expressed so frequently that it indi-
cates a real problem. What are we to do when two people, presented as experts in the same field, express opposite views? Not
everybody responsible for making decisions based on testimony can have the technical knowledge to evaluate it. We need
to find ways to recognize what the difference is and why it exists. We should start by examining the analyses presented by the
two experts, not by questioning their competence, although that
might come later.

Scientists express their expertise in several different settings:
in response to informal questions on the telephone or in letters,
in public lectures or discussions, in testimony before governmental bodies, or in sworn testimony in court trials. In all cases,
in judging the statements, it is important to put the most weight
on the evidence and the reasoning, not on the personal characteristics of the experts. Nevertheless, the trust that one places in
an expert witness will naturally be influenced by his manner of
presentation. An unusually clear example was provided by a
lawsuit in 1977 by the State of Illinois (plaintiff) against the City
of Milwaukee, Wisconsin (defendant) over the disposal of Milwaukee's sewage effluent. The complicated testimony covered
a great range of subjects centered on the effect of sewage effluent on lakes and involving concepts of ecology, of hydrody-
namics, and of the technology of sewage treatment. The judge's
decision (later overturned by the U.S. Supreme Court) would
have forced Milwaukee into a very expensive revision of its

sewerage that many people thought would be ineffective in accomplishing the worthy goals. In this way the case had some similarities to the argument about the EPA requirement that Seattle convert to secondary treatment at West Point. (See chapter 4.)

C. H. Mortimer gave the Milwaukee case a masterly review that includes a discussion of the process of environmental litigation and of the use of experts. The judge of the case made a frank evaluation of the effectiveness of the various expert witnesses and of his own problems in dealing with unfamiliar subject matter "such that my own experience and observations in life are of relatively little use to me." Mortimer states:

> Not intending to be "unkind or to denigrate anyone unnecessarily," Judge Grady classified the witnesses as follows: four (all plaintiff witnesses) were "outstanding," another five (3 defendant and 2 plaintiff) were "almost equally helpful" and six (5 defendant, 1 plaintiff) were "biased in the undesirable connotations of that term . . . combative and unwilling to concede points that they should have conceded because they were so obvious" and on occasion were "evasive and doctrinaire. . . ."
>
> Such commentary on expert witnesses, while displaying welcome candor on Judge Grady's part, also highlights a potential danger. The danger is that a judge's personal perception of the "credibility" of a witness may play an overly dominant role in a complicated technical decision, and *ad hominem* arguments will therefore be given too much weight. The key to reform, if necessary, appears to lie in better use of expert witnesses and in changes in the judge's interaction with them.

The attorney in charge of the case of the State of Illinois has given me his view of expert testimony:

> The strength of any expert witness' testimony lies in the expert's ability to address hostile cross-examination. The key to this is the expert's willingness to concede valid points of criticism and then to incorporate those valid points into his or her opinion. . . .
>
> As a lay lawyer who has had to work with scientific experts in dozens of environmental controversies, I have come to learn that science is afflicted as much with political bias and misperception as are any of the liberal arts. The cross-examination mechanism allows scientific bombast to be exposed for what it is, and permits sound scientific analysis to be tempered through critical adverse examination.

(Personal communication, Joseph V. Karaganis, Chicago)

Some difficulty arises from differences in procedures and standards of evidence in different professions. As Mortimer states:

> I suspect (and the *Illinois* vs. *Milwaukee* record shows) that there is often a mismatch between the modes of thought of the lawyer and that of the scientist or engineer. Lawyers are nurtured on rules of evidence and are more comfortable with clear-cut alternatives, while technical experts are conscious of the complexities of their narrow fields and tend to preface answers with "it depends." Such apparent lack of articulation does not make a "good" expert witness. . . .

Remember that the lawyer from Renton would not tell me the name of the "expert" he quoted on the radio because it would be like giving away his case before he went to court.

I can suggest some points to examine when experts disagree:

1. The disagreement may not be about the facts or data, but the experts may have reached different *conclusions* based on the same facts. This may be because they are using different priorities or subjective value judgments. I do not say that experts should not express opinions, but they should make clear which of their statements are clearly factual—reproducible by other scientists—and which are derived conclusions that involve some subjective factors. People who are dependent on statements by experts should beware of experts who do not make that distinction clear.

   Often this kind of dispute comes in connection with costs. "it will cost too much" is not a fact, it is a conclusion involving a judgment of relative values. The question of cost pervades discussions of environmental protection and restoration, often being presented as the only thing that really matters. In the debate about forming the Seattle Metro, opponents often said that it would cost too much, even before any real cost estimates had been prepared. For some purposes perhaps we should take advice from Justice Oliver Wendell Holmes who said: "I like to pay taxes. With them I buy civilization."

There were many examples of different conclusions in the detergent controversy covered in chapter 3. While there was plenty of scientific nonsense uttered during various testimonies about the function of phosphorus in lakes, several of the sanitary engineers understood phosphorus well enough but concluded that it would not be worth controlling detergents. Obviously this was an opinion based on costs and other criteria, not a fact. Using a different set of priorities, some people concluded that it would be worth doing. Part of the argument seemed to be factual because it involved numbers. For instance, the added per capita annual cost of chemical precipitation in the sewage treatment plants was given by various experts in a range from zero to about four dollars. Obviously they were making different assumptions about the process to be used and using different accounting systems of what should be counted as a cost. This particular example could be an interesting case to examine in detail to see why the estimates were so different.

2. Backwards thinking is often involved. Some people will decide that a particular action is desirable and will marshall a selection of arguments in favor of it. Everything they say may be true, but they will omit some other true things that, if considered, might lead to a different conclusion.

3. People are sometimes wrong about facts or reason poorly. First, they may be ignorant. There is nothing basically bad about ignorance; it is only lack of information. Ignorance can be corrected by learning. Ideally a person will recognize the limits of his knowledge, but not always. Second, they may be stupid. Some people are unable to assimilate information or think clearly. This does not prevent them from expressing opinions. Third, they may be dishonest. It appears that sometimes an expert will misrepresent facts deliberately, in a more deceptive way than in backwards thinking since it involves actual falsification rather than just omission of relevant facts. Deliberate ignorance is a form of dishonesty.

4. Maybe the expert is not really expert. People may feel free to express opinions about matters in which they have no experience or real knowledge. We saw an example of that in chapter 1 when the man at the research institute, with no real

knowledge of Lake Washington or eutrophication, gave mis-information to the Man from Renton. Some rely on their rep-utation for competence in something else to lend credibility. There were plenty of examples of this in the detergent de-bate when people with doctoral degrees in the physical chemistry of sewage treatment expressed unsupportable opinions about biological processes in lakes. The simple pos-session of a Ph.D. degree does not guarantee expertise in a broad field. In some fields of science, Ph.D. degrees are very narrow in focus and the research may even consist largely of grinding through part of the major professor's research pro-gram. It may help to know where the experts got their edu-cation, both undergraduate and graduate. An advanced de-gree in any case does not guarantee good judgment.

5. Examining motivation can be useful in identifying biases that could lead to faulty conclusions (although not for discredit-ing factual data). But effective action cannot stop there. One must show objectively what is wrong with the statements, whatever the motivation behind them. This last point is es-pecially pertinent to the evaluation of industrial propaganda and the activities of political or activist organizations which present arguments based on alleged expert advice. I can give as an example the situation developing in Yelm, the small town that produced the crowd of demonstrators against Metro sludge spraying described in chapter 4. It turns out that Yelm is the residence of a widely known psychic who claims to be in communication with ("channeling") Ramtha, a 35,000-year-old warrior. Several hundred followers have moved to the area and are taking an active interest in local affairs, especially en-vironmental matters. They dominated the caucus demon-stration against sludge spraying. They have been described as having a "maddening way of seeing only one side of an is-sue. It's this attitude they take, that there's only one way." (Goldsmith 1989) This explains much about their confronta-tional behavior, and helps us to evaluate the worth of their environmental concerns which apparently are based largely on a mystical appreciation of The Earth. Allegations of eco-nomic motivations have been made. It has been pointed out that the land owned by Metro would be very valuable if de-

veloped for residences. If Metro were to yield to this public outcry and sell the property, handsome profits could be made by somebody. And, incidentally, a real sewage disposal problem would be developed as well.

So, how to decide whom to believe? How to tell the experts from the phonies? Which organization to follow? All I can suggest is to look for elements of behavior that fit one or more of the categories above. My impression is that most of the cases in which experts appear to disagree are in the first category, where they are really talking about two different things or are using different criteria for judgment. In that case, ask for a full explanation of the facts that were considered and the line of reasoning that led to the disputed conclusions. Beware of the person who is unable to explain an environmental problem without using jargon or, if he uses jargon, cannot explain what it means. The way an expert handles complexity can be revealing, as in the detergent controversy when people cited irrelevant details about the large number of species of algae and many other things. When an expert tells you that something is too complicated for you to understand so just trust what he says, beware. Some experts will say that their opinion is as good as anybody's; but some points really are matters of fact, not opinion, and the expert may simply be wrong. One thing an expert must not do is to present a misleading statement deliberately, hoping to cause people to do the "right" thing. It may have a different effect if the trick is discovered; people will not believe anything the expert says. Finally, evidence of self interest or bias is not evidence that testimony is incorrect, but may direct attention to points that need careful scrutiny. The most effective advisory committees are made up of people who can examine evidence objectively, not people chosen because it is known how they will vote on a particular kind of issue.

In some fields, professional societies have programs of certification. For example, state licenses are needed to practice engineering. In the 1970s, a number of ecologists became disturbed by the kind of testimony being given by professional engineers about environmental problems, as in the detergent controversy. Committees of the Ecological Society of America

(ESA) studied the problem at great length. After much debate, a system of certification as Professional Ecologists was established. Opposition to the program was based on several points, one of which is that the comparison with engineers was false. Certified engineers have a clearly defined field of information and procedures, and their command of that can be determined by examination. Ecology is a different kind of field, and success is determined not by examination but by performance in original research.

The system finally adopted by ESA bases certification on experience in academic course work, professional employment, and two letters of recommendation. Thus it certifies that the person has an appropriate background to be regarded as a professional ecologist, but does not guarantee competent performance in any given circumstance. Likewise, lack of certification of an ecologist who has not bothered to apply cannot be used as evidence of incompetence. I am not a certified ecologist.

This brings up the question of where expert ecologists come from, and I want to comment about some aspects of graduate selection. It seems to me that the main requirements for serving effectively as an expert witness or adviser are brains and judgment. These cannot be created in a university. We hope that the admissions process selects for those qualities, because the university experience can develop a person's ability to use them. In preparing ecologists to participate in environmental problem solving we cannot just load them up with facts and concepts because new problems keep coming up. Somehow, students have to learn how to evaluate them, to formulate questions about them, and to learn how to find answers by appropriate techniques, including thought. With such background one can work effectively on a variety of problems including new ones. Thus, we should not expect professional ecologists to limit themselves to the field in which they did their Ph.D. research. In fact, there may be an advantage for students to have the experience of doing their dissertation research in a field with no immediate practical application. It gives them a broader, unbiased view. I can cite real examples. Most of my students have taken academic positions, but others have gone into applied work. I give two examples:

Dr. John Stockner, the man who is fertilizing Canadian lakes from an airplane, did his Ph.D. work at the University of Washington with me but not on eutrophication. I cannot imagine a more ivory-tower type of dissertation project than his (unless it was my own on sessile rotifers): a study of the community energetics of Ohanepecosh Hot Springs on Mt. Rainier. Warm, nutrient-rich water flowed out of the spring and ran in a stream down to the Ohanepecosh River. A thick mat of filamentous algae covered the bottom of the stream. This was difficult to sample, so Stockner made a wooden trough in part of one of the streams. The mat that developed could be sampled much more accurately. Stockner made a detailed study of the processes controlling the productivity of the mat and the invertebrate animals in it. The work was made possible by an unusual act of courtesy by the administration of Mt. Rainier National Park. They had plans to restore the springs to their original natural condition. This would have wrecked Stockner's research after it was well along, so they postponed rebuilding until the research had been finished. Doing the work gave Stockner experience with research, how to get relevant data, and how to handle ideas of community structure and productivity. He had no specific training in eutrophication or fishery biology, although he had some skill as an amateur salmon fisherman, but his background prepared him to take a position in the Eutrophication Section of the Freshwater Institute at Winnipeg from which he got into the lake fertilization project.

Another of my students, Dr. Robert A. Pastorok, did an equally ivory-tower dissertation on the ecology of an inconspicuous aquatic insect larva (*Chaoborus*), systematically testing the assumptions of optimal foraging theory, then a controversial topic in egghead ecology. As part of his graduate course studies, he spent a summer at Friday Harbor Laboratories at the University of Washington where he became familiar with marine communities. After finishing his Ph.D. degree he taught for a year and then joined an environmental consulting engineering firm. His job there involved a wide variety of problems, from techniques of restoring lakes, through helping with studies of the condition of Puget Sound, to a trip abroad to advise the government of Saudi Arabia about problems of monitoring the effects of oil spills.

So it is essential not to categorize people too early, putting them in little boxes where they must stay for the rest of their lives. It is just as important that they should know their limits so that they can develop new knowledge to meet new problems, and that may be the most important teaching goal of a good university.

One might ask, what are the jobs of a teacher and a student? It would be easy to say that the job of a teacher is to teach and that of a student is to be taught. I think that is wrong. The job of a student is to learn (the active part) and the job of the teacher is to help a student learn.

# Chapter 16

## Commentary

I n this chapter I comment on several topics that permeate the previous sections. Each could be developed greatly, but this is not the place to do it. Further, several topics involve matters that are beyond my present experience, and I can only mention some points that I would like to know more about.

### Environmental Problems and Natural Processes

A systematic examination of our major environmental problems and their causes exposes a striking uniformity in what at first appears to be a bewildering variety of difficulties. In almost every case the problem is produced by an increase or acceleration of a process that is a normal part of the operation of natural communities and the physical world. Usually it is possible to identify a human activity as responsible for the change. Sometimes doubt about the cause arises only because several conditions have changed at the same time.

Often we can find an exact or close parallel in the activities and effect of animal populations. An exception to this generalization concerns the disposal of nonbiodegradable trash in oceans and lakes. In the summer of 1988 that problem came to public attention when masses of hospital waste began to wash up on beaches widely distributed along the east coast of the United States; since some of the objects contained viruses, many beaches were closed to swimming. Plastic objects of various kinds have been responsible for deaths of many sea birds and mammals. This is a rather special problem, involving unpleasant aspects of human behavior and the resistance to decomposition of many of the products purposely manufactured to be resistant, and I will not deal with it further.

Let us first look at some of the chapters in parts 1 and 2 from this viewpoint, identifying the way natural processes were affected by human activity.

*Chapter 1.* Some pollution problems arise from the fact that more people live in an area than can be supported by the natural resources of that area. For example, the human population living in the watershed of Lake Washington could not possibly be sustained by local food production. All that is eaten is subjected to our physiological processes and the residue is flushed through the sewage treatment plants. Most of the phosphorus entering Lake Washington in 1964 had been imported in food from all over the world and concentrated in the local sewage effluent. The amount produced by the activities of the native American population two hundred years earlier must have been a trivial fraction of the later maximum.

Now there is nothing unnatural about eutrophication with sewage. All animals make wastes. Many are social, living in densely populated colonies. Guano islands have been built up by droppings of social sea birds. These birds rest and nest on the islands from which they range for dozens of miles at sea, catching fish that have been produced over a vast area. (Among ecologists this is known as central-place foraging.) Much is known about guano islands because they have been exploited as a rich source of agricultural fertilizer. Worker bees and ants forage widely from the nest, bringing back food for the resident population of larvae and reproductives. Much of their work consists of picking up around the nest and throwing out the garbage, feces and cast exoskeletons produced by the larvae; i.e., sewage and solid waste. Notice that this is all biodegradable material; ants do not make plastic exoskeletons, although chitin decomposes slowly.

Just as food must be imported to our cities, wastes must be exported. Waste is a regional problem. Suburban and rural dwellers cannot dismiss it as a problem that can be solved by clean living by the city people. Raw sewage or treated effluent has traditionally been poured into the nearest lake or river where it goes away. Of course there is no "away." It goes somewhere and is not noticed until the input becomes so large as to overload the receiving system. The liquid waste from the Seattle Metro can be sent into Puget Sound where it mixes with the waste from the other sound communities and fish farms. Sewage sludge poses special problems and there are legal restrictions on the place of disposal. It cannot go into Puget Sound.

*Chapter 3.* The disposal of secondary sewage effluent into a lake increases the input of phosphorus over that entering from natural sources, but that is not a qualitative change. The use of phosphate detergents simply increases further the amount of phosphate coming in. There is no chemical determination that can identify the source of a particular phosphate ion in the lake water.

*Chapter 4.* Two major points were made about Puget Sound. One was that the introduction of primary sewage effluent merely intensified the recycling carried out by the natural bacterial population in the water, releasing phosphorus and other elements from organic molecules. The other point was that some of the material put into the sewerage systems is toxic. But there are many places on earth where, for geological reasons, it is dangerous to drink the water because of a high content of arsenic or some other material. The mercury content of the air of cinnabar mines may exceed the legal limits permitted to industries.

Some of the toxic materials in Puget Sound are not natural in the sense that they are organic compounds produced in factories by processes that are not carried out by the enzymes of organisms. Some, like pesticides, were designed to be lethal. Others, like PCBs, just happen to be that way. These are human inventions. Nevertheless, we can compare them with antibiotics and other toxic materials that are produced by other organisms. Decomposing leaves of oak trees produce a substance that inhibits germination of competing plants. Many plants and animals produce poisonous compounds that damage others upon ingestion or by contact. Herbivorous mammals avoid some plants because of taste, or if they do not avoid them, die. Skunks protect themselves against predators chemically. Some millipedes can store deadly hydrogen cyanide and liberate it when attacked by a predator. The bombardier beetle has a structure in the abdomen in which it prepares a dose of repellent quinones to blow in the face of an enemy.

The promisingly productive use of sludge as a resource to fertilize commercial forest areas was also described in chapter 4. It was pointed out that there is not enough available commercial forest in the area served by Metro to absorb the amount of sludge produced (chapter 1)—any more than there is enough area to produce the food needed.

*Chapter 5.* The problem with Mono Lake was the changing lake level and the accompanying changes in salinity. Saline lakes are quite sensitive to climatic changes that affect precipitation and evaporation, with consequences for level and salinity. An increase in the diversion of water by Los Angeles would mimic a reduction in rainfall in the drainage area. Other natural processes can change the level of a lake. For instance, beavers, the Army Corps of Engineers of the animal world, are effective in damming streams, with major consequences for the area above the dam.

*Chapter 6.* In the chapter on the Panama Canal I emphasized the potential for introducing species of marine animals into communities where they had not been before. Man has certainly been responsible for a vast number of introductions, both deliberately and inadvertently, but there are many non-human agents of dispersal, such as migratory animals of all kinds, wind, and ocean currents. Rearrangements of river drainage by earthquakes and landslides have been responsible for changes in fish distribution.

*Chapter 7.* Of the atmospheric problems, acid precipitation based on sulfur is especially interesting because atmospheric sulfur compounds are produced abundantly both by organisms and by physical systems. The most spectacular sources are volcanos that distribute hydrogen sulfide over wide areas, but geysers, hot springs, and fumaroles are effective on a smaller scale. Recent discoveries of the magnitude of dimethyl sulfur liberated into the air by marine phytoplankton were surprising, and give new insight into the difficulty of identifying securely the effects of human activity. Likewise, all of the so-called "greenhouse" gases, of which $CO_2$ is the most prominent, are involved in interchanges between atmosphere and terrestrial and aquatic communities.

Several times in writing about pollution in chapter 14 I found myself contrasting "human effects" and "natural effects." However, I prefer to think of myself as part of the natural world, and would now say "human" and "non-human." Some people write as if the ideal world is one without any visible human effect. This is unrealistic. Our legitimate requirements as a species with the kind of nervous system we have will result in changes in the earth. This of course cannot serve as a basis for excusing careless, damaging, thoughtless behavior. Who wants to feel sick all the time because of low-level, but pervasive and multiple environmental contaminants? Our special intellect gives us a special responsibility to maintain our environment in more than barely livable condition. This makes sense for selfish reasons even if for no other.

## Endangered Species

Many human activities put particular species of plants and animals at risk of extinction. Some species are especially vulnerable to pollution, others to loss by hunting or fishing. A slight increase in death rate by hunting or a slight decrease in birth rate by pollution can result in a negative balance, and the species disappears, just as businesses go bankrupt if the profit rate drops slightly. Some species are at great risk now: elephants, whales, seals, and a host of less conspicuous animals and plants. One of the most spectacular examples of species extinction is the disappearance from North America because of overhunting of the passenger pigeon, a species once so abundant that flocks darkened the sky. One must not be deceived by the presence of a very large population; if the number is consistently decreasing and the trend continues, the species will not survive. People are sometimes misled by seeing a large number of whales, for instance, or an enormous tropical forest, not realizing that they are seeing a sample of a population one-tenth as large as it was a few years ago.

Modern technology has magnified the loss of heavily fished

marine populations. For example, a fairly recent development in the Pacific is the deployment of thirty-mile-long monofilament nylon nets (drift nets). One of the target species is squid, but the nets also catch dolphins which drown. Many tuna and salmon are caught as well. This mortality is unregulated and is not included in the calculations on which fishing quotas are based, and consequently valuable species will be reduced over large areas.

The relevance of this to ecology is that the study of population dynamics, the control of birth and death rates, is a major field of ecological research. It is the field that is involved in predictions of the effect of different rates of fishing, for instance.

I once heard a TV discussion of the problem of drift nets in which the question was raised about how many species might be driven to extinction. An official of the industry said, very confidently, as if it meant something: "In the past ten years we have not seen any species eliminated." Do we have to kill off a species before we recognize that it was in danger? How many species, before we recognize that we can do it?

### Lake Improvement: The Case of Green Lake

The effort to clean up Lake Washington is often cited as an example of lake restoration; that is, returning a lake damaged by human activity to an acceptable condition that it had earlier. However, not all conditions that bother people have been brought about by human activity. Algal nuisances or disturbing growths of rooted plants may result from natural conditions. When such lakes become surrounded by urban developments, the people in the neighborhood may want to modify their lake to make it conform to their standards for environmental amenities. A different approach has to be taken to the "improvement" of such lakes when there is no identifiable, divertable source of concentrated nutrients as there is with sewage pollution. In the first place, the people must recognize that they are imposing an unnatural change on the lake, not mending damage done by human activity.

In all cases of proposed restoration or improvement it is necessary to define the problem, establish a goal, and evaluate methods to accomplish it. This sequence can be expressed as a series of questions: Is there a problem? Exactly what is it? How severe is it? What would happen if no action were taken? What is the cause of the problem or condition? What are the goals of a solution? Are there tested techniques for reaching these goals? What are the advantages and disadvantages of each technique? What side effects can be expected? What are the costs? Cost cannot be estimated until the other questions are answered. In any case cost should not necessarily be the determining factor in a decision because a relatively cheap method may give an incomplete solution or have undesirable side effects. Finally there must be a decision either to attempt to change or not to take action.

Various methods have been developed to change the condition of a problem lake (Cooke et al. 1986). Each is designed to alter the specific part of the lake's production system that is involved in creating the problem. For example, when a planktonic algal nuisance is the problem, a considerable improvement can be made in many cases by interfering with the recycling of phosphate by the addition of alum (aluminum sulfate or similar compound). This material, when added to a lake, forms a flocculent precipitate that rapidly settles to the bottom, taking with it much of the phosphate and phytoplankton from the water. On the bottom the layer of precipitate continues to bind phosphate and greatly reduces its release from the mud back to the water, in turn reducing the production of phytoplankton. It is important to realize that when used for lake improvement alum does not act by toxicity. It simply reduces the production of algae in the lake. Treatment with alum has been successful in North America and Europe in many lakes that are used for fishing and swimming. The treatment is done in such a way as to maintain a sufficiently high pH to prevent the alum from dissolving. As mentioned in connection with acid rain, which can release aluminum from some kinds of soils, ionized aluminum is toxic to fish and some invertebrates. Dissolution of the floc would also destroy its effectiveness for reducing phosphate recycling. The addition of alum does not produce entirely unnatural conditions. Aluminum is one of the most abundant elements in soil, being a component of clays, and is present in all lake sediments. Clays are responsible for part of the phosphate-binding capacity of lake sediments.

A different method of controlling phytoplankton nuisances is to dilute the lake with water having a low concentration of limiting nutrients. This has two effects. The inflow displaces lake water containing phytoplankton, thus reducing its abundance in the lake. It also dilutes the dissolved nutrients, reducing the lake's capacity for further production. This method has been used less frequently than aluminum treatment because the large volumes of nutrient-poor water needed are rarely available.

A particularly interesting local case is developing in which the community responsible for a lake has an opportunity to choose between the two methods of control described above or take no action. It illustrates in an unusually clear way how a decision whether to modify a lake and how to do it depends on the balance of different interests and priorities, not necessarily on the availability of scientific evaluation. I introduce it here as a general illustration of a type of problem facing many communities. The case is that of Green Lake in Seattle, the same Green Lake that figured in chapter 3 because the soap and detergent people misrepresented data in presentations during U.S. Senate hearings.

Green Lake is the central feature of an attractive park in Seattle. It has a maximum depth of 29 feet (8.8 meters), but about three quarters of the bottom area is less than 10 feet deep (3.3 meters). Naturally there is a dense growth of rooted plants including milfoil. The lake was named early in the history of the city, before the area was urbanized, and its name is meaningful; it produces relatively dense crops of blue-greens, usually toward the end of summer.

The park is very popular. The lake is used by swimmers, boaters, and ducks and is valued by the terrestrial human population of strollers, joggers, and bicyclists for the scenic value of its two-mile perimeter. There has long been a desire by many people to improve its appearance. There has also been controversy about its actual condition. Some people have been quite satisfied with it, while others complain strongly about the occasional odors or cloudy appearance. In the early 1960s, after considerable study, the Seattle Parks Department instituted a program of flushing the lake with water from the city reservoirs. At that time the Cedar River, the main inlet to Lake Washington and the main source of drinking water for the city, could supply more water than was needed by the population of the service area, so this was like a partial diversion of the Cedar River into Green Lake. During a three-year period starting in 1962, a total of 6.5 billion gallons of water (25 million cubic meters) was put through the lake. This fell short of the ten million gallons of water per day that had been calculated to be needed for adequate control. Nevertheless, during that time the concentration of phosphorus was less and the lake produced smaller amounts of algae than before dilution (Oglesby 1969). Later the amount of city water was reduced and the condition of the lake was not as satisfactory.

During this same period public interest in improving the lake increased and led to yet another study, more detailed than previous efforts. There is still controversy about the degree of nuisance that exists. Some people are bothered, others think that the lake is good enough as it is and needs no action. Since city water now is far less available and more expensive, and the supply less dependable than it was, other methods of improvement have been explored. After much study and much argument the choice seems to have been resolved to the two clear actions, dilution or treatment with alum.

The effects of alum treatment are well enough known that a distinct improvement in the perceived condition of the lake could be expected. The cost for one treatment would be about $250,000. It is not certain how often alum would have to be applied, but a single treatment should last for several years. If for some reason the effect of the alum is not great enough, no permanent harm would be done. Even if some error should be made in the application, and aluminum were to be released from the mud into the water, the fish and invertebrate fauna might be damaged, but the effect would not be permanent.

The other alternative, in its original form, was to build a pipeline from Union Bay of Lake Washington to Green Lake, with a return pipe to the bay, and pump eleven million gallons (4.1 million cubic meters) of water per day. (Fig. 1.2 shows the relation between the two bodies of water, 2.5 miles [4.0 kilometers] apart.) There were two kinds of objections to that. First, the pipes would go through another pleasant, popular park—Ravenna Park, one of a number of Seattle parks, including the one at Green

Lake, designed by the same Olmsted brothers who designed Central Park in New York City. It was proposed to lay the pipes under Ravenna Creek at the bottom of the ravine that forms the park. While the plans called for restoration of the stream to its original condition, many people were skeptical that that could or would be done. The second objection is that Union Bay water has a higher nutrient concentration than city water, and there was some question that the maximum amount of water that could legally be pumped would be adequate. The phosphate concentration in Union Bay is variable and not controllable. Further, Union Bay too is an unusual amenity to find in the middle of a large city. It is a nature preserve, popular with bird watchers, boaters, and canoeists, and would certainly be altered by the return flow of such a large volume of water from Green Lake. A later proposition was to return the water to Lake Union rather than to Union Bay (fig. 1.2); Lake Union is essentially a commercial lake with marinas, shipping, and manufacturing operations, and does not have the environmental value of Union Bay.

The pipeline would cost about thirteen million dollars in public funds and would require a continuing annual expenditure of about $300,000 at present rates to pay for the electric power to run the pumps. Many people have questioned the prudence of that permanent commitment to a large use of electricity at a time when supplies of energy of all sorts are diminishing.

It might seem that the choice between these two options is obvious on the ground of expense alone. But some people seem to take seriously the idea of an effect of aluminum on health. Also, possibly dominating the thinking of some is the fact that the state Department of Ecology has offered to pay nearly six million dollars, about half the cost of the pipeline. This bait seemed irresistible, even though it required that an additional large amount of public funds be committed. Cost should not necessarily be the determining factor in choosing a method of improvement, but Green Lake solutions present the biggest differential in cost between two alternatives of any problem that I know.

As it happens, after a long period of study and debate, the pipeline was rejected for legal reasons. This seemed to force the decision to alum, but soon a third proposal was made as an alternative to simple, direct application of alum to the lake. A small water treatment plant would be built near Green Lake to take two million gallons per day of water from Green Lake, reduce the phosphate concentration to a low level, and return it to the lake. Ironically, the phosphate would be removed by precipitation with alum. While the proposal also provides for treatment of the lake itself with alum, that aspect continues to be vigorously opposed by a small group of inhabitants of the Green Lake neighborhood, and the discussion still continues.

As with the detergent controversy, this one has been clouded with irrelevancies, misunderstandings, and misrepresentations. Support for the pipeline was expressed largely by attempts to discredit alum treatment, thus leaving the pipeline as the only action available.

The treatment of Green Lake is controlled by provisions of the Seattle Master Shoreline Program, incorporated into the Seattle Municipal Code. There is no regulation about control of algae or use of algicides, but a section on aquatic weed control accepts as methods of control "hand-pulling, mechanical harvesting, or placement of aquascreens." It states further that "The use of herbicide or other chemicals to control aquatic weeds shall be prohibited." It seems clear from context that this prohibits the use of toxic chemicals for macrophyte control. It seems a weak basis for prohibiting the use of alum in Green Lake to control algae, but that happened. To use alum in Green Lake would now require a waiver from the city agency in charge of land use regulations. To define alum as an herbicide (weed killer) seems illogical. Gardeners who want their hydrangeas to have blue flowers put alum in the soil. It does not kill the plants. The purpose of adding alum to a lake is not to kill algae but to reduce their production by interfering with the nutrient supply. Alum is not expected to interfere with milfoil in Green Lake and other techniques will be needed for its control. Further, blue-greens cannot properly be called plants or weeds except by the loosest of popular usage. The main thing they have in common is photosynthesis. Structurally they are very different, and cannot be controlled by uprooting since they are minute and have no roots. This part of the land use code is clearly aimed at a very worthy goal, to reduce the liberal distribution of toxic material into lakes to control undesirable plants. It would have been more effective if it had been written with more regard to modern concepts of biology. The introduction of the word *toxic* before *chemicals* would have saved much argument.

In fact, one of the dominating themes in the anti-alum propaganda seems based on fear of "chemicals." The proponents do not accept the idea of adding a chemical (alum) to the lake, expressing fear for the health of swimmers or the benthic invertebrates. It is true that high concentrations of aluminum in drinking water should be avoided, but Green Lake is not used for drinking. Probably most of these people add chemicals to their food (salt and sugar). Many probably eat food containing alum (baking powder) or use antacids and anti-perspirants that contain aluminum compounds. They want to add water to the lake, apparently not regarding it as a chemical even though it is an effective solvent and is used as an active reagent in many industrial processes. Ironically, all water in the Seattle supply system is chlorinated, and the city water entering Green Lake contains about one-half part per million of chlorine, a toxic chemical added to kill bacteria. It is also fluoridated with another chemical to protect teeth.

The example of Green Lake illustrates all of the components of the decision process that are listed above as questions. Unlike the Metro decision, this one will not be made by public vote, but by the Seattle city council, working under legal restrictions of the shoreline act. They are also expected to be responsive to public opinion. Many public meetings have been held, many memoranda circulated, and letters written to department officials. At this time, some key issues have not been resolved, including the possibility of no action. The final decision has yet to be made.

## Biomanipulation

For many decades the control of plant and animal pests has been based on biological principles. Parasites or predators are introduced to reduce the abundance of the pest or even to eliminate it. Sometimes these efforts have been very successful, sometimes dismal failures because the introduced organisms had no effect, attacked desirable species as well as the target, or themselves became pests. The term biomanipulation has been introduced to describe techniques of biological control in lake restoration or improvement in which relatively small changes in the biological relations produce favorable changes in a lake. An example of inadvertent biomanipulation is the increased abundance of *Daphnia* in Lake Washington facilitated by flood control in the Cedar River.

A rather different but related use of biological activity is being investigated for environmental problems that are caused by chemical pollution. Oil spills at sea can damage a variety of organisms. The usual techniques for amelioration are to scrape or soak up as much of the oil as possible and to let the rest evaporate or decompose. Decomposition is a slow process because the bacteria that are able to use hydrocarbons are scarce and operate slowly in the low temperature of the ocean. Nevertheless there has been some progress toward developing ways in which massive local inoculations of bacteria can help break up oil slicks. Toxic organic molecules that are very stable offer special problems. By appropriate genetic techniques, strains of microorganisms have been developed that will break up PCB molecules. At the moment of writing it is not clear that these approaches will be practical, even for small spills.

An especially interesting case of chemical pollution is that of selenium. This metal is needed in very small amounts by some animals, but as with many other substances, higher concentrations are toxic. There are places in the world where selenium is so scarce that cattle are unable to develop hooves properly, as in parts of Australia. Selenium in excess is also damaging. For example, in the Ketterson Wildlife Refuge in California, continued evaporation of drainage from heavily fertilized fields concentrated the contaminating selenium. Birds that drink the water produce offspring without wings, with deformed beaks and other signs of damaged development. It has now been found that a particular fungus is able to convert the selenium into a nontoxic gas (dimethyl selinide) that passes into the air. The hope is to find a way to use it on a large scale (National Academy of Sciences 1989). It might be supposed that this would be merely a transformation of the problem into one of air pollution, but the quantities are relatively small and dispersal is wide. It is unlikely that dangerous concentrations can be produced elsewhere by chemical transformation to a toxic form and deposition in rain.

These developments represent really novel advances in controlling chemical pollution with biological agents. While they are directed at treating a damaged environment, possibly some can be modified and used for pretreatment to prevent entry of toxic material into the environment.

### Side Effects

Any action to use an environmental resource or to protect or restore one will almost certainly have side effects, sometimes unfortunate, occasionally favorable. It is common to refer to these as "unexpected" or "unforeseen" or "unintended costs." We should work out the foreseeable consequences of any action before it is taken so that a proper weighing of priorities can be made. But beyond that, the time has come when we should learn to anticipate the unforeseen. There has been so much experience now with many types of problems that there can be little excuse for making the same mistake repeatedly. For example, chlorination of drinking water has the desirable effect of killing bacteria, but under some circumstances it produces undesirable chlorinated organic compounds. Garbage incinerators may produce toxic dioxins which are emitted into the air. We should be able to generalize from these experiences.

A related point is that one decision will automatically force others. For example, the EPA blanket requirement to use secondary treatment forced the enlargement of the West Point treatment plant mentioned in chapter 4. In addition to all the problems associated with enlarging the plant in limited space, the sludge problem is magnified. There is an effective land disposal method in use now, but any system can be overloaded. And, the decision generated a great deal of public animosity that had nothing to do with the merits of the requirement.

### Monitoring

When people ask me "Are you still monitoring Lake Washington?" I say "No, but I am still studying it." The word monitoring has had an unpleasant connotation because of implications that it is an activity for accumulating data without a clear purpose or useful outcome. Actually, monitoring, properly done, is an essential part of environmental control. In environmental science, monitoring means making measurements of a particular set of environmental properties at appropriate intervals. There must be a clear reason for any monitoring program and it must incorporate measurements of properties that are related to the expected changes. For example, if a lake is showing signs of eutrophication or is recovering after treatment, a continuing census of blue-greens as well as nutrients should be obligatory. (Failure to get effective data on blue-greens vitiated some studies of the effect of detergent control.)

To be successful, a monitoring operation must be carried out with thought and attention, and there must be a way of reporting results so that a change will be recognized when it happens and action can be taken. An experience by the late Henry B. Bigelow of Harvard University is relevant. In World War I he had an assignment as navigation officer on an army transport ship. He was an oceanographer and thought that this would be a wonderful opportunity to get oceanographic data. He knew that every day one of the ship's officers was to read and record the temperature in the water intake. Since the ship had been criss-crossing the Atlantic Ocean many times, the ship's log should be a gold mine of information about the spatial and temporal variation of temperature. When Bigelow examined the log he found that all of the recorded temperatures were 40° F. So he went to look at the thermometer; the bulb had been broken off a long time before, leaving a column of mercury in the stem. Somehow it never occurred to the officer who made the readings that it was strange that the ocean was the same temperature all over at all times, and nobody checked the results.

It is appropriate to monitor a body of water that has received some protective treatment to find out whether the procedure was effective. It is also appropriate to monitor bodies of water subject to possible changes that could affect their condition. Metro has a consistent program of sampling the bays of Lake Washington, local small lakes, and streams to measure some of the chemical and biological properties that may be affected by accidents, land development, or changes in water supply. It also makes annual surveys of rooted plants in Lake Washington and in small lakes to determine any progressive changes.

An especially interesting example of the value of monitoring has to do with the invasion of the Great Lakes by the European *Bythotrephes*, which was mentioned in chapter 6. The first reported sighting of the small crustacean was in 1985 in stomach contents of fish collected from Lake Erie during a study of the food of different species of fish. When word got around, people at one of the EPA laboratories looked for the animal in their collection of routine plankton samples and found it in samples taken from Lake Huron in 1984, antedating the first observation and providing useful information on the introduction of the species, which is a keystone predator and has had a significant impact on the Great Lakes. One lesson from this; if you have a monitoring operation, do not discard the samples, at least not until you are sure that you have taken all the information from them that anybody will ever want. This situation provides a superb opportunity for basic research that will have practical applications. It is being well exploited (Lehman 1987).

A monitoring program must use methods of appropriate sensitivity and accuracy, with the caveat that improved methods should not be adopted without cross checking. Failure to do this confused interpretation of the effects of sewage pollution on Lake Michigan. Analyses at the city water intake in Milwaukee appeared to show that the silica concentrations decreased between 1926 and 1970. A tentative explanation was that increased input of phosphorus in sewage was permitting greater production of diatoms which remove silica from the water for use in their shells (Schelske and Stoermer 1971). Close examination of the data showed that the decrease in silica had not been gradual, but dropped sharply in 1948, when the responsibility for the analyses had changed from one agency to another and a different method of analysis was used (Shapiro 1983). Unfortunately, no comparison of methods was made, and this lapse led to some heated controversy about what had actually happened to the lake. Fortunately there are other sources of data on Lake Michigan and the other Great Lakes, but what might have been the longest record was invalidated by inadequate evaluation of procedures.

There is a difference between a scientific investigation and a monitoring program. A scientific investigation is directed at answering questions and comes to an end when those questions are satisfactorily answered. However, most studies uncover new questions as they go along, leading to new studies. A monitoring program can go on without change indefinitely until some reason develops for stopping it. By failing to design monitoring programs to get scientifically useful information, some good chances have been missed to improve ecological knowledge. Nevertheless, it may still be possible to use existing data imaginatively.

An excellent example of such imaginative use of data from a monitoring program for a purpose totally different from that for which they were collected is given by the study of special types of wave motion in Lake Michigan by C. H. Mortimer (1963), now at the University of Wisconsin-Milwaukee. Many towns and cities take their drinking water from the Great Lakes. The intake pipes are just long enough to get cool, alga-free water from the hypolimnion, but to save cost are no longer than necessary. Each water treatment plant constantly monitors the temperature of the water because the amount of chemicals needed to treat it depends on the temperature. For this reason, there is a long record of temperature at many points around the lakes, at a depth that is very susceptible to wind-induced motion. When wind blows steadily from one direction, the warm water of the epilimnion tends to pile up downwind, and cool water of the hypolimnion is drawn up toward the surface upwind. When the winds calm down, the water is released from the constraint of the wind and is set into complex wave motions including an up and down swinging called a *seiche*. There are also complex internal waves in the thermocline. From the recorded variation in temperature, Mortimer was able to learn many new things about the ways that water moves in lakes.

## Basic Research

I once heard the director of a large nuclear energy laboratory define basic research as "the research you do when you don't know why you're doing it." Yet everything going on in his laboratory could be traced back to research that was done simply to explore the nature of matter, with no thought of nuclear power or bombs. To be sure, many physicists talked about "harnessing the power of the atom," but they could not have had that thought until somebody had discovered the basic properties of matter.

Is there a difference between basic and applied research? I think that there is. As I see it, applied research starts with a definite goal: to solve a practical problem, to improve some product or process; and is completed when the immediate problem has been resolved. Basic research starts from some interesting condition or observation of a natural phenomenon and has as its goal an explanation of that phenomenon; there is no more specific goal at the beginning. The project may start from simple curiosity about the nature of the world and proceed stepwise from discovery to discovery, following wherever each leads. Applied research cannot be done effectively without a background of information developed by basic research, but the application is not merely a further development of the latter; it is qualitatively different. Some defenders of basic research seem to be saying that the good thing about it is that the results can be applied, but actually that is not its prime value. Nor, however, does the fact that basic research is sometimes called "pure research" mean that applied research is impure. We cannot do without it. My work on Lake Washington was designed as basic research aimed at increasing our understanding of the control of productivity and community structure in lakes, just because we want to know about those things. My applications to NSF for grants never described the work as being done for the purpose of pollution control. However, the information that I was getting and the predictions I had to make for the design of the sampling programs were exactly what was needed to evaluate the practical problem. In other words this was an example in which the results of basic research could be put to immediate application. But to find the answer to my questions we had to measure many more properties of the lake than would have been included in a normal engineering water quality study. An applied study probably would have been stopped as soon as the lake had reached the goal of apparent recovery in 1971. Even if the water quality study had been continued for a few years, the observations of a few *Daphnia* in 1973–75 would probably not have attracted attention. (See Edmondson and Litt 1982.)

Even if we regard applied and basic research as the two ends of a spectrum of ways of thinking rather than as a dichotomy, for solving our practical problems we must preserve the clearly basic end of the spectrum. Basic research must be actively encouraged, not merely permitted. We will not be able to solve the problems of the year 2090 with the knowledge of 1990; there will be problems then based on things we do not yet know. The utility of basic research often comes not from the application of results from a particular basic project, but from an unforeseen convergence of two basic projects that supplement each other, permitting solution of a practical problem (Koshland 1989). But beyond the underlying utility of basic research, our species has as part of its special requirements a need to use its mind freely. For this reason, we must be concerned that in many parts of the world where basic research has been cherished there are signs that it is losing financial support. Many of the few institutions where such research has been nurtured are being forced to turn to work that will show an immediate economic return. Such trends, unfortunately worldwide, will almost certainly damage the intellectual atmosphere of laboratories and reduce the value of the scientific work that can be accomplished.

## Public Action

Features of the Lake Washington affair that attracted much attention were the character of the campaign and the fact that the decision was made by the public vote described in chapter 1. Participation of the public has become much more common now, but it was most unusual thirty years ago. In addition to meeting the legal requirements for environmental impact statements, governmental agencies are now expected routinely to hold public discussions. Such discussions do not necessarily result in effective action. Often strongly polarized groups state extreme positions with vigor as if each knew that some middle position would have to be taken in the end. This usually means that a compromise is reached between the competing positions that accomplishes the goal of neither.

Public campaigns like the one for Metro do not happen automatically, and they are not carried out by unorganized aggregations of people, however interested. Someone must take the lead. The beginning of the Lake Washington-Metro campaign can be identified as the mayor's appointment of a committee of public-spirited citizens to study problems of urbanization in the Seattle area. A key part of that decision was the appointment of James R. Ellis as chairman. He seems to have had a knack of bringing out the best in everybody who participated.

Metro was not a one-shot affair. Mr. Ellis has remained active in community affairs ever since, and is credited with being the driving force behind other major public actions, such as the Forward Thrust campaign that created bond issues for development of parks and further improvement of sewage disposal, construction of a park in downtown Seattle built as a lid over part of a freeway, and a convention center also built over the freeway.

### Participation of Scientists in Public Debate

I chose not to take part in the debates about Metro in 1958, although I freely provided advice and opinion about Lake Washington. This does not mean that I think that scientists should avoid debates and let other people integrate information and make all the decisions. The scientist may be better able to evaluate the limits of knowledge and how to use it. What I would object to is having a scientist push his own plan of action based only on scientific issues without considering other issues that might be involved in a decision. Both sides of the question have been clearly presented in connection with the tobacco controversy by an official of the industry and a cancer research scientist (Resnick 1989; Cummings 1989).

### Participation of Industry in Environmental Protection

It is hard to write about this topic in the context of this book without sounding like a "rabid environmentalist." It is clear that many leaders of industry take a responsible attitude toward the environmental problems that their companies inevitably create. It is also clear that many others put environmental protection low on their list of priorities and some even knowingly engage in illegal practices. And, even though the CEO (chief executive officer) of a company may express the highest ethical standards in published statements, it does not follow that his associates and the employees in charge of factory operations will adhere to those standards. In chapter 4 I mentioned as an example the illegal disposal of toxic waste through concealed effluent pipes, a condition that could not be accidental or unknown to responsible officials.

It is generally understood that in our capitalistic society business administrators have an obligation to the stockholders to maximize profits, and this must involve minimizing expenses. It should be clear that the costs of limiting environmental damage must be included in the calculations, but the struggle for profits can overwhelm common sense. Most of the problems discussed in Part 2 are caused by industrial activities in which the avoidance or remedying of environmental pollution would reduce profits. That means that there is strong motivation for the industry to deny or even conceal damaging operations. Even the most altruistic business executive may feel that before taking any action he must be given strong evidence that damage has occurred, has been caused by his operation, and that it can be corrected without costing too much. A characteristic response of an industry to a challenge about its environmental damage is "show me" or even "prove it." This can lead to various kinds of denial and delaying action. This was well expressed by Dr. R. B. Wood, University of Coleraine, North Ireland in response to a question I asked about the usefulness of the Lake Washington experience in evaluating other eutrophication problems:

> The Lake Washington experience was certainly very useful in our efforts to persuade government here to do something about L. Neagh. They (the bad guys) went through the usual sequence of reactions—
> (a) there is no problem
> (b) there is a problem but we didn't cause it

(c) there is a problem, we did cause it but it is so bad we can do nothing about it

(d) perhaps there never was a man-made problem because the lake has always been like that, it's the way God made it.

One characteristic delaying action is to declare that not enough is known about the cause of a given problem and to call for a prolonged, elaborate research program. (Unfortunately such a proposal may be very appealing to some of the scientists and engineers working in the field.) Motivation for maintaining ignorance has been described by Dr. Gordon H. Orians (1986) of the University of Washington:

> Any person who is strongly identified with a particular position, particularly when that position has resulted in the allocation of considerable resources to the outcome advocated by that position, has a strong vested interest in not finding out if that position is incorrect. Shortage of critical information is the best way to guard the sanctity of strongly held views, and this is as likely to be true for persons on the environmental side as on the developmental side of disputes. Therefore, although we are all dedicated to better problem solving, we need to be ever mindful that in the arena we have chosen to tackle, *ignorance has a very large constituency.* [emphasis added]

This attitude seems to lead to excess skepticism about the danger of certain operations and may account for the unrealistic insistence of the tobacco industry on "scientific proof" of the cause of each and every individual cancer.

Not all such cases are caused by cupidity; sometimes naiveté or ignorance is responsible. Many examples have been publicized. Burying waste in tightly closed steel barrels underground out of sight might seem adequate, but eventually they corrode. It might even have been adequate if only a small amount were involved, but the amounts are tremendous. Building houses on reclaimed land over a garbage fill might seem to be an excellent way to develop housing projects. The trouble is that such dumps produce a great deal of methane gas which rises to the surface and accumulates in the basements of houses, sometimes reaching a concentration damaging to health or at which an explosion is a danger. Similarly, it may seem efficient to use tailings from uranium mines as a cheap source of building material, but the continued release of radon and other radioactive products can produce exposures to radioactivity that are dangerous because of the increased risk of cancer.

A result of both cover-up activities and simple mistakes is that a tremendous debt of environmental deterioration has been built up, since industry has paid only part of the real cost of doing business. By the term "real cost" I mean, among other things, doing business in such a way that wastes, especially toxic ones, do not accumulate and cause serious damage. The Love Canal situation is a well-publicized case in which a chemical company disposed of toxic wastes so that they were not evident until many years later, when odorous, poisonous material began to make its way to the surface from buried dumps, causing a large neighborhood to be evacuated. This type of activity has occurred abundantly all across the country, and the calculated cost of rectifying it is too large to comprehend, much less handle. The superfund concept appears to be too super to fund. The damage is far beyond that which we can rationally expect to absorb into normal activities. Of course, if the pollution had been cleaned up as it developed, profits would have been reduced. Companies that did a poor job of cleaning up would have been at a competitive advantage. They now have the largest "debt." This idea could be illustrated by any of several major industries. I select oil transportation and nuclear power.

The wreck of the oil tanker EXXON *Valdez* in Prince William Sound, Alaska on 24 March 1989 produced the largest and most damaging oil spill ever experienced in North America. The ship ran aground on a well-marked reef, evidently as a result of incompetent operation of the ship and poor personnel policy by the company. Ten million gallons of oil eventually spread over an area larger than the state of Rhode Island, going ashore on hundreds of miles of coastline where it severely damaged growths of seaweed and populations of shore-living invertebrates, birds, sea otters, and other animals. The spill occurred at the beginning of the salmon fishing season and put an immediate stop to fishing over a large area, idling hundreds of fishing boats and fishermen. Even though salmon were swimming freely toward spawning areas, fishing gear could not be used in many places because of oil floating on the surface.

The whole situation in which the wreck occurred provided a clear example of the conflict between environmental and economic interests and between different economic interests. Accounts of this case have been laid out richly in newspapers and magazines, and presumably books and governmental reports will appear. I recommend those sources for people who want details. In short, the oil field on the North Slope of Alaska was opened in 1974 by a consortium of oil companies called Alyeska. There had been a long controversy about the possible environmental effects of the pipeline that would convey the crude petroleum to a shipping terminal at Valdez on Prince William Sound. Supertankers carry the crude to refineries in the lower Pacific Coast states.

The exploitation of the oil field has been very successful, with profits to the operating consortium estimated at four billion dollars per year after taxes. Taxes benefitted the state of Alaska particularly, paying for schools, highways, and other amenities, including bonuses to each citizen.

Even before the oil shipping started, environmentalists and others realized that there were special environmental risks involved. No major oil shipping port has operated without inadvertent spills, and some ship operators have been very sloppy with the illegal disposal of oily bilge water at sea. The Alaskan region is an especially vulnerable area, being relatively enclosed and the site of commercially important salmon runs, salmon hatcheries, and national parks with a large variety of wildlife.

The response of the EXXON company to the accident was prompt: high officials went to Valdez and issued reassuring statements. They pledged that they would pay all reasonable costs and did in fact start disbursing large amounts. However, that word "reasonable" is subject to interpretation. A fisherman sitting on the dock rather than fishing and earning some thousands of dollars as he did the previous year can estimate the immediate loss of income, but not all the repercussions through the economy of the community can be so easily evaluated. And many of the people have chosen fishing primarily because they like the style of life. The psychological impact of seeing the damage and being forced into idleness cannot be recompensed. Indeed there have been reports of many cases of severe stress symptoms among the people affected by the spill. Furthermore, there is simply no way that the biological damage can really be repaired, much less paid for. Even if it were possible for EXXON to carry through its commitment to clean up the oil, it could only begin the healing process. Eventually the oil may disappear by evaporation, decomposition, and transport out of the area to the open sea. Some may settle among the rocks and form an impenetrable layer of asphalt-like material. Eventually the shores will be repopulated by some sort of community of plants and animals. Eventually the damaged salmon runs will rebuild. But nothing can replace the animals that were killed and their descendants. The replacement population will have a different history of colonization and interaction.

Given the carnage in Prince William Sound, it is important to use it to build our understanding of marine communities and how they operate and what they need for maintenance. A genuine ecological study of the consequences and "recovery" of the damaged community must be carried out for however long it takes for some kind of equilibrium or climax community to become established. Who will fund such a study?

From the beginning, attempts made to minimize the risks were strongly opposed by effective lobbying by the oil consortium. In 1976 the Alaskan legislature passed a bill requiring tankers to be equipped with double hulls and various safety devices. There were requirements to maintain oil cleanup gear and provide a fund for paying costs of cleaning up spills. The oil companies challenged the bill, it was declared unconstitutional, and the state did not appeal. On the federal level, the late Senator Warren G. Magnuson introduced a bill to require oil tankers to have double hulls, but it did not pass. He was more successful in limiting the activities of tankers in Puget Sound by his usual tactic of attaching a rider to an appropriations bill, thus infuriating many people (including former supporters). Even the minimal system of safeguards that was set up at Valdez in the beginning was permitted to deteriorate over the years:

There has been no emphasis on environmental compliance since the late 1970s. . . . The oil-spill contingency plan was a joke from the start. A few people tried to point this out, but every time they hollered, we called them environmentalists. Nobody listened. We all pretended everything was fine. (Richard Fineberg, adviser to Alaskan Governor Steve Cowper, as quoted by Anderson 1989.)

It appears that EXXON and perhaps other members of the consortium took a calculated risk by cutting expenses as much as possible, building tankers cheaply with single hulls and without special equipment that would have been required by the proposed Alaskan law and operating them with crews of inadequate size and qualification. This seems to violate a principle of engineering, the margin of safety. Usually structures are built with components designed to carry loads much larger than the maximum expected. In the case of the EXXON procedures, the margin of safety, if any, seems grossly inadequate in relation to the predictable consequences of failure. The equipment available could not have dealt effectively with even a much smaller spill. However much EXXON pays for cleanup, the cost will possibly be less than the cost would have been of maintaining adequate safety measures, especially since they probably can deduct much of the expense from taxes as "ordinary and necessary business expenses." I wonder if the word "necessary" could be challenged.

This case is not just industrialists vs. environmentalists, for the salmon fishery is a multimillion dollar industry. What we have here is a rather cavalier treatment of the needs of one industry by another industry. The fishery has some very clear environmental needs that are incompatible with sloppy oil transport.

As I write this, the story is still developing. There has been a rising incidence of complaints by the Alaskan government and others that EXXON's response was too slow and not effective enough. One of EXXON's responses was to file a lawsuit against the state of Alaska, alleging that the state had interfered with the cleanup effort. Eventually we will have a clearer idea of what the response actually has been, what direct costs were reasonable enough to be paid off, and, just as important, what kinds of costs were refused by EXXON as being unreasonable. It seems to me that it is futile to propose that EXXON's response was neither soon nor great enough. The accident should not have happened. Even if the protective gear had been available immediately, I doubt it is technically possible to contain a spill of that magnitude. Any large industrial operation has some risk, and the precautions against accident must have some relation to the probability of damage. It appears in this case that preparations were simply inadequate to match the consequences. EXXON took chances, not just with its own well-being but with a much wider target.

Nothing I have read or heard about this unfortunate episode illustrates the power of the profit motive better than a comment I heard on a TV news program by the operator of a service station who was asked why he had raised gasoline prices only hours after the spill was reported. The answer was something like "Of course we are out to make a profit. That is our business."

Finally, I comment about the nuclear power industry, which has special problems. Many people have felt that energy from nuclear power would improve environmental conditions by substituting for fossil fuels which produce acid emissions. Also it would reduce pressure to dam more rivers for hydroelectric power, thus benefitting the fisheries. Many accounts of the development of the nuclear power industry in the United States have emphasized the seriousness and care with which the industry approached the problem of safety: extraordinary efforts were made to design plants with effective safety features. Unfortunately it appears that the actual performance fell far below the goal, as has the performance of some of the operators of the plants. It must be frustrating for people who were eager for the transformation to nuclear power to see the relative lack of success that it has had in the United States. It seems to me that in large part the failure results from faults in the management of a complex technology.

Without question there are special dangers in nuclear power because of the intense radioactivity and the serious consequences of a major malfunction. A mistake with a nuclear reactor that would be comparable to the one that wrecked the EXXON Valdez could injure and kill many people, make large areas of land uninhabitable for a very long time and require costly clean-up efforts.

Nobody should take pleasure from the fact that the first serious internationally damaging nuclear reactor accident took place at Chernobyl in the USSR, rather than in the United States. We have come close enough, as with the partial meltdown at Three Mile Island, Pennsylvania in March 1979. Some people have taken the fact that such accidents have not resulted in direct fatalities as indications that the safeguards are working well. The contrary view is that such accidents indicate inadequate technology or inadequate management and personnel. In any case there has been very great damage although without fatalities. Some examples:

In October 1966, a partial meltdown in the Enrico Fermi plant near Detroit resulted in permanent inactivation of the plant before it had gone into full operation. The problem started when some metal parts inside the cooling system were torn loose by the flow of coolant and clogged the flow to part of the core, which then started to melt. The parts had been added as safety measures after the plans had been drawn, and evidently had not been given adequate engineering (Fuller 1975; Webb 1976). There were no injuries and no radiation was released, but many millions of dollars and months of effort were wasted. And the reputation of the nuclear industry was damaged.

Perhaps the most grotesque example of human error took place in March 1975, at the Brown's Ferry reactor in Alabama. The walls of the room through which the control cables pass were being sealed. A workman was checking for air leaks with a lighted candle [sic]. It set fire to plastic sealing material which spread and set fire to the insulation of the cables, inactivating most of the control and safety systems. A meltdown was averted, but total damage was reported to be about 100 million dollars. There are several astonishing things about this one. How was it possible that the reactor was designed with such easily flammable insulation? Who determined that a candle was an appropriate instrument for tracing air leaks? Earlier a similar fire had been started but put out in time. Nothing was learned from that experience. Further, it turned out that the cables of the backup safety system were in the same place as the main control cables, permitting both to be damaged by a single fire. The explanation that I heard on a TV news program for this was that a design that separated the cables would have been "prohibitively expensive." At about the same time I heard on another program an official assert that the industry would spare no expense to assure public safety. Here is a case in which proponents of nuclear power can say that the system worked well; no one was killed or hurt, and it provided a valuable learning experience. (Surely no one would test for leaks with a candle a third time.) Others may have a different standard for judging performance.

At lower levels of operation, incompetence of one sort or another has had spectacular results. More than once we have read that pumps or valves in a nuclear power plant under construction were installed backwards and had to be replaced at great expense. Sometimes tools or pipes have been left inside where they jammed pumps or valves. Nobody was injured, but the time of technicians and engineers and much money were wasted, and the credibility of the industry eroded further. Are nuclear plants so complicated that conventionally trained construction engineers cannot interpret the plans? Were the plans incorrectly drawn?

Another aspect of nuclear power is the fact that inevitably people will be exposed to radioactive substances in the plants or by inadvertent release. There has been much dispute about the degree to which this might increase the incidence of cancer. Proponents of nuclear power can argue that everybody eventually dies of something, sometimes cancer, and that the early development of cancer in a relatively few people is a small social cost for the social benefits that can be accrued from the use of nuclear energy rather than environmentally more damaging fossil fuel. Even so, it is necessary for them to minimize the dangers. This motivation has led to extensive studies of the biological effects of radiation and widely different interpretations of the results. The literature on the controversy is similar in many ways to that about the effects of smoking tobacco, but the tobacco industry does not have much of a case for social benefit.

It should be clear that the foregoing discussion applies to the use of nuclear energy for useful production of power, not nuclear weapons. That is an entirely different matter. It is weapons production that produces the greatest waste disposal problems and the most serious political problems.

Proponents of nuclear power have blamed extreme environmentalists for imposing impossibly high standards of safety. It does appear that the technology has been priced out of the range that most Americans are willing to accept, not because it has been made so safe but because the performance has been so bad.

## Participation of Environmentalists
## in Environmental Protection

From the foregoing comments, it is clear that industrial activities can create severe environmental damage, much of it unnecessary except as a component of a program to maximize profits. It appears that few if any major industries operate voluntarily with an effective balance between production and protection. Much of the protection accomplished has been imposed by law, and evasion of legal restraints is common. It is only natural that people with an active interest in maintaining acceptable living conditions should react against such activities. They are called environmentalists. (They are not to be confused with people who oppose the capitalistic system for political, moral, or religious reasons.) Some of their reactions will take the form of reasoned talks or written articles. It is inevitable that some environmentalists who hold strong opinions may take much more vigorous action than sober talks or writing; they are known, pejoratively, as environmental extremists or activist environmentalists (Ray 1990). Sometimes instead of discussion, debate and evaluation of priorities, there is a confrontation. Groups may make their point by waving signs and chanting slogans as in political rallies. I have been embarrassed by such activities, especially when the people are identified as ecologists. But while some of the antics are indeed childish and extreme, they may be the only technique the people know for a problem they consider important. Some of their protests are against extreme activities by industry, but I do not recall ever seeing the term "industrial extremist" for somebody who maximizes profits for his company by permitting severe environmental damage. If there is a major industry that, within itself, produces a balance between profits and environmental protection, it is not conspicuous. Some major industries publish informational advertisements about the social benefits of their products and their care for the environment. Some of these are effective, others are clearly one-sided, self-serving propaganda and raise questions about what information has been omitted and what other viewpoints exist.

It is understandable that an industry will present the most favorable account of its activities—often by the omission of important information, an action that some seem to accept. I have seen this attitude described, in a different context: "[they] aren't objective because of their profit motive. That's not dishonesty, but simply the way the free enterprise system works." It may be that one function of serious environmentalists is to provide the missing information.

A key difference between a serious environmentalist and an extreme environmentalist is that the former tries to assure that environmental considerations get proper consideration and is willing to consider alternative solutions. The latter will push specialized environmental considerations at the expense of all others, often in a confrontational way. Sometimes a pseudo-environmentalism is introduced, for example, in connection with the location of waste disposal facilities. Here the real motivation may be the familiar "not in my backyard" syndrome rather than a real concern for environment, as shown by the reactions to the proposed relocation of the West Point treatment plant and the demonstrations against sludge spraying.

# Chapter 17

# Prospects

I have not dealt with the most serious problem we face, the population problem. It is too big and complex to treat adequately here, but since it has a strong ecological basis I want to indicate some connections with the problems I have discussed.

The question is, in ecological terms, what is the carrying capacity of the earth for *Homo sapiens*? In other words, how large a human population can be sustained indefinitely by the earth's resources? I think that it is essential to qualify this question by including a phrase like "in a state of good physical and mental health" as part of the special requirements of mankind.

Various predictions have been made of the possible upper limit of the human population of the earth and the consequences of exceeding it. People in favor of unlimited growth may point out that an 18th century prediction by T. R. Malthus failed to occur, usually after misquoting what Malthus actually said (as pointed out by G. E. Hutchinson in his remarkable book on population biology [1978]). Predictions are always made on the basis of some assumptions such as "if nothing changes" or "assuming the present rate of increase continues" or "if the data on so and so are correct." Malthus had no way of predicting the Industrial Revolution nor the capacity for increasing agricultural productivity. This seems to have misled some people into thinking that there is no end to technological advances. But common sense seems to show that there must be a limit to the size of the human population that can be maintained in a decent state of health and happiness.

I will limit this discussion to some ideas of population ecology based on laboratory experiments with *Daphnia*, Lake Washington's useful little crustacean. This animal has been widely used to study the relation between food supply and carrying capacity. Many experiments have been done in such a way as to discover basic principles that can be generalized to other species. *Daphnia* can be cultured easily in small bottles, perhaps a half pint (250 ml), containing pond water with a suspension of a suitable algal food. From the experimenter's viewpoint, *Daphnia* has the convenient property of parthenogenesis; normally the population consists of females that produce eggs which do not need to be fertilized. Thus one can start a population in one of the microcosms with just one animal, Eve without Adam. Each day the experimenter transfers the mothers and offspring to a new vessel containing the same amount of food as before.

Following the history of the population by counting the animals each day, the experimenter sees a clear demonstration of control by food supply. At first, feeding by the mother and a few offspring removes only a small fraction of the food and an excess remains. Within a few days the population grows so large that it reduces the abundance of algae to a low level by the end of the day, before the food is replenished. The same amount of food is now being shared by many animals. In a few more days the population is so large that the food is depleted in a few hours, and the animals spend most of their time without food. Each animal gets less and less food each day, and its physiological condition deteriorates. Mothers make fewer eggs, live a shorter time, and the population stops growing. If the experimenter now increases the food supply fivefold, the population again starts to grow but in time levels off again, fluctuating around a size about five times as large as before. Thus there is a clear relation between the *rate* of food supply and the number of animals that can be sustained.

This kind of experiment has been done with many kinds of animals with similar results. In all cases, the population expands until the food is consumed, leaving a large number of animals living a marginal existence. The details vary with circumstances and the kind of animal. Rats and mice become very aggressive under crowded conditions and life is shortened by fighting. Some people object to relating animal studies to hu-

man conditions. However, no one can doubt that there is a relation between food and human health, and that in some parts
of the world local food production is inadequate to support the
population while the importation of adequate amounts is, for
various reasons, impossible under present or foreseen conditions.

The relation between food and population size of *Daphnia* described above seems perfectly clear and natural to me. Thus I was
puzzled by a reaction I got when I described it to a man I met
some time ago. He asked me what I was doing, and one thing
led to another, and I described the *Daphnia* experiments. I could
see that something was wrong; he seemed not to understand my
point or not to believe me. A little more conversation straight-
ened that out. It turned out that he was a sociologist working with
a society where the poorest people had the most children because the parents needed help with work, and the wealthier
people had smaller families. The sociologist was so fixed on this
relation that he could hardly accept a different one for *Daphnia*.
Apparently he had never seen a *starving* human population.

I relate this anecdote for two reasons. One is that it shows how
communication between people in different disciplines can fail
for unexpected reasons. The other is that it emphasizes that *Homo
sapiens* is indeed different from other species of animal; *Daphnia*
does not have conversations like that and has no way of managing its population size. But it is important to know that man,
like all other animals, does indeed have limits. We also have the
ability to affect the condition of the earth more powerfully than
any other species, for better or worse.

Almost all of our environmental problems are closely related
to population, the number of people on earth. They are exacerbated by the patchy distribution of resources and climate. More
people in densely populated industrial societies burn more fuel
and accelerate the greenhouse effect, changing conditions for
people all over the globe. Systems that could recycle the output
of a smaller population are overloaded by a larger one. Eutrophication, toxic waste, acid precipitation, and solid waste production all vary in intensity with the number of people, and dump
sites are finite. None of those problems can be controlled if the
population grows indefinitely. Only to a limited extent can per

capita rates of use of some materials and hence production of wastes be reduced. Control of the size of a population that is getting out of hand can be exceedingly unpleasant, as the Chinese have found out by mandating a very stringent birth control program. Of course we can debate about how best to control the human population, but if we do not begin to control it somehow, our talk about solving environmental problems will be futile. Much of the current discussion is clouded with sentimentality, religious dogma, and incomprehension of the physical limits on the production and transportation of resources. Unfortunate political decisions have been made on questionable bases. For instance, the Reagan administration's policy toward aid to third world countries prohibited aid to those that used certain techniques of population control.

Professor Preston Cloud of the University of California at Santa Barbara reviewed the population problem from the viewpoint of a geologist who understands the non-renewable resources of the earth. The title of his paper:

"Is There Intelligent Life On Earth?"

# References

Sources of information for each chapter are listed. In addition to those specifically cited in the text using the author-date system, references are given to more general publications for readers who desire additional information.

I appreciate the efforts of those people cited below who have taken the trouble to make available in print the results of their work and thought. Isaac Asimov (personal communication) put it this way:

"It was a shame that when a bright, creative individual died, his brain, with all its knowledge and ideas died with him. In my case, however, . . . it wouldn't matter, for every idea I had ever had I wrote down and published."

## Preface

The title of the lecture series was "Environmental Problem-Solving and Ecological Research." Edited videotapes of the three lectures are available in the Media Center of the Odegaard Undergraduate Library of the University of Washington under the call number Videorecord TV 007-009. The titles are (1) "What Happened to Lake Washington: How and Why"; (2) "Lessons from Lake Washington: Puget Sound and Other Problems"; (3) "Long Term Environmental Research: Why and How."

## Chapter 1

Bagley, C. B. 1916. *History of Seattle from the earliest settlement to the present time.* 2 vols. Chicago: S. J. Clarke Publishing Co. Published in the year of the opening of the Lake Washington ship canal.

Bird-borne aquatic weed has moved to Union Bay. *Seattle Times,* 25 July 1976.

Brown and Caldwell, Civil and Chemical Engineers. 1958. *Metropolitan Seattle sewerage and drainage survey.*

Caldwell, L. K., L. R. Hayes, and I. M. MacWhirter. 1976. *Citizens and environment: Case studies in popular action.* Bloomington: Indiana University Press. Refers to the All-American City Award to Metro.

Change in image of botanist urged. *Seattle Post-Intelligencer,* 25 August 1969.

Chasan, D. J. 1971. The Seattle area wouldn't allow death of its lake. *Smithsonian* 2 (July), 6–13.

Chrzastowki, M. 1983. *Historical changes to Lake Washington and route of the Lake Washington Ship Canal, King County, Washington.* Water Resources Investigations WRI 81-1182. U.S. Geological Survey. The report includes a map at scale 1:24,000 showing the shoreline of Lake Washington before and after the ship canal was opened.

Collier, A., G. M. Finlayson, and E. W. Cake. 1968. On the transparency of the sea (Observations made by Mr. Cialdi and Mr. Secchi). *Limnology and Oceanography.* 13:391–94.

Davis, M. B. 1973. Pollen evidence of changing land use around the shores of Lake Washington. *Northwest Science* 47:133–48.

Dornbusch, D. M. and Company, Inc. 1976. *The impact of water resource quality improvements on residential property prices.* Report for the National Commission on Water Quality, Washington, D.C.

Edmondson announces pollution may ruin lake. *University of Washington Daily,* 13 October 1955.

Edmondson, W. T. 1968. Water quality management and lake eutrophication: The Lake Washington case. In *Water resources management and public policy,* ed. T. H. Campbell and R. O. Sylvester, 139–78. Seattle: University of Washington Press. A review of eutrophication, somewhat out of date. This paper was translated into Hungarian by Dr. Olga Sebestyén, under the title Visminöségi ügyvetés és a tavak eutrofikációja: A Lake Washington ügy Tihany.

———. 1969. Eutrophication in North America. In *Eutrophication: causes, consequences, correctives,* 124–49. National Academy of Sciences Publication No. 1700. Washington, D.C.: National Academy of Sciences.

———. 1970. Phosphorus, nitrogen, and algae in Lake Washington after diversion of sewage. *Science* 169:690–91. This is the source of data for fig. 3-1. Reprinted in *Readings in aquatic ecology,* ed. R. F. Ford and W. E. Hazen, 373–74. Philadelphia: Saunders, 1972.

———. 1972. Nutrients and phytoplankton in Lake Washington. In Nutrients and eutrophication, ed. G. Likens, 172–93. American Society of Limnology and Oceanography, Special Symposia. No. 1.

———. 1973. Lake Washington. In *Environmental quality and water development,* ed. C. R. Goldman, J. McEvoy III and P. J. Richardson, 281–98. San Francisco: Freeman.

———. 1977. *Trophic equilibrium of Lake Washington: Final report on EPA project R 8020 82-03-1.* (EPA-600/3-77-086) Corvallis, Oregon: Environmental Research Laboratory, Environmental Protection Agency.

———. 1989. On the modest success of *Daphnia* in Lake Washington in 1965. In *Algae and the aquatic environment,* ed. F. E. Round, 225–43. Bristol: Biopress. Contains a specific description of the approach I have used in the work on Lake Washington, combining descriptive and experimental approaches.

Edmondson, W. T. and S. E. B. Abella. 1988. Unplanned biomanipulation in Lake Washington. *Limnologica* 19:73–79.

Edmondson, W. T. and J. T. Lehman. 1981. The effect of changes in the nutrient income on the condition of Lake Washington. *Limnology and Oceanography* 26:1–29.

Edmondson, W. T. and A. H. Litt. 1982. *Daphnia* in Lake Washington. *Limnology and Oceanography* 27:272–93.

Higman, H. W. and E. J. Larrison. 1951. *Union Bay: Life in a city marsh.* Seattle: University of Washington Press.

Infante, A. and S. E. B. Abella. 1985. Inhibition of *Daphnia* by *Oscillatoria* in Lake Washington. *Limnology and Oceanography* 30:1046–52.

Infante, A. and W. T. Edmondson. 1985. Edible phytoplankton and herbivorous zooplankton in Lake Washington. *Archiv für Hydrobiologie. Ergebnisse der Limnologie* 21:161–71.

Infante, A. and A. H. Litt. 1985. Differences between two species of *Daphnia* and the use of ten species of algae in Lake Washington. *Limnology and Oceanography* 30:1053–59.

Lake Stinko. *Seattle Post-Intelligencer,* 5 October 1963.

Lake Washington brown—That's algae, not mud and it'll be there for the next 10 years. *Seattle Post-Intelligencer,* 3 July 1962.

Lampert, W., W. Fleckner, H. Rai and B. E. Taylor. 1986. Phytoplankton control by grazing zooplankton: A study on the spring clear-water phase. *Limnology and Oceanography* 31:478–90.

Larson, S. B. 1975. *Dig the ditch! The history of the Lake Washington ship canal.* Boulder, Colorado: Western Interstate Commission for Higher Education. A very detailed account of all aspects of the background of the canal with abundant quotations and references.

Lehman, J. T. 1986. Control of eutrophication in Lake Washington. In *Ecological knowledge and environmental problem-solving,* 301–16. Washington, D.C.: National Academy of Sciences Press. This is an excellent, concise account of the Lake Washington story presented as one of a number of case histories of environmental problems and their ecological basis.

McDonald, L. 1979. *The Lake Washington story.* Seattle: Superior Publishing Co. Eutrophication is discussed on 149–52.

McDonald, R. K. and L. McDonald. 1987. *The coals of Newcastle: A hundred years of hidden history.* Seattle: Dove Graphics & Litho. An account of coal mining in the region of Lake Washington in the 19th century.

McNulty, R. H., R. L. Penne, and D. R. Jacobson. 1986. *The return of the livable city: Learning from America's best.* Washington, D.C.: Acropolis Books. A concise description of the basis of Seattle's reputation for livability, including an account of Metro and Forward Thrust.

Milfoil takes over lake. *University of Washington Daily,* 26 September 1977.

Murtaugh, P. A. 1981. Selective predation by *Neomysis mercedis* in Lake Washington. *Limnology and Oceanography* 26:445–53.

Paine, R. T. 1969. A note on trophic complexity and community stability. *American Naturalist* 103:667–85.

———. 1980. Food webs: Linkage, interaction strength and community infrastructure. *Journal of Animal Ecology* 49:667–85.

Purvis, N. H. 1934. History of the Lake Washington canal. *The Washington Historical Quarterly* 25:114–27, 210–13.

Scheffer, V. B. and R. J. Robinson. 1939. A limnological study of Lake Washington. *Ecological Monographs* 9:95–143.

Shapiro, J., V. Lammara, and M. Lynch. 1975. Biomanipulation: An ecosystem approach to lake restoration. In *Proceedings of a symposium on water quality management through biological control*, ed. P. L. Brezonik and J. L. Fox, 85–96. U.S. EPA Report. No. ENV-07-75-1.

Shapiro, J. and D. I. Wright. 1983. Lake restoration by biomanipulation. *Freshwater Biology* 14:371–83.

Sockeye run called biggest in 11 years. *Seattle Times*, 12 July 1988.

Superior Court, State of Washington, King County. Cause No. 636660. 1965. This was the lawsuit by Metro to establish the cost of easements for an underwater sewage pipeline.

U.S. Army Corps of Engineers. Seattle District. 1979. *Eurasian watermilfoil: Information pamphlet*. A succinct discussion of the benefits and detriments of milfoil and how to control the growth.

U.S. National Oceanographic and Atmospheric Administration. Chart 18447 (Formerly 690-SC). Lake Washington Ship Canal (scale 1:10,000) and Lake Washington (scale 1:25,000).

Williams, H. 1985. The mysteries of Lake Washington. *Pacific* (magazine supplement to the Sunday edition of the Seattle Times/Post-Intelligencer), 4 August 1985. Includes "The healing of the lake," a section on eutrophication and subsequent events, 18–21.

## Chapter 2

Bartsch, A. F. 1970. Accelerated eutrophication of lakes in the United States: ecological response to human activities. *Environmental Pollution* 1:133–40.

Bramwell, A. 1989. *Ecology in the 20th century: A history*. New Haven: Yale University Press. I include this reference only because the title may mislead readers of my preface. Possibly there is a field of human thought for which this book is a useful summary, but the modern science of ecology is not that field.

Brock, T. D. 1985. *A eutrophic lake: Lake Mendota, Wisconsin*. Ecological Studies, vol. 55. New York and Berlin: Springer-Verlag.

Burgis, M. J. and P. Morris. 1987. *The natural history of lakes*. Cambridge and New York: Cambridge University Press. An excellent non-technical background for this book.

Carmichael, W. W., ed. 1981. *The water environment: Algal toxins and health*. New York and London: Plenum Press.

Elser, J. J., E. R. Marzolf and C. R. Goldman. 1990. Phosphorus and nitrogen limitation of phytoplankton growth in the freshwaters of North America: a review and critique of experimental enrichments. *Canadian Journal of Fisheries and Aquatic Sciences*. 47:1468–77.

Franko, D. A. and R. G. Wetzel. 1983. *To quench our thirst: The present and future status of freshwater resources of the U.S.* Ann Arbor: University of Michigan Press. A non-technical discussion of problems of water supply.

Hutchinson, G. E. *A treatise on limnology:* Vol. 1 (1957) *Geography, physics and chemistry;* Vol. 2 (1967), *Introduction to lake biology and the limnoplankton;* Vol. 3. (1975), *Limnological Botany.* New York and London: John Wiley & Sons. A very detailed compilation. Volume 1 was written before some of the major concepts used in this chapter had been fully developed.

———. 1969. Eutrophication, past and present. In *Eutrophication: causes, consequences, correctives,* 17–26. Washington, D.C.: National Academy of Sciences Press. See also Rodhe. These two reviews of the same field in the same book were written independently.

Krebs, C. 1985. *Ecology: The experimental analysis of distribution and abundance.* 3d ed. New York: Harper and Row.

Margalef, R. 1983. *Limnología.* Barcelona: Omega. An excellent moderately technical book accessible to those with only a modest knowledge of Spanish.

Marsden, M. W. 1989. Lake restoration by reducing external phosphorus loading: the influence of sediment phosphorus release. *Freshwater Biology* 21:139–162.

Norvell, W. A. 1977. Rapid changes in the composition of Linsley and Cedar Ponds (North Branford, Connecticut). *Archiv für Hydrobiologie* 80:286–96.

Odum, E. P. 1989. *Ecology and our endangered life-support systems.* Sunderland, Massachusetts: Sinauer Associates.

Rawson, D. S. 1939. Some physical and chemical factors in the metabolism of lakes. In *Problems of lake biology,* ed. F. R. Moulton, 9–26. American Association for the Advancement of Science Publication No. 10. An informative discussion of the effects of external factors on lakes.

Rodhe, W. 1969. Crystallization of eutrophication concepts in northern Europe. In *Eutrophication, causes, consequences, correctives,* 50–64. Washington, D.C.: National Academy of Sciences Press. This presents trophy in terms of production of organic matter.

Schindler, D. W. and E. J. Fee. 1974. Experimental lakes area: Whole-lake experiments in eutrophication. *Journal of the Fisheries Research Board of Canada* 31:937–53.

Vallentyne, J. R. 1974. *The algal bowl: Lakes and man.* Miscellaneous special publication 22. Ottawa: Department of the Environment, Fisheries and Marine Service. The title is a reference to the "dust bowl" of the 1950s.

Vollenweider, R. 1976. Advances in defining critical loading levels for phosphorus in lake eutrophication. *Mem. Ist. Ital. Idrobiol.* 33:53–83.

———. 1989. Global problems of eutrophication and its control. In *Conservation and management of lakes,* ed. J. Salánki and S. Herodek,

19–41. Symposiae Biologicae Hungaricae, 38. Budapest: Akadémiai Kiadó.

Welch, E. B. with T. Lindell. 1980. *Ecological effects of wastewater.* Cambridge and New York: Cambridge University Press.

Wetzel, R. G. 1983. *Limnology.* 2d ed. Philadelphia: Saunders. A technical text book.

Whiteside, M. C. 1983. The mythical concept of eutrophication. *Hydrobiologia* 103:107–11. (Reprinted in *Paleolimnology*, ed. P. Huttunen Mariläinen and R. W. Battarbee. Developments in Hydrobiology, No. 15. The Hague and Boston: W. Junk, Publishers.)

## Chapter 3

Abelson, P. H. 1957. Organic constituents of fossils. *Geological Society of America Memoirs* 67:87–92.

———. 1970. Excessive emotion about detergents. *Science* 169:1033.

Allen, H. L. 1972. Phytoplankton photosynthesis, micronutrient interactions, and inorganic carbon availability in a soft-water Vermont lake. In *Nutrients and eutrophication: The limiting-nutrient controversy*, ed. G. E. Likens, 63–83. American Society of Limnology and Oceanography Special Symposia, vol. 1. Lawrence, Kansas: Allen Press. Note: The fact that this lake had been fertilized with phosphate is mentioned on p. 81.

Burns, N. M. 1985. *Erie: The lake that survived.* Totowa, New Jersey: Rowman and Allanheld.

Cordone, A. J. and S. J. Nicola. 1970. Influence of molybdenum on the trout and trout fishing of Castle Lake. *California Fish and Game* 56:96–108.

Derr, P. F. See U.S. Federal Trade Commission 1971 and U.S. House of Representatives 1970a for quoted comments.

Edmondson, W. T. 1968. Water quality management and lake eutrophication: The Lake Washington case. In *Water resources management and public policy*, ed. T. H. Campbell and R. O. Sylvester. Seattle: University of Washington Press.

———. 1970. Phosphorus, nitrogen and algae in Lake Washington after diversion of sewage. *Science* 169:690–91. Reprinted in *Readings in aquatic ecology*, ed. R. F. Ford and W. E. Hazen, 373–74. Philadelphia: Saunders, 1972.

———. 1972. Nutrients and phytoplankton in Lake Washington. In *Nutrients and eutrophication*, ed. G. Likens, 172–93. American Society of Limnology and Oceanography Special Symposia, vol. 1. Lawrence, Kansas: Allen Press.

———. 1974. Review of *The environmental phosphorus handbook*, ed. E. J. Griffith et al. *Limnology and Oceanography* 19:369–75.

Einsele, W. 1941. Die Umsetzung von zugeführtem, anorganischen

Phosphat im eutrophen See und ihre Rückwerkung auf seinen Gesamthaushalt. *Zeitschrift für Fischerei* 39:407–88.

Fitzgerald, G. P. 1970. Aerobic lake muds for the removal of phosphorus from lake waters. *Limnology and Oceanography* 15:550–55.

FMC Corporation. 1970. *Eutrophication: Technical reviews on proposed causative factors and corrective actions [in four sections].*

———. *The eutrophication problem: A review and critical analysis (The Nonrole of detergent phosphates in eutrophication).* 24 pages.

———. [Untitled]. 10 pages.

———. *Lack of correlation between phosphorus and algal growth.* 4 pages.

———. *Stream aeration demonstrations.* 8 pages. See U.S. House of Representatives 1970a, which reproduces the whole booklet on pages 1478–1520 and part of it on 877–902.

Fogg, G. E. 1956. The comparative physiology and biochemistry of the blue-green algae. *Bacteriological Reviews* 20:148–65.

Gilbert, F. A. See U.S. Federal Trade Commission 1971 and U.S. House of Representatives 1972, for quoted comments.

Goldman, C. R. 1960. Molybdenum as a factor limiting primary productivity in Castle Lake, California. *Science* 132:1016–17.

———. 1967. Molybdenum as an essential micronutrient and useful watermass marker in Castle Lake, California. In *Chemical environment in the aquatic habitat,* ed. H. L. Golterman and R. S. Clymo, 229–38 Koninklijke Nederlandse Akademie van Wetenschappen. Amsterdam: North Holland Publishing Co.

Griffith, E., J. A. Beeton, J. M. Spencer, and D. T. Mitchell. 1974. *The environmental phosphorus handbook.* New York and London: Wiley-Interscience.

Hayes, F. R. 1955. The effect of bacteria on the exchange of radiophosphorus at the mud-water interface. In *Proceedings of the International Association of Theoretical and Applied Limnology* 12:111–16. Stuttgart: E. Schweizerbart.

Hutchinson, G. E. 1957. *A treatise on limnology.* Vol. 1. New York and London: Wiley.

Kerr, P. C., D. F. Paris, and D. L. Brockway. 1970. *The interrelation of carbon and phosphorus in regulating heterotrophic and autotrophic populations in aquatic ecosystems.* Water Pollution Control Research Series 16050 FGS 07/70. Washington, D.C.: U.S. Government Printing Office.

Krieger, J. H. 1975. Symposium scores misuse of scientific data. *Chemical and Engineering News* 53:17–18.

Krumrei, W. See U.S. Federal Trade Commission 1971, U.S. House of Representatives 1972 and U.S. Senate 1970 for quoted comments.

Kuentzel, L. E. 1969. Bacteria, carbon dioxide and algal blooms. *Journal of the Water Pollution Control Federation* 41:1737–47.

———. 1970. Bacteria-algae symbiosis—a cause of algal blooms. In *Proceedings of the National Symposium on Hydrobiology: Bioresources of shallow water environments,* ed. W. G. Geist, Jr. and P. E. Green, 321–34. Urbana, Illinois: American Water Resources Association.

———. 1971. Phosphorus and carbon in lake pollution. *Environmental Letters* 2:101–20.

Lange, W. 1967. Effect of carbohydrates on the symbiotic growth of planktonic blue-green algae with bacteria. *Nature* 215:1277–78.

Legge, R. F. and D. Dingeldein. 1970. We hung phosphates without a fair trial. *Canadian Research and Development* 3 (March/April 1970):19–42. This series of articles was followed by extensive rebuttal and comment in three subsequent issues of the magazine, May/June 1970, July/August 1970, and March/April 1971. The last contains "The controversy bubbles on," Legge's review of the National Academy of Sciences's symposium on eutrophication.

Likens, G. E., ed. 1972. *Nutrients and eutrophication.* American Society of Limnology and Oceanography Special Symposia, vol. 1. Lawrence, Kansas: Allen Press.

Likens, G. E., A. F. Bartsch, G. H. Lauff, and J. E. Hobbie. 1971. Nutrients and eutrophication. *Science* 170:873–74. A review of a symposium; see National Academy of Sciences, 1969.

Michalski, M. F. P. and N. Conroy. 1973. The "oligotrophication" of Little Otter Lake, Parry Sound District. In *Proceedings of the 16th conference, International Association of Great Lakes Research,* 934–48.

Mortimer, C. H. 1954. *Fertilizer in fishponds: A review and bibliography.* Fishery Publication No. 5, 1954. London: Colonial Office and Her Majesty's Stationery Office. See also Neess.

National Academy of Sciences. 1969. *Eutrophication: Causes, consequences, correctives.* Publication 1700. Washington, D.C.

Neess, John C. 1946. Development and status of pond fertilization in central Europe. *Transactions of the American Fisheries Society* 76:335–58. Published in 1949.

Oswald, W. J. See U.S. House of Representatives 1970a and 1972 for quoted comments.

Paerl, H. W. 1984. Transfer of $N_2$ and $CO_2$ fixation products from *Anabaena oscillatorioides* to associated bacteria during inorganic carbon sufficiency and deficiency. *Journal of Phycology* 20:600–608.

Parker, M. 1977. Vitamin $B^{12}$ in Lake Washington, USA: Concentration and rate of uptake. *Limnology and Oceanography* 22:527–38.

Parker, R. A. 1976. *Phosphate reduction and response of plankton populations in Kootenay Lake.* U.S. EPA-600/3-76-063. Washington, D.C.: Environmental Protection Agency.

Patrick, R., T. Bott, and R. Larson. 1975. *The role of trace elements in management of nuisance growths.* U.S. EPA-660/2-75-008.

Patrick, R., B. Crum, and J. Coles. 1969. Temperature and manganese as determining factors in the presence of diatom or blue-green algal floras in streams. *Proceedings of the National Academy of Sciences of the U.S.* 64:472–78.

Provasoli, L. 1969. Algal nutrition and eutrophication. In *Eutrophication: Causes, consequences and correctives*, 574–93. Publication 1700. Washington, D.C.: National Academy of Sciences.

Rodgers, W. H., Jr. 1973. *Corporate country: A state shaped to suit technology*. Emmaus, Pa.: Rodale Press, Inc. Chapter 6, "The washday miracle," is about the detergent controversy.

Ryther, J. H. and W. M. Dunstan. 1971. Nitrogen, phosphorus, and eutrophication in the coastal marine environment. *Science* 171:1008–13.

Sawyer, C. N. 1947. Fertilization of lakes by agricultural and urban drainage. *Journal of the New England Water Works Association* 61:109–27.

———. 1952. Some new aspects of phosphates in relation to lake fertilization. *Sewage and Industrial Wastes* 24:768–76.

———. 1954. Factors involved in disposal of sewage effluents to lakes. *Sewage and Industrial Wastes* 26:317–25.

———. 1965. Problem of phosphorus in water supplies. *Journal of the American Water Works Association* (November 1965):1431–39.

Schindler, D. W. 1974. Eutrophication and recovery in experimental lakes: Implications for lake management. *Science* 184:897–99.

Shapiro, J. and R. Ribiero. 1965. Algal growth and sewage effluent in the Potomac Estuary. *Journal of the Water Pollution Control Federation* 37:1035–43.

Steinfeld, J. L. 1973. Behind the great phosphate flap. *Readers Digest* (November 1973), 170–74.

Strøm, K. M. 1928. Recent advances in limnology. In *Proceedings of the Linnaean Society of London* 140:96–110.

Stumm, W. 1985. Clean shirts and clean water. *Environmental Science and Technology* 19:1013.

Swingle, H. S., B. C. Gooch, and H. R. Rabanal. 1963. Phosphate fertilization of ponds. In *Proceedings of the 17th annual conference, Southeastern Association of Game and Fish Commissioners*, 213–18. Publishing place varies.

Sylvester, R. O. and G. C. Anderson. 1964. A lake's response to environment. *Journal of the Sanitary Engineering Division, Proceedings of the American Society of Civil Engineers* 90:1–22.

U.S. Federal Trade Commission. 1971. Hearing on labelling and advertising requirements for detergents. File No. 215–32. The testimony was not published, but I obtained copies from the commission under the Freedom of Information Act. It is the source of quotations from P. F. Derr, W. Krumrei, and F. A. Gilbert.

U.S. House of Representatives. 1968. *Views of the governors on saving America's small lakes. (Water Pollution Control and Abatement)*. House Report No. 1571, Twenty-sixth report by the Committee on Government operations.

———. 1970a. *Phosphates in detergents and the eutrophication of America's waters: Hearings before a subcommittee of the Committee on Government Operations.* (Conservation and Natural Resources Subcommittee). Ninety-first Congress, First Session. December 15 and 16, 1969. The source of quotations from P. C. Derr, F. A. Gilbert, W. C. Krumrei, and W. J. Oswald. It also reproduces the FMC pamphlet mentioned above.

————. 1970b. *Phosphates in detergents and the eutrophication of America's waters.* Committee on Government Operations. Twenty-third report. (House report No. 91-1004). This report is based on the hearings (1970a). It presents statements of the S & D position followed by vigorous rebuttals.

————. 1972. *Phosphates and phosphate substitutes in detergents: Hearings before a subcommittee of the Committee on Government Operations.* Ninety-second Congress, First Session. October 20, 27, 28 and 29, 1971. The source of quotations from W. C. Krumrei and W. J. Oswald. See also Shapiro's discussion of Lake Washington.

U.S. Senate. 1970. *Water Pollution—1970.* Hearings before the Subcommittee on Air and Water Pollution of the Committee on Public Works. Ninety-first Congress, Second Session. April 20, 21 and 27, 1970. Parts 1–5. The source of quotations from W. C. Krumrei. It contains a description of the Lake Washington situation by the late Senator Warren G. Magnuson.

————. 1971. *Advice to consumers on laundry detergents: A report to the Senate Committee on Commerce.* 92nd Congress, First session.

Vallentyne, J. R. 1974. *The algal bowl: Lakes and man.* Miscellaneous special publication 22. Ottawa: Department of the Environment, Fisheries and Marine Service. The title refers to the "dust bowl" in western U.S. in the 1930s.

Welch, E. B., C. A. Rock, R. C. Howe, and M. A. Perkins. 1980. Lake Sammamish response to wastewater diversion and increasing urban runoff. *Water Research* 14:821–28.

Welch, E. B., D. E. Spyridakis, J. I. Shuster, and R. R. Horner. 1986. Declining lake sediment phosphorus release and oxygen deficit following wastewater diversion. *Journal of the Water Pollution Control Federation* 58:92–96.

Zicker, E. L., K. C. Berger, and A. D. Hasler. 1956. Phosphorus release from bog lake muds. *Limnology and Oceanography* 1:296–303.

## Chapter 4

Barinaga, M. 1990. Fish, money and science in Puget Sound. *Science* 247:631.

Burns, R. 1985. *The shape and form of Puget Sound.* Seattle: Washington Sea Grant Program and University of Washington Press.

Chasan, D. J. 1981. *The water link: A history of Puget Sound as a resource.* Seattle: Washington Sea Grant Program and University of Washington Press.

Cheney, D. P, and T. F. Mumford, Jr. 1986. *Shellfish and seaweed harvests of Puget Sound.* Seattle: Washington Sea Grant Program and University of Washington Press. A detailed account of the commercially important species.

Crutchfield, J. A. 1989. Economic aspects of salmon aquaculture. *The Northwest Environmental Journal* 5:37–52.

Culliney, T. W. and D. Pimentel. 1986. Effects of chemically contaminated sewage sludge on an aphid population. *Ecology* 67:1665–69.

Downing, J. 1983. *The coast of Puget Sound: Its processes and development.* Seattle: Washington Sea Grant Program and University of Washington Press.

Glude, J. 1989. Aquaculture for the Pacific Northwest, a historical perspective. *The Northwest Environmental Journal* 5:7–21.

Malins, D. C. et al. 1987. Field and laboratory studies of the etiology of liver neoplasms in marine fish in Puget Sound. *Environmental Health Perspectives* 71:5–16.

Nelson, R. T. 1987. Set aside for solitude. *Pacific* (magazine supplement to the Sunday edition of the Seattle-Times/Seattle Post-Intelligencer), 4 October 1987, 12–25. Account of Discovery Park.

Puget Sound Water Quality Authority. 1988. *State of the sound: 1988 report.* The PSWQA has issued many informative reports and position papers on the problems of Puget Sound. Address: 217 Pine Street, Suite 1100, Seattle, Washington 98101.

Rensel, J. E., R. A. Horner, and J. R. Posterl. 1989. Effects of phytoplankton blooms on salmon aquaculture in Puget Sound, Washington: Initial research. *The Northwest Environmental Journal* 5:53–69.

Schiewe, M. H., J. T. Landahl, M. S. Myers, P. D. Plesha, F. J. Jacques, J. E. Stein, B. B. McCain, D. D. Weber, S. L. Chan, and U. Varanasi. 1989. Relating field and laboratory studies: Cause-and-effect research. In *Proceedings of the first annual meeting on Puget Sound research,* 577–84. Seattle: Puget Sound Water Quality Authority.

Strickland, R. M. 1983. *The fertile fjord: Plankton in Puget Sound.* Seattle: Washington Sea Grant Program and University of Washington Press. A non-technical but complete account of biological conditions including the effects of pollution.

Sun, M. 1989. Mud-slinging over sewage technology. *Science* 246:440–43. A review of current developments in sewage treatment for coastal marine waters including disagreements about the EPA requirement for conventional secondary treatment.

Winter, D. F., K. Banse, and G. C. Anderson. 1975. The dynamics of phytoplankton blooms in Puget Sound, a fjord in northwestern U.S. *Marine Biology* 29:139–75.

## Chapter 5

Botkin, D., W. S. Broecker, L. G. Everett, J. Shapiro, and J. A. Wiens. 1988. *The future of Mono Lake.* Report No. 68. Riverside, California: University of California Water Resources Center.

Chasan, D. J. 1981. Mono Lake vs. Los Angeles: A tug-of-war for precious water. *Smithsonian* 11 (February):42–51

Cooper, S. D., D. W. Winkler, and P. H. Lenz. 1984. The effect of grebe predation on a brine shrimp population. *Journal of Animal Ecology* 53:51–64.

National Academy of Sciences. 1987. *The Mono basin ecosystem: Effects of changing lake level.* Washington, D.C.: National Academy Press.

Sun, M. 1987. Trouble ahead for exotic Mono Lake. *Science* 237:716–17. A summary of the NAS report.


## Chapter 6

Glynn, P. W. 1982. Coral communities and their modifications relative to past and prospective Central American seaways. *Advances in Marine Biology* 19:91–132.

Jones, M. L. and R. B. Manning. 1971. A two-ocean bouillabaisse can result if and when sea-level canal is dug. *Smithsonian* 2 (December), 11–21.

Lehman, J. T. 1987. Palearctic predator invades North American Great Lakes. *Oecologia* 74:478–80.

Mooney, H. A. and J. A. Drake, eds. 1986. *Ecology of biological invasions of North America and Hawaii.* (Ecological studies, Vol. 58. Analysis and synthesis.) New York and Berlin: Springer-Verlag. Much information about the cases of invading species and the conditions for their success.

Roberts, L. 1990. Zebra mussel invasion threatens U.S. waters. *Science* 249:1371–72.

Rubinoff, I. 1970. The sea-level canal controversy. *Biological Conservation* 3:33–36.

Zaret, T. M. and R. T. Paine, 1973. Species introduction in a tropical lake. *Science* 182:449–55. The effect of introducing a keystone predator into Gatun Lake.


## Chapter 7

### *Atmospheric ozone*

Kerr, R. A. 1988. Stratospheric ozone is decreasing. *Science* 239:1489–92.

National Academy of Sciences. 1983. *Causes and effects of changes in stratospheric ozone: Update 1983.* Washington, D.C.: National Academy Press.

Roan, S. L. 1989. *Ozone crisis.* New York: Wiley. A detailed treatment with an extensive bibliography.

Shell, E. R. 1988. Probing the ozone hole. *Smithsonian* 18, (no. 11):142–55.

Tolba, M. K. 1987. The ozone agreement—and beyond. *Environmental Conservation* 14:287–90.

## Atmospheric carbon dioxide

Houghton, R. A. 1987. Terrestrial metabolism and atmospheric $CO_2$ concentrations. *BioScience* 37:672–78.

National Academy of Sciences. 1983. *Changing climate: Report of the carbon dioxide assessment committee.* Washington, D.C.: National Academy Press.

———. 1987. *Responding to changes in sea level.* Washington, D.C.: National Academy Press.

Tangley, L. 1988. Preparing for climate change. *BioScience* 38:14–18.

## Acid Deposition

Howells, G. P. 1983. Acid waters—the effect of low pH and acid associated factors on fisheries. *Advances in Applied Biology* 9:143–255. A conservative review of the problem.

Mohnen, V. 1988. The challenge of acid rain. *Scientific American* 259(2):30–38.

National Academy of Sciences. 1986. *Acid deposition: Long term trends.* Washington, D.C.: National Academy of Sciences Press.

Schindler, D. W. 1988. Effects of acid rain on freshwater ecosystems. *Science* 239:149–57. A comprehensive review with extensive bibliography.

U.S. Congress. Office of Technology Assessment. 1984. *Acid rain and transported air pollutants: Implications for public policy.* Washington, D.C.: U.S. Governmental Printing Office.

## Smoking Tobacco

National Research Council. 1986a. *Environmental tobacco smoke: Measuring exposures and assessing health effects.* Washington, D.C.: National Academy Press.

———. 1986b. *The airliner cabin environment: Air quality and safety.* Washington, D.C.: National Academy Press.

Tollison, R. D. 1986. *Smoking and society: Toward a more balanced assessment.* Lexington and Toronto: D. C. Heath Co., Lexington Books.

———. 1988. *Clearing the air: Perspectives on environmental tobacco smoke.* Lexington and Toronto: D. C. Heath Co., Lexington Books.

U.S. Department of Health and Human Services. 1986. *The health consequences of involuntary smoking: A report of the Surgeon General.* U.S. Government Printing Office.

## Chapter 8

Bormann, F. H. and G. E. Likens. 1981. *Pattern and process in a forested ecosystem.* New York and Berlin: Springer-Verlag.
Likens, G. E., ed. 1985. *An ecosystem approach to aquatic ecology: Mirror Lake and its environment.* New York and Berlin: Springer-Verlag.

## Chapter 9

Goldman, C. R. 1981. Lake Tahoe: Two decades of change in a nitrogen deficient oligotrophic lake. In *Proceedings of the International Association for Theoretical and Applied Limnology* 21:45–70.
————. 1985. Lake Tahoe: A microcosm for the study of change. *Bulletin of the Illinois Natural History Survey* 33:247–60.
Goldman, C. R. and E. R. Byron. 1987. *Changing water quality at Lake Tahoe: The first five years of the Lake Tahoe interagency monitoring program.* California State Water Resources Control Board. Davis, California: Tahoe Research Group, Institute of Ecology, University of California, Davis.
University of California Extension Media Center. 1987a. *Tahoe: Two decades of change.* 1987b. *Tahoe: Moving beyond the conflict.* Two 16 mm color films produced in cooperation with C. R. Goldman. (Available from the center at 2176 Shattuck Avenue, Berkeley, California 94704).

## Chapter 10

Allen, J. E., M. Burns, and S. C. Sargent. 1986. *Cataclysms on the Columbia.* Portland, Oregon: Timber Press.
Carmichael, W. W. 1981. *The water environment: Algal toxins and health.* New York and London: Plenum Press.
Dog deaths blamed on algae bloom. *Columbia Basin Daily Herald,* 26 October 1982, 3.
Kadis, S., A. Ciegler, and S. J. Ajl, eds. 1971. *Microbial toxins.* Vol. 7. *Algal and fungal toxins.* New York: Academic Press.
Sheppard, J. C. and W. H. Funk. 1975. Trees as environmental sensors monitoring long-term heavy metal contamination of Spokane River, Idaho. *Environmental Science and Technology* 9:638–42.
Soltero, R. A. and D. G. Nichols. 1981. The recent blue-green algal blooms of Long Lake, Washington. In *The water environment: Algal toxins and health,* ed. W. W. Carmichael, 143–59. New York and London: Plenum Press.
Thomas, S. R. and R. A. Soltero. 1977. Recent sedimentary history of a eutrophic reservoir: Long Lake, Washington. *Journal of the Fisheries Research Board of Canada* 34:669–676.
Toxic bloom reappears. Algae poisons Lake Spokane. *The Spokesman-Review* (Spokane), 19 July 1977, 1.

## Chapter 11

Anderson, G. C. 1958. Seasonal characteristics of two saline lakes in Washington. *Limnology and Oceanography* 3:51–68.

Edmondson, W. T. 1963. Pacific Coast and Great Basin. Chapter 13 in *Limnology in North America*, ed. D. G. Frey, 371–92. Madison: University of Wisconsin Press.

———. 1984. Volcanic ash in lakes. *The Northwest Environmental Journal* 1:139–50.

Edmondson, W. T. and G. C. Anderson. 1965. Some features of saline lakes in Central Washington. *Limnology and Oceanography* 10(supplement): R87–R96.

Edmondson, W. T. and A. H. Litt. 1984. Mt. St. Helens ash in lakes in the lower Grand Coulee, Washington State. In *Proceedings of the International Association for Theoretical and Applied Limnology* 22:510–12. Stuttgart

Hairston, N. G., Jr. 1978. The adaptive significance of carotenoid pigmentation in two species of *Diaptomus* (Copepoda). *Limnology and Oceanography* 24:15–37.

———. 1981. The interaction of salinity, predators, light and copepod color. *Hydrobiologia* 81:151–58. Reprinted in *Salt lakes: Proceedings of an international symposium on athalassic (inland) salt lakes*, ed. W. D. Williams. Developments in Hydrobiology 5. The Hague and Boston: W. Junk, Publisher.

Luecke, C. 1986. The effect of the introduction of cutthroat trout on the benthic community of Lake Lenore, Washington. Ph.D. dissertation, Department of Zoology, University of Washington.

Walker, K. F. 1975. The seasonal phytoplankton cycles of two saline lakes in central Washington. *Limnology and Oceanography* 20:40–53.

Wiederholm, T. 1980. Effects of dilution on the benthos of an alkaline lake. *Hydrobiologia* 68:199–207.

## Chapter 12

Donaldson, J. R. 1967. The phosphorus budget of Iliamna Lake, Alaska, as related to the cyclic abundance of sockeye salmon. Ph.D. dissertation, College of Fisheries, University of Washington.

Hairston, N. G., Sr. 1989. *Ecological experiments: Purpose, design and execution.* Cambridge: Cambridge University Press.

Hyatt, K. D. and J. G. Stockner. 1985. Responses of sockeye salmon (*Onchorhynchus nerka*) to fertilization of British Columbia coastal lakes. *Canadian Journal of Fisheries and Aquatic Science* 42:320–31.

Johnson, W. E. and J. R. Vallentyne. 1971. Rationale, background, and development of experimental lake studies in northwestern Ontario. *Journal of Fisheries Research Board of Canada* 28:123–28.

Nelson, P. R. 1958. Relationship between rate of photosynthesis and growth of juvenile red salmon. *Science* 128:205–206.

————. 1959. Effects of fertilizing Bare Lake, Alaska, on growth and production of red salmon (*Onchorhynchus nerka*). *Fishery Bulletin* 159(vol. 60):59–86.

Nelson, P. R. and W. T. Edmondson. 1955. Limnological effects of fertilizing Bare Lake, Alaska. *Fishery Bulletin* 102(vol. 56):413–36.

Soltero, R. A., D. G. Nichols, A. F. Gasperino, and Michael A. Beckwith. 1981. Lake Restoration: Medical Lake, Washington. *Journal of Freshwater Ecology* 1:155–65.

Stockner, J. G. 1987. Lake fertilization: The enrichment cycle and lake sockeye salmon (*Onchorhynchus nerka*) production. In *Sockeye salmon (Onchorynchus nerka) population biology and future management,* ed. H. D. Smith, L. Margolis, and C. C. Wood, 198–215. Canadian Special Publication of Fisheries and Aquatic Science, 96. Ottawa: Department of Fisheries and Oceans.

## Chapter 13

Callahan, J. T. 1984. Long-term ecological research. *BioScience* 34:363–67. Describes the operation of the Long Term Environmental Research (LTER) program of the National Science Foundation.

Franklin, J. F., C. S. Bledsoe and J. T. Callahan. 1990. Contributions of the long-term ecological research program. *BioScience* 40:509–23.

Lehman, J. T. 1989. Review of *Complex interactions in lake communities,* ed. S. R. Carpenter. *Limnology and Oceanography* 34:487–89.

Likens, G. E. 1983. A priority for ecological research. *Bulletin of the Ecological Society of America* 64:234–43. A thoughtful discussion of the characteristics and requirements of genuine long-term research.

Likens, G. E., ed. 1989. *Long-term studies in ecology: Approaches and alternatives.* New York and Berlin: Springer-Verlag.

Magnuson, J. J. 1990. Long-term ecological research and the invisible present. *BioScience* 40:495–501.

Magnuson, J. J. and C. J. Bowser. 1990. A network for long-term ecological research in the United States. *Freshwater Biology* 23:137–43.

Matzuzan, G. T. 1988. *The National Science Foundation: A brief history.* Washington, D.C.: National Science Foundation.

National Science Foundation. 1977. *Long-term ecological measurements: Report of a conference.*

————. 1978. *A pilot program for long-term observation and study of ecosystems in the U.S.: Report of a second conference on long-term ecological measurements.*

————. 1979. *Long term ecological research: Concept statement and measurement needs.*

————. 1988. *Proposal evaluation at NSF: Perceptions of principal investigators.* NSF Report No. 88-4.

Paine, R. T. 1989. Review of *Complex interactions in lake communities,* ed. S. R. Carpenter. *Limnology and Oceanography* 34:486–87.

Roe, A. 1953. *The making of a scientist.* Dodd, Mead & Co.
Strayer, D., J. S. Glitzenstein, C. G. Jones, J. Kolasa, G. E. Likens, M. J. McDonnell, G. G. Parker and S. T. A. Pickett. 1986. *Long-term ecological studies: An illustrated account of their design, operation, and importance to ecology.* Occasional Publication of the Institute of Ecosystem Studies, no. 2. Millbrook, New York: New York Botanical Garden. Mary Flagler Cary Arboretum. An excellent, detailed description of many case histories of long-term studies and an analysis of factors for success, based on a symposium. Available from the arboretum at Box AB, Millbrook, New York 12545.
Swanson, F. J. and R. E. Sparks. 1990. Long-term ecological research and the invisible place. *BioScience* 40:502–508.

## Chapter 14

Kerr, R. A. 1989. Nyos, the killer lake may be coming back. *Science* 244:1541–42.
Kling, G. W., M. A. Clarke, H. R. Compton, J. D. Devine, W. C. Evans, A. M. Humphrey, E. J. Koenigsberg, J. P. Lockwood, M. L. Tuttle, and G. N. Wagner. 1987. The 1986 Lake Nyos gas disaster in Cameroon, West Africa. *Science* 236:169–75.
Stager, C. 1987. Silent death from Cameroon's Killer Lake. *National Geographic* (Sept. 1987), 404–18.

## Chapter 15

Goldsmith, S. 1989. Uproar over the guru of Yelm. *Seattle Post-Intelligencer*, 12 October 1989.
Mortimer, C. H. 1981. *The Lake Michigan pollution case: A review and commentary on the limnological and other issues.* Milwaukee: Sea Grant Institute and Center for Great Lakes Studies, University of Wisconsin. (WIS-SG-81-237).

## Chapter 16

Anderson, R. 1989. The 'screw-ups' that led to 'Alaska's Chernobyl', *Seattle Times*, 31 March 1989.
Bloch, E. 1986. *Basic research: The key to economic competitiveness.* National Science Foundation Publication 86-21.
Cooke, G. D., E. B. Welch, S. A. Peterson, and P. R. Newroth. 1986. *Lake and reservoir restoration.* Ann Arbor Science. Stoneham, Massachusetts: Butterworth.
Cummings, K. M. 1989. Public policy involvement is the duty of all scientists. *The Scientist* (2 October 1989), 11, 13.
Davidson, A. 1990. *In the wake of the Exxon Valdez: The devastating impact*

*of the Alaska oil spill.* Vancouver, B.C. and Toronto: Douglas & McIntyre.

Easterbrook, G. 1989. Cleaning Up. *Newsweek* (24 July 1989), 26–42. An extended review of current problems.

Edmondson, W. T. and A. H.. Litt. 1982. Daphnia in Lake Washington. *Limnology and Oceanography* 27:272–93.

Ehrlich, P. R. and A. H. Ehrlich. 1970. *Population, resources, environment: Issues in human ecology.* W. H. Freeman and Company.

Fuller, J. G. 1975. *We almost lost Detroit.* New York: Reader's Digest Press.

Koshland, D. E., Jr. 1989. The cystic fibrosis gene story. *Science* 245:1029. An excellent example of the convergence of different fields of basic research permitting solution of an important practical problem.

Lehman, J. T. 1987. Palearctic predator invades North American Great Lakes. *Oecologia* 74:478–80.

Linden, E. 1989. Playing with fire: Destruction of the Amazon is one of the great tragedies of history. *Time Magazine* (18 September 1989), 134(12):76–85.

Mason, W. H. and G. W. Folkerts. 1979. *Environmental problems.* 2d ed. Dubuque: W. C. Brown. Although dated, this is a very convenient catalog of environmental problems with editorial comments and explanations. It includes samples of anti-environmentalist writing.

Mortimer, C. H. 1963. *Frontiers in physical limnology with particular reference to long waves in rotating basins.* University of Michigan Great Lakes Research Division Publication 10:9–42.

Murdoch, W. W., ed. 1975. *Environment: Resources, pollution and society.* 2d ed. Sunderland, Massachusetts: Sinauer. A non-technical review of many environmental problems.

National Academy of Sciences. 1969. *Irrigation-induced water quality problems: What can be learned from the San Joaquin Valley experience.* Washington, D.C.: National Academy of Sciences Press.

National Science Foundation. 1980. *How basic research reaps unexpected rewards.*

Ogelsby, R. T. 1969. Effects of controlled nutrient dilution on the eutrophication of a lake. In *Eutrophication: Causes, consequences, correctives*, 483–93. Washington, D.C.: National Academy of Sciences Press.

Orians, G. H. 1986. Cumulative effects: Setting the stage. In *Cumulative environmental effects: A binational perspective*, 1–6. Washington, D.C.: National Science Foundation.

Owen, O. 1985. *Natural resource conservation: An ecological approach.* 4th ed. New York: MacMillan. A massive source of information about many kinds of problems.

Raven, P. H. 1987. *The global ecosystem in crisis.* MacArthur Foundation Occasional paper. A concise description of the environmental problems of the tropics resulting from over-exploitation of the forest resources.

Ray, D. L. 1990. *Trashing the planet: How science can help us with problems of acid rain, global warming, nuclear power and many other issues.* Washington: Regnery Gateway.

Resnick, F. E. 1989. Scientists have no business trying to sway public policy. *The Scientist* (2 October 1989), 11.

Scheffer, V. B. 1989. Environmentalism: Its articles of faith. *The Northwest Environmental Journal* 5:99–109.

Schelske, C. L. and Stoermer, E. F. 1971. Eutrophication, silica depletion and predicted changes in algal quality in Lake Michigan. *Science* 173:423–24.

Schmidt, F. H. and D. Bodansky. 1976. *The energy controversy: The fight over nuclear power.* San Francisco: Albion Publishing Company.

Shapiro, J. 1983. Lessons from the silica "decline" in Lake Michigan. *Science* 221:457–59.

Tolba, M. K. 1989. Our biological heritage under siege. *BioScience* 39:725–28. A concise through detailed account of many of the problems considered in this book. Tolba is the Executive Director of the United Nations Environment Programme.

U.S. Environmental Protection Agency. 1988. *Lake and reservoir restoration guidance manual.* L. Moore and K. Thorton, eds. Corvallis: Environmental Research Laboratory.

Webb, R. E. 1976. The accident hazards of nuclear power plants. Amherst: University of Massachusetts Press.

Wilson, E. O. and F. M. Peter, eds. 1988. *Biodiversity.* Washington, D.C.: National Academy Press. A very comprehensive and detailed discussion of the significance of the diversity of living things as a global resource and the consequences of reducing it by imprudent exploitation.

## Chapter 17

Cloud, P. 1973. Is there intelligent life on earth? In *Carbon and the biosphere,* ed. G. M. Woodwell and E. V. Pecan, 264–80. Proceedings of the 24th Brookhaven Symposium in Biology. U.S. Atomic Energy Commission.

Council on Environmental Quality. 1982. *The global 2000 report to the president.* New York: Penguin Books. A very detailed summary of environmental data with analysis and projection of possible future conditions.

Hutchinson, G. E. 1978. *An introduction to population ecology.* New Haven: Yale University Press.

# Index

Abelson, Philip H., 128
Acid deposition, 177–82, 195–96
Acidification of lakes, 178–82
Acid rain, 195
AEC. *See* Department of Energy
Algae: in lakes, 62–63, 65, 69; as cause of phosphate, 122. *See also* Blue-greens; Blooms, algal
Alkalinity: in Lake Washington, 52, in lakes, 178
Alum: use of in lakes, 228, 275, 277, 278–80; on hydrangeas, 279
American Association for the Advancement of Science (AAAS) symposium, 127
American Society of Limnology and Oceanography (ASLO), symposia, 95, 122, 224
*Anabaena*, toxic blooms of, 53, 202
Anderson, George C., 13, 211, 218
Andrew W. Mellon Foundation, 248
Antifouling paint, 142
Aquatic communities, 57–86
Arcachon, Bay of: pollution of oyster beds, 142
Artemia, 160
Atomic Energy Commission, 220. *See* Department of Energy
Autotrophic, 61, 63

Bacteria, 62, 63, 106–9
Barber, Richard T., 122
Benthos, 61, 63
Bhopal, 259
Bigelow, Henry B., 283
Bioaccumulation, 141
Bioassay, 82–85, 206, 227
Biogeochemical cycling, 195
Biological communities, 61–63
Biological oxygen demand (BOD), 80
Biomanipulation, 40, 56, 280–82
Blooms, nuisance algal: vivid

description of, 71–72; even more vivid description of, 120; toxic, 53, 72, 142–43, 202–5
Blue-greens: definition, 63; in lakes, 63–64; nuisance blooms, 71–72; as weeds, 279; and organic matter, 117–18, and vitamins, 112. *See also* Bacteria
Bormann, F. H., 195
*Brachionus plicatilis*, 210
Brine fly (*Ephydra*), 160
Brine shrimp (*Artemia*), 159
Brown and Caldwell, 21, 28
Bureau of Reclamation (U.S.), 217
*Bythotrephes*, 166, 284

California-Tahoe Regional Planning Agency, 201
Canadian Fisheries and Marine Services: lake fertilization program, 233
Carbon dioxide, 65–66, 168–169, 174–77
Carnivores, 62
Cause and effect, 82
Cedar River, 5–6; salmon run, 43–47; revetment benefits, 46–47, 55–56
Central place foraging, 270
*Chaetoceros elmorei*, 211–12
Channelling, 264
Chemicals, fear of, 280
Chesapeake Bay, 132
Chlorofluorocarbons (CFCs), 172
*Chrysochromulina*, 143
*Cladophora*, 13
Clean Water Act, 255
Clinton, Gordon, 21
Cloud, Preston, 303
Columbia Basin Project, 215
Comita, Gabriel W., 211
Communities, biological, 61–64
Consumers, 61–62

W. T. EDMONDSON, Professor Emeritus of Zoology at the University of Washington, is widely known for his work in aquatic ecology, particularly in the areas of lake productivity and population dynamics.

He was born in Milwaukee, Wisconsin, and a very early photograph shows him enjoying the shore of Lake Michigan. The gift of a simple microscope when he was about twelve reinforced a growing enchantment with the creatures that inhabit the water, by then reduced to the ponds and streams of southern Indiana. A gift a year later of Ward and Whipple's *Freshwater Biology*, the standard technical manual for the identification of freshwater organisms, necessitated an accompanying carrying case because the book was too heavy for a small boy to carry around. This experience came full circle when, many years later, he was asked to prepare a second edition of the work, which appeared in 1959.

His interest in aquatic organisms and in their environment led to a B.S. and a Ph.D. under G. Evelyn Hutchinson at Yale, with an emphasis on limnology, the study of inland waters. His first scientific paper was published when he was still in high school. His first teaching job was at Harvard. During the Second World War he did oceanographic research, as a civilian, for the Navy, mainly at Woods Hole Oceanographic Institution. He has been on the faculty of the University of Washington since 1949.

Professor Edmondson's work has been a model of the use of science in public policy. His study of Lake Washington, begun soon after he arrived in Seattle, has produced both scientific knowledge and practical consequences. In 1955 he pointed out that the increasing supply of treated sewage was acting as a chemical fertilizer and would result in rapid deterioration of the quality of the lake. His detection of the first signs of trouble, and this warning, facilitated the vote that established the Municipality of Metropolitan Seattle (Metro), organized initially to enable different communities to act together in cleaning up the lake. This led in turn to the eventual diversion of treated sewage from Lake Washington and to prompt recovery. His long-term studies were the first to predict the course of events in the eutrophication of a lake by pollution and to follow its subsequent recovery, during which the early predictions were proved to be remarkably accurate. A wager with one of the unbelieving European scientists provided him with the payoff, a bottle of fine Swiss Kirschwasser.

Professor Edmondson has served on many editorial boards and on many advisory panels, among others to the National Science Foundation and the Office of Naval Research. His research has brought him many honors. He was named Eminent Ecologist by the Ecological Society of America. He is a Fellow of the American Association for the Advancement of Science, a charter member and past president of the American Society of Limnology and Oceanography, and a member and former officer of various other professional organizations. He was elected to the National Academy of Sciences in 1973 and has served on the

Academy's Environmental Studies Board. He has received the National Academy Award for Environmental Quality (Cottrell Award), the G. Evelyn Hutchinson Medal of the American Society of Limnology and Oceanography, and the Naumann-Thienemann Medal of the International Society for Theoretical and Applied Limnology, the highest international honor in the field of limnology. In 1987 he was awarded an Honorary Doctor of Science degree by the University of Wisconsin-Milwaukee.